Layton Talbert demonstrates from
about vindicating the complete int� ⌐
All of God's words are reliable. God always keeps his words.

ANDREW DAVID NASELLI
Associate Professor of Systematic Theology and New Testament,
Bethlehem College & Seminary, Minneapolis, Minnesota
Author of several books including *How to Understand and Apply
the New Testament* and *40 Questions About Biblical Theology*

God can be trusted. All of the time. His Word is reliable and authoritative;
and He keeps all His promises. Layton Talbert explains clearly, and in an
engaging way, that if we do believe what God says, we bring glory to Him;
and we enjoy the confidence in his sovereignty that enables us to 'laugh at
the days to come' (Proverbs 31:25). This book provides immense pastoral
wisdom on a foundation of firm biblical truth.

SHARON JAMES
The Christian Institute, UK
Author of several books including *The Lies We Are Told, the Truth We Must Hold*

*The Trustworthiness of God's Words: Why the Reliability of Every Word
From God Matters* spotlights the complete reliability of all that God says
despite His use of fallible writers and human language. Hermeneutically
nuanced. Theologically sound. Pastorally sensitive. Layton Talbert offers
both the church and the academy a valuable service here. I heartily
recommend it to God's people as an antidote to unbelief in God's Word.

A. PHILIP BROWN II
Professor of Bible and Theology, Graduate Program Director,
God's Bible School and College, Cincinnati, Ohio
Co-author of *A Reader's Hebrew and Greek Bible*

Layton MacDonald Talbert has produced a very useful work which is not
a conventional defence of the complete trustworthiness of God's Words
encapsulated in Scripture, but more of a series of applications for believers.
It belongs with the works of pastoral theology rather than apologetics,
although it delves into both fields. The book rests on the foundation that
God's word is true, and is to be trusted, and that faith is intellectual,
emotional and volitional. The result is a most stimulating work.

PETER BARNES
Minister, Revesby Presbyterian Church, Revesby, New South Wales, Australia
Lecturer in Church History, Christ College, Sydney

'People are ultimately unknowable apart from their words,' says Layton Talbert, author of *The Trustworthiness of God's Words*. If you want to come to know God, His words are essential to the process. And the strength of Talbert's book—like his strength as a classroom teacher—is that he marshals so many of God's words as he teaches about their trustworthiness. In other words, Talbert does not merely list the usual prooftexts (though there'd be nothing wrong with that!) and draw out their implications; no, he demonstrates in concrete text after text within Scripture that God's words are trustworthy. Talbert not only trusts God's words, he models that truth by rooting it in careful examination of those words.

MARK WARD
Editor of Faithlife's Bible Study Magazine
Author of *Authorized: The Use and Misuse of the King James Bible*

Can we rely on God to keep His word? All Christians would answer this question positively, but too often we live as if we don't really believe what we affirm. Layton Talbert helps to strengthen our wavering faith by showing us how and why God's words are absolutely trustworthy. The author then shows how a clear understanding of God's trustworthiness affects our everyday lives. This book is thoroughly biblical and deeply theological, but it is also highly readable. I would have no hesitation in handing Talbert's book to an ordinary church member—and I probably will!

KEVIN BAUDER
Research Professor of Systematic Theology, Central Baptist Theological
Seminary, Plymouth, Minnesota
Author of several books including
Baptist Distinctives and New Testament Church Order

In *The Trustworthiness of God's Words* Layton Talbert focuses on the importance of trusting the very words of God. The result is a book that teaches, encourages, challenges, and exhorts believers to trust everything God has said, and to respond to God with lives that say Amen! to all His words. Written in a very accessible style with helpful practical applications, this book (which includes an outstanding summary of the Kingdom of God on earth for worldview context), ought to be in the library of every Christian and re-read at least annually.

CRAIG HARTMAN
Director of Shalom Ministries, Brooklyn, New York
Author of *Through Jewish Eyes*

If God is a God of truth, then surely his words must be true and truthful (John 17:17). This new book by Layton Talbert emphasizes the integrity of the spoken words of the Living God. Christians may find comfort in these words and can do so because God always speaks truth; whatever He says can be counted on to be true. This helpful study shows that the very integrity of God is at stake in the veracity of His words. They are true because he is true. There is great comfort in the truthfulness of God's words!

JEFF STRAUB
Independent scholar and semi-retired professor
of Historical Theology, Plymouth, Minnesota

Christians recognize that God is jealous for his glory, but we sometimes forget that God is also jealous for his integrity. In *The Trustworthiness of God's Words*, Layton Talbert helpfully reminds us that God's glory is at stake if we don't trust what God has said, since the person of God is inseparable from his words. Yet Talbert does not try to guilt us into trusting God; rather, he meticulously shows from Scripture itself that God is true to his word, and that great blessings and comfort come to those who trust him. Deeply biblical and thoroughly pastoral, this book is a must-read for every Christian.

SCOTT ANIOL
Executive Vice President and Editor-in-Chief of G3 Ministries
Author of several books including *By the Waters of Babylon:
Worship in a Post-Christian Culture*

What Layton writes is intended for you to firmly plant your faith on the solid, immoveable rock of God's Word. Amen!

STEVE PETTIT
President of Bob Jones University, Greenville, South Carolina

The

TRUSTWORTHINESS
of GOD'S WORDS

*Why the Reliability of Every Word
from God Matters*

LAYTON TALBERT

Scripture quotations have been taken from the *Holy Bible, New King James Version,* copyright © 1982 by Thomas Nelson Publishers. Used by permission. All rights reserved. See following abbreviations list below indicating other versions of the Holy Bible employed where appropriate.

Paperback ISBN 978-1-5271-0790-8
Ebook ISBN 978-1-5271-0864-6

10 9 8 7 6 5 4 3 2 1

Published in 2022
by
Christian Focus Publications Ltd,
Geanies House, Fearn, Ross-shire,
IV20 1TW, Great Britain.

www.christianfocus.com

A CIP catalogue record for this book is available
from the British Library.

Cover design by
Rubner Durais

Printed by
Bell & Bain, Glasgow

Contents

Abbreviations

CJB   The Complete Jewish Bible (1998)

ESV   English Standard Version (2007 update)

HCSB Holman Christian Standard Bible (2004)

KJV   King James Version

LXX   Septuagint (Brenton, 1986)

NASB New American Standard Bible (1995 update)

NCV   New Century Version (2005)

NET   New English Translation (2005)

NIV   New International Version (2011)

NJB   New Jerusalem Bible (1985)

NKJV New King James Version (1982)

NLT   New Living Translation (1996)

1
What This Book Is (and Isn't) About

This is not a book about the inspiration of the Bible. It is not an apologetic defense of the books of the canon. It is not a book about how we can know the Bible is the Word of God. Those are all important topics that have been ably addressed elsewhere.[1] The focus of this book, though related and complementary to all those themes, is different.

This is a book about God's jealousy for His integrity, His passion to be believed on the basis of His words alone. It is about the trustworthiness of God's words in the Bible. Throughout Scripture God expresses His determination to be known as the God who keeps His words. He has resolved that every person and nation will see and confess that all His words are reliable down to every last syllable, jot, and tittle. Learning to trust a God who is sovereign and in control, especially in the ache and throb of life, means hanging on to the conviction that every word He speaks is utterly dependable.

Open the Bible and the first thing that tumbles out is a presupposition, a foundational assumption: 'In the beginning, God ....' The Bible never argues rationally or philosophically for the existence of God; it simply assumes it. Similarly, this book makes no attempt to argue that the Bible communicates the words of God; it is written from the presupposition that the Bible is God's Word—or, as I prefer

---

1. Just to give a recent example for each category, see Kevin DeYoung, *Taking God at His Word: Why the Bible Is Knowable, Necessary, and Enough, and What That Means for You and Me* (Crossway, 2014); Michael Kruger, *Canon Revisited: Establishing the Origins and Authority of the New Testament Books* (Crossway, 2012); John Piper, *A Peculiar Glory: How the Christian Scriptures Reveal Their Complete Truthfulness* (Crossway, 2016).

to express it, God's *words*. That language is my way of making the general specific, and I will stick to it throughout the book. If you are not already persuaded of the divine origin and content of the Bible, it is not my purpose to persuade you of that here. Again, many other books designed to argue that very point are already available. My purpose here is to persuade believers not only to believe the *logos* (the revelation or message) of God but to trust the *rhemata* (the revelations or sayings) of God, the individual statements He makes in that revelation, all the words within the Word—in short, to actually live by every word that proceeds from the mouth of God (Matt. 4:4).

So, my intended audience is not the unbeliever, though I think God could use much of this book convincingly in an unbeliever's life. Nor am I targeting academicians, though I hope what I've written will profit such an audience since I have labored to make it academically informed and competent. I am writing for the Church, the people of God at large—the housewife who finds herself doubting God's assurances to provide for the needs of His people, the young father wrestling with the character of God when his child is diagnosed with a terminal illness, the senior wondering about God's promised presence to the end of her days, the high school student whose faith is intimidated when unbelieving teachers mock Scripture, the undergraduate or seminarian tempted to follow scholarly interpretations that undermine the words that God chose to express Himself.

For me as a teacher, documentation and explanation are non-negotiable. I have, however, traded the extensive endnotes of my previous books for fewer and (usually) briefer footnotes, and a simplified documentation system. I have tried to cite works that are generally more accessible than abstruse volumes of interest only to scholars, though the latter are cited when necessary. Corroborative or elaborative material that would clutter the text but is still important to interested readers is incorporated in brief appendixes.

Also, I am not of the opinion that the teacher's (or writer's) job is always to 'put the cookies on the bottom shelf.' To quote C. S. Lewis, 'I do not think the average reader is such a fool.' On the other hand, to place them out of reach is in no one's interest either. So I try to aim for the middle shelf. My experiences as a teacher convince me that a learner—whether sitting in class at a desk or in an armchair with a book—is best served by being stretched a little. I don't think readers resent being treated like adults and challenged to understand the Bible and its Author better.

The contents are arranged into three major divisions. Part 1 lays down essential scriptural foundations. What, exactly, do we mean by trust and is it distinguished in any way from belief (Chapter 2)? Where and how does God express this 'jealousy' for His integrity (Chapter 3)? In what ways and passages does God demonstrate the value He places—and that He expects us to place—on His words (Chapter 4)? How do we know that God is trustworthy, and how does that relate to His other attributes (Chapter 5)? What does Jesus have to say about the trustworthiness of God's words (Chapter 6)?

Part 2 then explores specific practical applications of the trust-worthiness of God's words, like what it means to trust God's testimony of past history (Chapter 7), God's assurances about His own character (Chapter 8), and even God's most astonishing promises (Chapter 9). What does trusting God's words look like in real life (Chapter 10) and how has it played out in the experience of God's people historically (Chapter 11)?

Part 3 invites the reader to a wide-angle view of the Bible. Chapters 12-14 unfold God's overarching narrative of reality in terms of His primary metaphor for that reality throughout Scripture: the kingdom. The only proper response to the truth this book seeks to display is captured in a single biblical word (Chapter 15). Finally, the Review & Reflect questions at the end of most chapters are suggestive, optional opportunities to process, recover, apply, or expand on principles or passages covered in the chapter, whether in a personal or group study setting.

I will confess that in the writing of this book I was often torn by opposing impressions. At times it seemed that what I was writing was, on one level, so simple and so obvious it hardly needed to be written. But that sense was always quickly countered by the sudden awareness that God jealously defends His integrity in so many ways and places, that the integrity of His words is obviously deeply important to God, and that this theme therefore has the profoundest implications for the glory of God.

God charges His prophets, '… let him who has my word speak my word faithfully' (Jeremiah 23:28 ESV). Or to be pedantically literal, *let him who has my word, word my word faithfully*. However imperfect my efforts, that's my ambition as a teacher and as a writer. My aim in this book is a simple one: to magnify God's integrity and His zeal to be known as the God who keeps His words, and to magnify those twin themes in a way that encourages and nourishes in His people a confident trust in every word that proceeds from the mouth of God.

God has tucked into every dell and dingle of the Bible this emphasis on the trustworthiness of His words. He is passionate about displaying and sharing His glory with His people. That, as Jonathan Edwards put it, is 'the end for which God created the world.'[2] Part of God's passion for His glory is His passion for His integrity—that He means what He says, that He has said exactly what He meant to say, and that He will unfailingly do all that He has said. We glorify God and vindicate His integrity when we trust His words entirely—all of them.

> 'Tis so sweet to trust in Jesus,
> Just to take him at his word,
> Just to rest upon his promise,
> Just to know, 'Thus saith the Lord.'[3]

Trusting Jesus is not a vague, indefinable spiritual experience. Trusting Jesus has specific, identifiable content. To trust in Jesus is to trust His words, to rest on His promises, to be confident in every 'thus says the Lord.'

Oh, for grace to trust Him more.

---

2. The most accessible version of Edwards's magisterial essay, 'The End for Which God Created the World,' is in John Piper's *God's Passion for His Glory: Living the Vision of Jonathan Edwards* (Crossway, 2006).

3. Lyrics by Louisa M. R. Stead, published in 1882, after her husband drowned trying to rescue a drowning boy.

PART ONE:
Theological Foundations

2
Trusting God's Words

I trust in Your word.
Psalm 119:42

Inner peace. An internet search of that phrase turns up over twenty million results. Everyone wants it. The most popular sites list five, or seven, or seventeen steps for attaining this coveted yet elusive condition. Most of these steps orbit like moons around the planet Self—loving yourself, valuing yourself, being good to yourself, being proud of yourself, doing things that make you happy. Self is the sinner's substitute for God. You are your own biggest idol.

In a sense, this is a book about inner peace. It would probably sell better if I had put those words in the title, but that would create a misimpression. Because important as our inner peace is—not just to us, but to God—it is a by-product, not an end. The end is something far more grand and satisfying.

What Does It Mean to Trust?

The Bible is God's own testimony to past occurrences, present conditions, and future events. It is our only window into God's perspective of reality. When we talk about the concept of the trustworthiness of God's words, the theological term for this is the Bible's *infallibility*. Put simply, infallible means un-fail-able. God's words

> **Infallible**—unfailing; unable to fail.

never misinform us about past occurrences, they never misrepresent present realities, and when it comes to future promises or prophecies they will never malfunction.

The assertion that God's words are trustworthy is only a clinical canon in a catechism, however, until it impacts my personal *response* to those words. God's trustworthiness means that I am invited, obliged, and compelled not merely to *believe His* words but also to *trust* them. What does that mean?

Learning from the Reformers

Protestant theologians understood that all believing is not the same—a conclusion that is both intuitive and biblical.[1] Sometimes they used Latin words (in brackets below) to distinguish between different components of faith.[2]

Faith is, first of all, a kind of knowledge [*notitia*]. The assumption that faith is the opposite of knowledge is demonstrably mistaken. Everyone, down to the most anti-supernaturalistic atheist or evolutionist, believes things he has never personally witnessed, experienced, or calculated out—and operates on those beliefs as a form of knowledge. The reliability of that knowledge depends on two things: (a) the accuracy of the evidence itself, and (b) the correctness of one's interpretation of that evidence. Many legal court cases demonstrate not only that 'evidence' can be planted, twisted, or partial but also that juries and judges weighing the same evidence can come to very different conclusions.

In the case of biblical faith, the content of belief is not what I desire to be true, nor is it defined by my personal imagination of what is or ought to be true. The content of biblical faith is defined by the words of God, the Scripture itself. Paul implies this component of faith as he recollects the beginning of the Thessalonian church, 'when you received the word of God, which you heard from us' (1 Thess. 2:13). Faith begins with knowledge: acquaintance with certain necessary facts. In Jesus' parable of the soils, the first kind of hearer—the hardened wayside soil—doesn't even make it this far. He 'hears the

---

1. There is a kind of faith that justified Abraham (James 2:23), a kind of faith that that does not save (James 2:14), and even a kind of faith possessed by demons (James 2:19).

2. Cf. Turretin 1994, pp. 560-64; à Brakel 1993, pp. 263-66, 270ff. For a more accessible summary, see Sproul 1995, pp. 75-91.

word' but 'does not understand it' (Matt. 13:19) because it lies atop an unreceptive, uninterested heart and penetrates no deeper. So 'the devil comes and takes away the word out of their hearts, lest they should believe and be saved' (Luke 8:12).

Second, biblical faith doesn't stop with merely knowing what God says; it also acknowledges (assents) that what God says is so [*assensus*]. Paul implies this component of faith when he adds that the Thessalonians who heard God's word from the apostles 'accepted it not as the word of men but as ... the word of God' (1 Thess. 2:13 ESV). You can see the progression from knowledge to acknowledgement, from awareness to assent. Another example of this level of response is the second kind of soil in Jesus' parable, represented by 'the ones on the rock ... who, when they hear the word, receive it with joy. But these have no root; they believe for a while, and in time of testing fall away' (Luke 8:13 ESV). There is an immediate and even emotional reception of what they hear. The 'rock' is a reference not to stony soil but to a shelf of stone just beneath the surface; that's why they 'have no root,' no depth of commitment. [3] The response, though emotional, is shallow, superficial, and temporary. Jesus indicates that this kind of response falls short of genuine or lasting faith.

A third component of biblical faith is a personal persuasion that acts [*fiducia*]. Full-grown faith is confident in the reliability of God's words to the point that it operates on the basis of what God says. That's why Paul caps off his Thessalonian reminiscence by noting that the word of God— which they heard [*notitia*] and acknowledged as divinely authoritative [*assensus*]—'performs its work in you who believe' (1 Thess. 2:13 NASB). That's *fiducia*, when one acts on what he has both heard and acknowledged, by putting his faith in (entrusting himself to) God and His word. (That's why older theologians used to refer to a genuine Christian believer as a *fiduciary*.) Returning to Jesus' parable, the fourth example is 'good soil.' These, Jesus says, are 'the ones who, after hearing the word, cling to it with an honest and good heart, and bear fruit with

---

3. The translation 'rocky' (NASB, NIV) is unfortunate. The text literally reads 'the ones upon the rock [singular],' describing a thin layer of soil sufficient for the seed to sprout initially but not to survive (Cranfield 1985, p. 149).

steadfast endurance' (Luke 8:15 NET). Personally and whole-heartedly embracing God's words—that's trust. And that's life-changing.

In the context of salvation, it's not some higher sense of complete trust [*fiducia*] that saves apart from knowing truth [*notitia*] and acknowledging its truthfulness [*assensus*]. 'None of these elements, even *fiducia*, taken alone or separately, is a sufficient condition for saving faith. All three are essential to it' (Sproul 1995, p. 75). All three are necessary components of a faith that saves.

Components of Biblical Faith

Knowledge	Assent	Trust
Notitia	*Assensus*	*Fiducia*
One can have knowledge without assent or trust	One can have assent without correct knowledge or personal trust	One can have trust without correct knowledge or complete assent

So is faith intellectual? Or emotional? Or volitional? The answer is yes. Saving faith is more than just knowledge or even assent; both knowledge and assent must find their way to *activating the will to choose to trust* what is known and assented, 'to cling to it with an honest and good heart'. In that sense, faith is ultimately seated in the will (à Brakel 1993, p. 278). The will is like the third number to the combination lock of the human heart. It is possible to dissect the process of faith in order to isolate and differentiate between our faculties of intellect, emotion, and volition, so that we can better understand the individual role played by each; but they cannot be 'fully distinguished when man is operative' because in reality they all function together.[4]

How is a field tilled? By the farmer, the plow, or the horse? (Or, if you prefer a more modern image, by the farmer, the disc, or the tractor?) None of them individually, nor even any two of them together, can till the field; the field is plowed only when all three work in unison.

---

4. 'Applying this to faith, this means that the believing soul is engaged in understanding, willing, and desiring. When a man believes, all his faculties function simultaneously' (à Brakel 1993, pp. 270-71).

Moving from Saving Faith to Sanctifying Faith

Theological discussions of the nature of faith have historically focused specifically on defining saving faith. The same is true, however, of what might be called sanctifying faith. Understanding the components of faith is just as important for Christian living as it is for becoming a believer in the first place.

> **Sanctification**—set apart to God and made more like Christ.

Unfortunately, becoming a believer doesn't mean that I automatically now fully trust everything I read in the Bible. I should; but often I don't. Believers still struggle with coming to trust all of God's words and living out that trust in their daily experience. Because even as a believer I still carry around inside me a fallen nature (what the New Testament calls 'the flesh') that is incurably disinclined to trust God. Faith is not a static, inanimate commodity. Faith needs to grow (see Luke 17:5; 2 Cor. 10:15; 2 Thess. 1:3).

> *Trust is defined by our choices and revealed in our behavior.*

Believers never permanently plateau so that they always make decisions and react to situations in a way that displays a steady, unbroken trust in God. Even the mighty Elijah tumbled from the summit of an intrepid trust in God (1 Kings 18) to bolting at the impotent threats of an irate queen (1 Kings 19).[5] When Elijah fled for his life into the wilderness, God's response was frank and succinct: 'What are you doing here, Elijah?' The question was pregnant with innuendo: *You can trust me to rescue you from hundreds of pagan prophets but not from one wicked woman? You can trust me to deliver a bolt out of the blue to ignite wet wood and lick up ditchwater, but not to douse a little pagan indignation?* How could Elijah fall so far so fast, from fearless trust to fright and flight? Because, as James reminds us, he was only human just like us (James 5:17).

We have an internal barometer that measures our trust (or lack of it). Its reading registers the condition of our spirit on a spectrum

---

5. For a different take on this chapter in Elijah's life see Davis 2007, pp. 253-70. Davis' thoughtful and text-focused exposition is a good corrective to some excesses, though I don't find all of his analysis convincing.

ranging from peace to panic, revealing our soul's sense of security or anxiety. Those internal readings inevitably transmit to our attitude, our demeanor, even our countenance. Consider two brief illustrations.

The first illustration comes from the New Testament. The Apostle Paul, on his way to Rome as a prisoner, was convinced that any attempt to sail on into the tail end of the year would be fraught with danger, damage, and probably loss of life (Acts 27:10). Sure enough, the ship sailed into a storm so terrific that 'all hope that we would be saved was finally given up' (27:20). But the Lord sent an angel to assure him that though the ship itself would be lost, no lives would be (27:23-24). Paul's personal belief in those words from God (27:25) had a powerful impact not only on his own spirit, emotions, and actions, but on those of the ship's crew and passengers as well. On the basis of his own confidence in God's words, he urged them not to be afraid (27:24) but to take courage (27:22, 25). After two tempestuous weeks at sea, Paul pressed them to eat some food and assured them that 'not a hair will fall from the head of any of you' (27:34). Then, giving 'thanks to God in the presence of them all,' Paul began to eat (27:35), as though they were in no more danger than if they were sitting safely ashore. The basis of Paul's trust was the words of God. The effect of Paul's trust? 'They were all encouraged, and also took food themselves' (27:36). The whole passage is richly colored with the emotional impact of trust; it shows up in hues of confidence, security, relief, and reassurance.

When we are truly trusting God's words, it has a transforming impact inside and out.

The second illustration comes from the Old Testament. When the barren Hannah went to the tabernacle to pray for a son, she was miserable, tearful, grieved, and in bitterness of soul over her childlessness (1 Sam. 1:6-8, 10, 15). But when Eli the high priest blessed her with the assurance that God would grant her petition (1:17), she 'went her way and ate, and her face was no longer sad' (1:18). Hannah did not merely believe that God *could* (i.e., was able to) give her a child; she was persuaded that God *would* hear and grant her prayer for a child, based on bona fide word from God's priestly spokesman. Her trust totally transformed not just her spirit

22

but even her countenance, *even though nothing in her circumstances had changed*. When we are truly trusting the words of God, it has a transforming impact inside and out.

'Believing' and 'Trusting' the Bible

The fact that even English uses two different words with distinct nuances—sometimes interchangeably, but sometimes not—confirms our innate understanding that there *can* be a difference between belief and trust. Believing and trusting are twins; and like twins, there are distinctions as well as similarities.

Nuance—shade of meaning.

As in English, the Hebrew Old Testament has two different words to highlight the potential distinction between believing and trusting. The Greek Septuagint recognized and preserved the difference between those two Hebrew words. It routinely renders the primary Hebrew word for *believing* (*'āman*) with the primary Greek word for *believing* (*pisteuō*). But the Old Testament word for *trusting* (*bātach*) God

Septuagint—a pre-Christian Greek translation of the Hebrew Old Testament.

is always rendered with the Greek word for *hoping* (*elpizō*)—a word that the Bible usually uses to denote not just optimism but confident anticipation (Oswalt 1980, I:101-02). The Greek New Testament collapses the ideas of *believe* and *trust* into a single word (*pisteuō*).[6] The fact that the New Testament routinely merges both nuances doesn't mean that the emotional component of trust is dropped but, rather, that it is folded into what becomes the primary New Testament expression for our response to God's words.

Believing (*'āman*) is predominantly an act of *thinking* and deals with processing information (facts or claims). Trusting (*bātach*) is the choice to act on that knowledge; in that sense it is an exercise of the

---

6. Though the NT predominantly relies on *pisteuō* to convey both *believing* and *trusting*, it also occasionally employs distinctive language for trust including words for *hope* (*elpizō* and cognates—John 5:45; 2 Cor. 1:10; Eph. 1:12; 1 Tim. 4:10, 5:5; 1 Pet. 3:5) and *persuasion* or *confidence* (*peithō* and cognates—Luke 18:9; 2 Cor. 1:9, 3:4).

will, as I mentioned earlier. But trusting also denotes an emotional experience, 'that sense of well-being and security which results from having something or someone in whom to place confidence,' and 'stress[es] the feeling of being safe or secure' (Oswalt 1980, I:101). That's the inner peace I talked about at the beginning of the chapter.

You can genuinely believe something factually and yet refuse to trust it personally. It's not at all uncommon to use 'believe' in a technical, impersonal, creedal sense that doesn't match my actions or attitudes. Some people believe that airplanes can and do fly safely and successfully every hour of every day, but they would never dream of actually getting on one. Their refusal to set foot on an airliner does not mean that they don't *really* believe that planes can fly; they *know* they can. It's an issue of trusting personally what they believe factually.

Greek scholar Daniel Wallace describes how his once vibrant, personal relationship with the Lord was gradually replaced by a kind of clinical orthodoxy.[7] He got in the habit of approaching the Bible from a purely professional and academic perspective that eventually depersonalized his relationship to God's word and, consequently, to God Himself. It took the providential piling up of painful trials in his family life for Wallace to discover that there was no solace in the mere technicalities of the biblical languages. God graciously used affliction to reawaken in him a thirst for a relationship with God Himself. That relationship is the heart of genuine Christianity; and the heart of that relationship is the Scripture. The Bible is a profoundly relational document. But when it is isolated from God as an object for icy exegetical dissection, he says, 'our stance changes from "I trust in" to "I believe that"' (Wallace 2005, p. 9). Believing and trusting are not necessarily the same thing. And the difference can be life-altering.

So, is believing inferior to trusting? No, that's not the point. But it is possible to believe without trusting—like the guy who sees planes overhead all day long yet refuses to fly, or the housewife who fusses

---

7. Wallace describes this personal experience in his preface to *Who's Afraid of the Holy Spirit?* See Wallace 2005.

and frets over the bills even though she believes that God provides for His own, or the father who subscribes to the doctrine

Trusting completes believing.

that God sovereignly rules over the affairs of men and yet is constantly out of sorts over the prosperity of the wicked in society. Believing is incomplete without trusting. Trust *completes* belief.

Trusting is a willingness to *rely* on what is believed that produces a sense of *confidence, safety, security, optimism*. In fact, those are the very words used to translate the Hebrew noun *trust* (*betech*). They are all words of *feeling*; but they are feelings that are properly grounded in thinking and believing the right things. Our sense of confidence, safety, security, and optimism registers the degree to which we not only believe the word of God but trust the words of God.

So, trust is both an action and a result. It is deciding to lean all your weight on a word from God; that's the action. And it is the serenity, security, and confidence you experience when you do; that's the result.

Trusting What, Exactly?

This sense of security or optimism is not, however, merely an abstract, subjective, nebulous, indefinable 'mood.' Our ground for trusting God is not what we think Him to be, or assume He should be. Our only ground for trusting God is what He says He is like and what He says He will do. The process works like this, from the bottom:

Trust/Confidence/Security in God

↑

Belief in God

↑

Revelation of God

↑

Character of God

Trusting God is the fruit of believing God; and the only way to believe God is to believe His revelation—what He says about Himself and about everything else. And the ultimate basis for believing and trusting God's words is His character (ultimately, His trustworthiness).[8] 'Unlike pagan religions where unremitted anxiety was the rule, the Hebrew religion knew a God whose chief characteristic was faithfulness and trustworthiness' (Oswalt 1980, I:102). The Christian religion is the sequel and heir to the Hebrew religion, authored by the same God. That's why this book is focused on finding your safety and security, your confidence and optimism, in the God whose *words* are trustworthy because He is.

Soteriology—what the Bible teaches about salvation.

It may help to return to the context of salvation for an illustration. In soteriological terms, believing God's words secures salvation, whereas trusting God's words produces *assurance* of salvation.

SALVATION	
Belief → *Deliverance*	Trust → *Assurance*
Result: Factual Security	Result: Felt Confidence

Someone objects, 'Belief isn't really belief if I'm anxious or apprehensive about the proposition I say I believe.' If that's true, then anyone who ever wrestles with assurance of salvation cannot be saved, because 'belief isn't belief if I'm anxious or apprehensive'; and if they don't believe, then by definition they aren't saved. But both Scripture and experience suggest that something else may be going on in such cases; and often it is a disconnect between belief and trust.

Yet the objection makes a valid point because, as I argued above, saving faith *does* involve trust. Sometimes, however, such faith can develop a hairline fracture between trusting the propositions of the gospel (that God *can* save and this is how He does it) and trusting the personal effect of the gospel (that God really has saved *me*). Hairline fractures are slight, but they can still be intensely painful and debilitating. Also known as stress fractures, these fatigue-induced fractures are caused by repeated stress over time. That's a pretty

---

8. This is explored in detail in Chapters 3 ('God's Jealousy for His Integrity') and 5 ('The Theological Foundation for God's Trustworthiness').

accurate way to describe the spiritual phenomena that can contribute to doubting one's salvation.[9]

That's why some people who truly believe the gospel can wrestle with doubts about their salvation, sometimes for years. John Bunyan did; just read his autobiography *Grace Abounding to the Chief of Sinners*. Lots of things can contribute to this, but one is a failure to *trust* in the truth of the Gospel despite *belief* in the facts of the Gospel. It is one thing to believe God's Word—mentally, intellectually, and quite genuinely. It can be quite another to trust God's words, to lean all your weight on the specific statements of God about what He has done, what He will do, and what He is like. When you do that, you experience the rest, security, confidence, and peace that comes from the persuasion that He truly is what He says and that He will really do what He says. Both of those are wrapped up in a biblically robust understanding of faith. But it is possible to have one without the other. Put another way, it's one thing to believe that God *can* but another thing altogether to believe (trust) that He *will*. We'll explore that concept further in a later chapter.

The larger point here is that the ultimate object of belief and trust is God. But the crucial link between my belief/trust and God is the *words* of God. Why? Because they are the only means by which I can know God Himself.

So the ultimate object of trust is the person and character of God; but the immediate object of trust is the words of God by which He communicates His person and character. This book is devoted to fleshing out that idea. For the sake of present illustration, however, one passage will serve: Psalm 56.

A Madman's Trust in God's Words

While hiding from King Saul, David decided to hole up in the Philistine city of Gath (Goliath's hometown). It was a brilliant strategy because it was the last place Saul would ever expect David to go. But it was

---

9. Those phenomena, usually patterns of action or thinking over time, may include tolerance of sin, an excessive tendency towards introspection, a misunderstanding of the total grace of the gospel, or any number of other causes.

also risky; he might be identified as the guy who knocked off their champion. Sure enough, someone recognized him.

David had to react in a heartbeat. 'So he changed his behavior before them, feigned madness in their hands, scratched on the doors of the gate, and let his saliva fall down on his beard' (1 Sam. 21:13). It was a crazy idea (literally). But it worked!

We might be tempted to credit David's hair-breadth escape to quick wits and consummate theatrical skill. The narrative makes no attempt to interpret David's deliverance to divine intervention, direct or indirect. That interpretation is left for Psalm 56. And David had no doubts about it: it was God.

The ancient subtitle to Psalm 56 links this Davidic poem to the time 'when the Philistines captured him in Gath.' Listen to the refrain he folds into this hymn of praise for God's protection:

> When I am afraid, I put my trust in You. **In God, whose word I praise, in God I trust**; I shall not be afraid. What can flesh do to me? (56:3-4 ESV)

> Then my enemies will turn back in the day when I call. This I know, that God is for me. **In God, whose word I praise, in the LORD, whose word I praise, in God I trust**; I shall not be afraid. What can man do to me? (56:9-11 ESV).

David blends his trust (the word is *bātach*) in God with his praise for God's words. What's the connection? The *object* of his trust is God Himself, but the *content* of his trust is God's word (Kidner 1973, p. 203).

| *Trust replaces fear.* | Because God is known for keeping His promises, 'to praise God's word is to praise the very attribute that the one praying is depending on for his deliverance'—His trustworthiness to do |

what He has said (Tanner 2014, p. 484). And the praise he trumpets for God's word in 56:4 he repeats *twice* in 56:10.

By the way, notice what his trust replaces: 'In God, whose word I praise, in the LORD whose word I praise, in God I trust; **I shall not be afraid.**' Fear is not primarily an intellectual experience but an emotional experience. Why will he not be afraid? Because he doesn't just believe in God, he *trusts* God. And the emotion of trust replaces the emotion of fear.

> Putting his fear aside, the psalmist praises the promises of the Lord. After all, trusting in the Lord requires a prior commitment to the revelation of God in his Word. ... He rests on the promises of the Lord, as he praises the Lord of promise (VanGemeren 1991, 5:399, 401).

You can hear the explicit connection between trust and God's words—'the revelation of God in his Word ... the promises of the Lord'. What promises? At the very least, David had God's promise that he would succeed Saul as the next king of Israel (1 Sam. 16:1-13). It was God's words that informed and fed his trust in God.

'You just need to trust in the Lord,' someone may exhort. Fine, but how do I do that? What about Him do I trust? Who is He? What is He like? What has He done? What does He promise to do? There is only one way to know and one place to find the answers to any of those questions—the words of God Himself. We trust God by trusting His words. Trust in God that is not grounded in the words of God is fantasy.

What Does It Mean Not to Trust God's Words?

What is the alternative to trusting God's words? The opposite of trusting God is not trusting nothing. No one trusts nothing. Life is not livable without trust. Everyone trusts someone or something—it's either God, or self, or someone else. The opposite of trusting God is trusting the wrong thing.

No one trusts nothing.

C. S. Lewis captures the spirit of self-trust in *The Last Battle*. Jaded by a series of charades, the dwarves are determined never again to be 'taken in' by (in other words, trust) anyone. They've even become agnostic about the reality of Aslan himself, withdrawing like turtles into a shell of inflexible skepticism. Their mantra is, 'The dwarves are for the dwarves!' There is hardly a sadder image in Lewis's final chronicle of Narnia than the dwarves' self-willed blindness that mistrusts everything and everyone *except* their utterly blind and erroneous selves.

> 'You see,' said Aslan. 'They will not let us help them. They have chosen cunning instead of belief. Their prison is only in their own minds, yet they are in that prison; and so afraid of being taken in that they cannot be taken out' (Lewis 1970, p. 148).[10]

'Cunning instead of belief.' The Bible has a great deal to say not only about trusting God but also about the wrong things we are inclined to trust instead of God. The potential objects of misplaced confidence are legion. Some of them we can relate to immediately—like trusting in wealth (Mark 10:23), or your own righteousness (Ezek. 33:13). Others, at first glance, may not seem to apply to us.

For example, the Bible prohibits trust in Egypt, chariots, idols, swords, and bows. Trusting in these is not a big temptation for us. Or is it? The reason that these seem so exotic and inapplicable to us is because God was making very direct application to His original audience in their time and culture. The details may differ for us, but the underlying issues are still the same because people are still the same; so we're inclined to put our trust in, not the same things, but the same *kinds* of things.

These days you'd be crazy to put your trust in Egypt (Isa. 36:9), but we can still be inclined to put our confidence in the weaponry (Isa. 31:1, 'horses and chariots') and military might of countries that seem to us to be invincible (Hosea 10:13 ESV, 'the multitude of your warriors'). You've probably never felt convicted about trusting in 'fortified' cities (Deut. 28:52). But what about other things you've put in place to protect yourself from physical danger or material loss? Locks and bolts, state-of-the-art security systems, the Glock 9mm in the bedside table drawer, salary, employment, bank accounts, insurance

---

10. Not all failure to trust takes the form of 'cunning instead of belief.' But if you want a biblical example of that same phenomenon, read Isaiah 7. King Ahaz, a wicked king but under the protections of the Davidic covenant, was in danger of a conspiracy to dethrone him. God graciously promised him deliverance, and offered Ahaz his choice of a miraculous confirmatory sign. The king's reply was 'cunning' cloaked in the garb of humility: 'I will not ask, and I will not put the LORD to the test' (7:12). In reality, he had no interest in trusting God. He already had his own strategy for dealing with the threat; he was trusting in a bribed military alliance with Assyria.

policies, retirement investments. None of these are wrong. But relying on any of them as the basis of your confidence and security is wrong. That's what God is saying when He challenges the locus of our trust in a passage like Deuteronomy 28:52.

Locus—the place where something is situated.

Probably no one in our Western culture thinks of himself as an idolater; that's only for pagans in poverty-stricken, education-deprived foreign countries. But trusting in idols (Isa. 42:17) is merely shorthand for finding our security in anything other than, or more than, God—especially anything devised, created, and guaranteed by fellow fallen mortals to protect us and provide our needs. In the end only God does that. We in the educated, industrialized West are just as idolatrous as anyone else anywhere else. Our idols, where we ground our trust and find our confidence, are just more sophisticated and less obvious.

Scripture has a great deal to say about trusting in the wrong things. As in all application, therefore, the key is to identify the point(s) of contact between the historical particular and the modern parallel. In the list of passages below, the concept of trust is central; God warns people about the things they tend to trust instead of Him and His words. Can you identify with any of these as things from which you derive your security or peace of mind?

The opposite of not trusting God is not trusting nothing, but trusting the wrong thing.

- Wealth—Ps. 49:6, 52:7; Prov. 11:28; Mark 10:23; 1 Tim. 6:17

- Successful business practices that are shady or extortive—Ps. 62:10

- A 'cancel culture' mentality that shuts down those who speak truth and practices deceit—Isa. 30:12[11]

- Slick excuses and self-justification of sin—Isa. 59:4

- The absence of chastisement that makes you think that your sin is okay with, or overlooked by, God—Isa. 47:10

---

11. The context of Isa. 30:12 is both religious and political, and surprisingly modern. See Isa. 30:1-11.

- Lies of prophets, preachers, or anyone who contradicts God's words—Jer. 7:4, 8, 28:15, 29:31

- Influential people—Ps. 118:9, 146:3

- Powerful nations—Isa. 30:2, 36:9

- Military might—Isa. 31:1

- Your own plans or assets—Hosea 10:13

- Your own skill or strategies—Ps. 44:6

- Your own idols and ideas—Isa. 42:17; Jer. 13:25; Pss. 115:8, 135:18; Hab. 2:18

- Your own righteousness—Ezek. 33:13

- Your own understanding—Prov. 3:5

- Your own gifts, success, or prosperity—Ezek. 16:15; cf. Jer. 49:4; Amos 6:1

- Your own self-protective measures—Deut. 28:52; Jer. 5:17

- Yourself—Prov. 28:25-26; 2 Cor. 1:9

- People—Ps. 118:8; Jer. 17:5; cf. Jer. 9:4, Micah 7:5

A few of these objects of trust are evil in themselves, but most are not. The point is not that it is always wrong to make use of any of these things, but that it is always wrong to ground your trust and find your security in any of them.[12]

Any decision to trust anything or anyone other than God is a decision to mistrust God. Any decision to mistrust God's words is only a decision to trust someone else's words instead. And no one else deserves that honor.

What Does It Look Like to Trust God's Words?

In Psalm 56, David sketches out the concept that trusting God means trusting God's words. In Psalm 37, he inks it in with color and action. What does the life of a person trusting in God's words look like? How

---

12. '[T]he fact is, all trust, except that reposed in the Lord, is trusting that which is without rhyme, reason or reliability' (Motyer 1993, p. 485).

does it impact not just his choices and actions but his attitudes and emotions?

Remember, *trusting* God and His words is inherently emotional. That doesn't mean that trusting God is just a 'feeling' we conjure up. But truly trusting God will have a powerful, settling impact on our emotions and attitudes, especially when we are threatened or battered by life in a fallen world.

David's verbs in Psalm 37 capture trust's emotional dimension. When confronted, frustrated, or even threatened by the apparent success of evil and evil men, three times David counsels against a very natural emotional reaction: 'Don't fret' (37:1, 7, 8). That's easy to say. But how? By choosing to 'trust in the LORD' instead (37:3, 5). Trust replaces the instinct to fret. What does that look like? What practical steps move your soul in that direction? David fills that out with a number of other actions.

Trusting the Lord means *delighting* in the Lord (37:4) rather than agitating over all the surrounding sin. It means *committing your way* to the Lord (37:5) rather than trying to manipulate your circumstances. It means *resting* in the Lord (37:7) rather than ruminating over evil, and *waiting patiently* for Him to act in His way and time (37:7) instead of rashly taking things into your own hands. It means *ceasing from anger* and *forsaking wrath* (37:8) rather than stewing over wrongs and injustices.

Delight, commit, rest, wait patiently, cease from anger, forsake wrath—do you hear how emotionally oriented all these actions are? They all describe that 'inner peace' I talked about at the beginning of the chapter, the sense of well-being, confidence, and security that come from trusting God. And the only way to trust God is by trusting His words. The psalmist's five-step program for real inner peace beats anything you'll find on the internet.

Believing God's Word is the general. Trusting God's words is the specific. Learning how to move our souls from the general (believing God's Word) to the specific (trusting God's words) is a choice but also a process. Learning to trust God's words is the path to the peace and security we crave, and to giving God the full glory that He deserves.

Just how serious and invested is God in defending the reliability of His words? Keep reading.

Review & Reflect

1. What are the three components of biblical faith?

2. The fact that we have two different words—believe and trust—which do not always mean exactly the same thing indicates that there can be a difference between believing and trusting. How would you describe that difference?

3. What is the relationship between believing and trusting?

4. What is the specific object of a believer's trust?

5. What is the opposite of trusting God?

6. What are some of the things you tend to trust rather than God or God's words?

7. Do you relate to anything in the list of objects of misplaced trust? What do the connected passages (and their context) contribute to your understanding of how God feels about trusting in those objects, and why?

8. What are some of the terms that Psalm 37 uses to describe what trusting God looks like? What are some of the opposites of trusting mentioned in the psalm?

3
God's Jealousy for His Integrity

I, the LORD, have spoken it and I will do it.
Ezekiel 36:36

God has resolved to display His glory to every being in every dimension of creation. That's not merely the philosophical conclusion of theologians who want to champion a particular image of God. It's an emphasis that emerges from divine declarations that punctuate the pages of the Bible.

God's 'glory' is the sum of His perfections, all the attributes that make Him the unique and only God.[1] He alone possesses an infinite and inexhaustible supply of energy (omnipotence), a complete awareness of all realities and possibilities past, present, and future (omniscience), and the capacity to be present everywhere at all times (omnipresence).[2] He is unfailingly pure, righteous, and just, yet also patient, compassionate, merciful, and gracious. He is wise and generous, utterly sovereign and yet infinitely self-sacrificial. And He is entirely truthful, reliable, and trustworthy. And in all these qualities and abilities, He never changes (what theologians call immutability).

---

1. For a practical and accessible discussion of the 'glory of God' see Berg 2002, p. 29ff.

2. I have not included passages to support these divine attributes, first because it is beyond the scope and purpose of this book and, second, because there are many books entirely devoted to this subject. See any of the standard systematic theologies by Millard Erickson, Wayne Grudem, Robert Reymond, John Frame, and many others.

His trustworthiness, however, is at the root of our confidence in all His other attributes. We would know almost nothing about Him if He did not tell us. Romans 1:18-20 teaches that creation itself furnishes both internal and external evidence for the existence of a Being of omnipotence and deity. According to Psalm 19:1-4, the sky itself bears eloquent and universal testimony that this Being is glorious. But little else about His actions or character is discernible on the basis of creation alone (what theologians refer to as general revelation).

God's trustworthiness is at the root of our confidence in all His other attributes.

For example, one might infer from all the beauty of the world that this Being must be good, while another observes all the cruelty and suffering in this world and concludes otherwise. Only additional explicit and authoritative revelation from God Himself ('special revelation') can inform us how to correctly interpret everything we see around us—including what He's like. Such additional 'special revelation' (as the theologians call it) need not be exhaustive, but it does need to be reliable.

If this Being is not 'a God of truth' (Deut. 32:4), if what He tells us about Himself is not trustworthy, then we do not know God and cannot know God. We're left to cobble together our own thoughts and hopes into a god of our own devising to join the countless knick-knack deities that cram every nook and cranny in humanity's pantheon.

> A firm belief in God's trustworthiness is essential to any correct theology, for only this can supply the foundation for understanding God's revelation and God's redemptive acts, and for certain and assured faith (Trueman 2002, p. 191).[3]

That's why the Lord zealously displays and jealously guards the integrity of His words. His reputation and His glory rest upon it. This chapter surveys just a few of the passages where God showcases the reliability of His words and explains why it matters so much to Him.

---

3. Trueman is here describing Calvin's view, but its validity extends beyond Calvin.

Narrative Testimony to God's Integrity

We will explore the Bible's testimony in some detail under two broad categories of passages: narrative and prophecy. Narrative passages include assertions of divine integrity from both God and man.

Divine Testimony in Narrative

Historically, God has expressed a compelling interest in demonstrating the integrity of what He says. The panorama of Scripture is spangled with statements and insinuations of God's dependability, and of His determination to prove it, to be known and renowned for it.

Declaring, then Doing

God does not merely act in silence so He can demonstrate His omnipotence. God speaks first, and then acts according to His words 'that you may know that I am the LORD.' This language punctuates the events in the book of Exodus like the refrain to a hymn.

- Moses invites Pharaoh to name the day that he wants God to destroy a plague of frogs. When Pharaoh says, 'Tomorrow,' Moses agrees, 'that you may know that there is no one like the LORD our God' (Exod. 8:10).

- God informs Moses (8:20) that when He sends the plague of flies on Egypt He will exempt Goshen, where His people are, 'that you may know that I am the LORD in the midst of the land' (8:22).

- God tells Moses to inform Pharaoh that He will unleash more plagues on Egypt, 'that you may know that there is none like Me in all the earth' (9:14).

- God explains to Moses that He has hardened Pharaoh's heart in order to display His glory, with the intent 'that you may tell in the hearing of your son and your son's son the mighty things I have done in Egypt and My signs which I have done among them, that you may know that I am the LORD' (10:2).

- God states His intent to defeat Pharaoh and his armies so 'that the Egyptians may know that I am the LORD' (14:4).

God does not merely act and then take credit afterward. He announces what He will do before He does it so that Moses, Pharaoh, the Egyptians, the Israelites, and Israel's future generations will know who He is—the God of all the earth who says what He will do, and then does what He says.

Covenanting, then Keeping

Covenants are one of God's basic building blocks in constructing communicative relationships with His creatures. Built into the covenant concept is the essential ingredient of reliability. Covenants put trustworthiness to the test. Throughout the Old Testament, God constantly demonstrates and reiterates His absolute loyalty to the covenants He has made.

The Noahic Covenant, the first and only covenant expressly made with creation itself (including the animals, Gen. 9:8-17), is also one of the few covenants to incorporate a sign as a visible reminder of the covenant obligation. The sign in this case (the rainbow) is a visual reminder not only to man but also to God: 'and I will look on it to remember the everlasting covenant between God and every living creature of all flesh that is on the earth' (Gen. 9:16). Thousands of years have passed since then, filled with provocative human wickedness, torrential downpours, and local floods on a massive scale; yet God has kept His word never again to destroy the earth and all its creatures by flood (Gen. 9:11). He will again destroy the earth, next time finally and decisively, though it will not be by water but by fire. In his own inimitable way, Charles Schulz (creator of the *Peanuts* comic strip) memorialized the trustworthiness of God's words in this very covenant. Staring out the window at the pouring rain, Lucy wonders if it might eventually flood the whole world; but Linus reminds her that can't happen because of God's promise in Genesis 9. When Lucy expresses her great relief, Linus replies, 'Sound theology has a way of doing that.' And sound theology begins with the trustworthiness of God's words.

> *Covenants are public tests of personal trustworthiness.*

After four decades of drifting through the desert, the Jews stood on the threshold of their promised land. That's when Moses assured them, God 'will not forsake you nor destroy you nor forget the covenant of your fathers which he swore to them' (Deut. 4:31). At first glance you might assume he's referring to the covenant God made with their fathers at Sinai, but it is largely because of that covenant that their

> *The reliability of God's Words is the heart and soul of sound theology.*

fathers (and mothers) are all dead. Their parents' refusal to trust God's words and enter the land forty years earlier was a mutiny against their sworn covenant obligations to Yahweh (Num. 13-14). Moses has just threatened this new generation with the same kind of judgment under the same covenantal terms (Deut. 4:1-28). But the nation's survival and recovery from such punishment under the conditional Sinai covenant is guaranteed by the unconditional Abrahamic covenant.[4] In 4:29-31, Moses is explaining how those two covenants relate and work together.

> Israel as the seed of Abraham constituted an indispensable element of the promise and for that reason could never fail to exist before God. For him to forget Israel would constitute a violation of the oath he swore to the fathers (Gen. 15:12-21; 17:1-8). This, of course, is theologically inconceivable (Merrill 1994, p. 129).

More than that, it is theologically impossible. Because God is utterly trustworthy, so are His words. That's why He cannot forsake Israel or forget the promises He made in covenant with their fathers (Abraham, Isaac, and Jacob). Those promises include the perpetuity of the nation and the possession of the land, and they form the foundation for every other covenant He will make with them, including the Mosaic, the Davidic, and the New covenants. The inviolability of God's covenant

---

4. The Abrahamic covenant is a unilateral, unconditional promise to Abraham and his descendants that God will never forsake them and will bring them into the land He promised to give them; nothing can cancel the fulfillment of those divine promises (cf. Jer. 31:35-37). The Sinai covenant is a conditional arrangement that lays down the terms on which Israel, as a nation, can expect to experience either the prosperity or punishment of God.

words to the patriarchs is a running theme throughout Deuteronomy.[5] Covenants are public tests of personal trustworthiness. Whatever God covenants He keeps, because all His words are trustworthy.

Defending, then Demonstrating

After the amazing grace the Israelites had experienced in Egypt, we are flabbergasted to hear them whining in the wilderness about a miracle God was performing on a daily basis for their survival. They were tired of manna. They wanted meat (Num. 11:10, 13). We would never react like that, would we?

God responds: 'The people despise Me and My provision. They crave meat? Tell the people I will give them meat. Nothing but meat. For a whole month. Starting tomorrow. Go tell them, Moses!' (11:16-20, paraphrase). Moses has no stomach for this assignment: 'Lord, there are 600,000 of us men, plus all the women and children. You say you'll give us meat for a month, but how? Are we to slaughter all our livestock? Or will you gather all the fish from the sea and dump them out here in the desert?' (11:21-22, paraphrase).

Listen carefully to the conversation. Moses isn't listening to God, he's looking at the problem. The size of the crowd makes God's proposal seem utterly implausible (as if God had forgotten how many people He had just brought out of Egypt and through the Red Sea). And Moses fixates on the unimaginable; the only way he supposes God could do what He says just doesn't make sense (as if his imagination were God's limitation). Finally he protests, 'Yet **You have said**, I will give them meat!' (11:21). Do you hear the focus on God's words?

God's reply? 'Has the Lord's arm been shortened?' (an idiom for overpromising). 'Now you shall see whether **what I say** will happen to you or not' (11:23). Do you hear the focus on God's words again? God doesn't merely defend His omnipotence. He doesn't say, 'Now you shall see whether or not I am powerful enough to do a great miracle.' God defends His integrity, His reliability to do exactly what He said: 'Now you shall see **whether my word to you will come true or not!**' (11:23 NET).

---

5. Deuteronomy 7:8, 12-13; 8:1, 18; 9:5; 11:9, 21; 13:7; 27:3; 28:11; 29:13; 30:20.

He had gone on record, publicly and verbally, stating what He would do; and once again, He did exactly what He said (see 11:31-34). But it wasn't goat or lamb or fish on the menu. It was something they never would

Lilliputian—tiny, miniscule; based on the diminutive inhabitants of the island nation of Lilliput in Jonathan Swift's *Gulliver's Travels*.

have imagined: fowl. We discredit God when we measure the reliability of His words by our lilliputian imagination.

It's easy to overlook the fact that this conversation wasn't with the people of Israel, but with Moses! We are often snookered into thinking that if we could actually see God perform just one bona fide miracle, we would never doubt Him again. But Moses had witnessed one jaw-dropping wonder after another—by this time at least twenty-five, in fact[6]—first in Egypt and now in the wilderness. Despite all the miracles he had seen, and all the times God had done exactly what He said, Moses just couldn't comprehend how God would manage *this* one. Send ten national plagues to bring the mightiest nation on earth to its knees? Been there. Split open a path through the sea, and then close it on top of a pursuing enemy? Seen it. Miraculously provide bread in the wilderness daily for weeks on end? Certainly. But deliver a one-month supply of meat in the desert? How could the Lord possibly do *that*? After every other word He had kept, how could He not?

Directly witnessing divine miracles may allay doubt temporarily, but it does not cure it. Doubt has a high recidivism rate in humans. We are capable of boundless unbelief, especially

Doubt has a high recidivism rate in humans.

whenever God says things that over-reach our meager imaginations. But God is intent on proving the reliability of every word He speaks. And He's willing to push the envelope to make His point.

Human Testimony in Narrative Passages

In the previous examples, God personally showcases the trustworthiness of His words in different ways. But there are also human testimonies

---

6. See Crockett 2013, Appendix B 'Chart of Biblical Miracles,' pp. 335-60.

to this same truth. The book of Joshua concludes the record of Israel's conquest with a sweeping declaration:

> the LORD gave to Israel all the land **of which He had sworn to give to their fathers**, and they took possession of it, and dwelt in it. The LORD gave them rest all around, **according to all that He had sworn to their fathers**. And not a man of all their enemies stood against them; the LORD delivered all their enemies into their hand. **Not a word failed of any good thing which the LORD had spoken to the house of Israel. All came to pass** (Josh. 21:43-45).[7]

As if that weren't a sufficiently emphatic exoneration of God's integrity, at the end of his career Joshua personally calls on the consciences of his countrymen to bear witness to the reliability of all God's words to them:

> Behold, this day I am going the way of all the earth. And you know in all your hearts and in all your souls that **not one thing has failed of all the good things which the LORD your God spoke concerning you**. All have come to pass for you; **not one word of them has failed** (Josh. 23:14).

These statements raise a question or two. When the book ends, didn't Israel still have more land left to conquer? How can these two statements make such unqualified claims? My purpose here is to underscore God's desire to magnify His integrity and the trustworthiness of His words, not to wade into technical debates. Still, defending that thesis with integrity requires addressing valid questions that surface along the way.

First, we can rule out error or ignorance on the part of the writer. He himself noted that there remained yet more land to be taken (16:10; 17:12-13; 23:4-5), but he clearly saw no conflict between that fact and the statements of God's faithfulness to do everything He had said He would do.[8]

---

7. 'To say that not one of these [promises] was forgotten or given in vain is no exaggeration. The Lord always fulfills His promises' (Goslinga 1986, p. 152).

8. 'Too often biblical criticism fails to realize that the biblical writers had at least as much sense as we do and could certainly observe contradictions and inconsistencies when they saw them' (Davis 2008, p. 156). For more detail, see

Second, their enjoyment of God's promises was conditioned on their obedience (1:2-9). For His part, God *gave* to them all the land He had promised; their part was to fight and take it. Even though there remained pockets of populations to be conquered, they had clearly achieved hegemony over the whole region (21:43). God delivered into their hands every enemy that had stood against them, so that they no longer stood in danger of attack from any more nations or confederations (21:44). Against all odds, God had done for them everything He had promised (21:45). In these two passages, the writer of Joshua exclaims

> praise to Yahweh for complete, thorough, persistent fidelity to his promises.... Only when we see the barriers Yahweh smashes, only when we see his promise trampling all apparent obstacles put in its way, only then will we appreciate how tenacious our God's fidelity is to his promise and his people (Davis 2008, pp. 156-57).

Prophetic Testimony to God's Integrity

Prophecy is God's platform of choice for proving the reliability and integrity of what He says. It is here that His zeal to display the trustworthiness of His words is most acute. There's a great deal to explore in this area, but for now we'll survey just a few passages where God is jealous to establish His integrity, especially when His international reputation is at stake.

Isaiah

Isaiah 40–48 is arguably God's most magisterial self-revelation in all of Scripture. Dominating this self-revelation of theology proper is His declaration not merely that there is no other God like Him, but that there is no other God, period.[9] He weaves into His case a running commentary on the inanity of idolatry.[10]

Magisterial— majestic, stately, august.

Goslinga 1986, pp. 21-22.

9. See, for example, Isa. 40:18, 25; 43:10-11; 44:6, 8; 45:5-6, 14, 18, 21, 22; 46:5, 9.

10. See Isa. 40:18-24; 41:7; 44:9-20; 45:20; 46:1-2, 5-7.

In Isaiah 41, God articulates a series of prophetic promises to Israel: their former enemies will be ashamed and disgraced (41:11-13), God will use Israel to overcome and judge their surrounding enemies (41:14-16), and God will provide for Israel and cause her to flourish as never before (41:17-19). These are not rewards for her deserving conduct; they are gracious promises to a graciously chosen nation (41:8-10). To what end?

> So that people may see and know, may consider and understand,
> that the hand of the LORD has done this, that the Holy One of
> Israel has created it (Isa. 41:20 NIV).

The verbal pile-up (*see, know, consider, understand*) is not poetic redundancy. There is a progression from *seeing* the events, to *recognizing* who's actually doing it, to *pondering* the ramifications, to fully *grasping* the significance of what all these events say about God.

The ultimate criterion of deity is prophecy.

How will people know that this was God's doing and not just another swing of the pendulum in the fates of nations? Because His words spell out ahead of time exactly what He will do. The verses that follow continue the argument. God challenges all wannabe deities to prove their godhood by saying ahead of time what will happen (Isa. 41:21-24). Predictably, none of them are up to the challenge. But God says, 'Look, my earlier predictive oracles have come to pass; now I announce new events. Before they begin to occur, I reveal them to you' (Isa. 42:9 NET). It is a continuation of God's policy of declaring, and then doing.

> It is insufficient for Yahweh merely to make a claim to direct
> world history—all the gods would have registered the same
> claim. It is therefore essential to offer some proof. [God]
> proposes a test case: to predict an event and then demonstrate
> control of the historical processes. The idol gods fail this test
> but the Lord succeeds (Motyer 1993, pp. 314-15).[11]

---

11. Motyer actually states that 'Isaiah proposes a test case.' I highly esteem Motyer, but his language here is unfortunately imprecise and disappointingly common in commentary literature. The proposed test case does not originate with the prophet, but with God. Isaiah is merely quoting God (see 41:21). The

As this extended oracle in Isaiah unfolds, God's Exhibit A is a person named Cyrus. A century and a half before his birth, God named him and foretold how he would equip and empower this future Medo-Persian ruler to have dominion over the nations (45:1-5) and to be the instrument through whom He would bring the as-yet unconquered people of Judah back out of captivity (44:28). To what end?

> That men may know from the rising to the setting of the sun that there is no one besides Me. I am the LORD, and there is no other (Isa. 45:6 NASB).

And how does the Lord distinguish Himself from all the other counterfeit gods of all the other nations? By

> declaring the end from the beginning, and from ancient times the things that are not yet done, saying, '**My counsel shall stand,** and I will do all My pleasure'.... Indeed, **I have spoken it; I will also bring it to pass.** I have purposed it, I will also do it (Isa. 46:10-11).

Prophecy is the ultimate criterion of deity. At the core of prophecy is a threefold cord: knowledge of the future (divine omniscience), combined with control over the future (divine omnipotence), expressed in an accurate communication of the future (divine veracity, integrity). Without the last component—the expression beforehand—there is no prophecy. But the Lord specializes in prophecy.

> **I have declared** the former things from the beginning;
> **They went forth from My mouth** and I caused them to hear
> it. Suddenly I did them, and they came to pass (48:3).

He uses prophecy to preclude people (especially His people) from crediting events to false gods or other forces.

---

difference is not pedantic in my opinion; it seems to me to fall short of giving God full and sole credit in an area that He expressly claims as an exclusive domain for His glory (Isa. 48:11).

> Even from the beginning **I have declared it to you;**
>> Before it came to pass **I proclaimed it to you,**
> Lest you should say, 'My idol has done them,
> And my carved image and my molded image
> Have commanded them' (Isa. 48:5).

He uses prophecy to preclude people (especially His people) from claiming that certain events were predictable.

> I have made you hear new things from this time,
> Even hidden things, and you did not know them.
> They are created now and not from the beginning;
> And before this day you have not heard them,
> Lest you should say, 'Of course I knew them.'
> Surely you did not hear,
> Surely you did not know;
> Surely from long ago your ear was not opened.
> For I knew that you would deal very treacherously,
> And were called a transgressor from the womb
>> (Isa. 48:6-8).

This is a matter of supreme importance to God, because at issue is the very identity and glory of God.

> For My own sake, for My own sake, I will do it;
> For how should My name be profaned?
> And I will not give My glory to another (Isa. 48:11).

Prophecy is the premier showcase of God's glory.

Prophecy is the premier showcase of the glory of God. And the heart and soul of prophecy is the trustworthiness of God's words. God's zeal for making Himself known hangs on saying what He will do and then doing exactly what He says.

That is why God asserts an unbreakable, two-way linkage between what He says and what His prophets say. We think of the prophet affirming what God says, and so he does. But in a stunning reversal, God also affirms and fulfills whatever His prophets say: 'Thus says the LORD ... Who confirms the word of His servant, and performs the counsel of His messengers' (Isa. 44:24, 26)—not because He is their servant, but because they are His.

Jeremiah

As part of Jeremiah's induction into the prophetic ministry, the Lord showed him an object and asked him a question; the connection between the picture and the point rests on a word-play (from Jer. 1:11-12 ESV):

> 'Jeremiah, what do you see?' ... 'I see an **almond** [*shāqēd*] branch.'... 'You have seen well, for I am **watching over** [*shōqēd*] my word to perform it.'

God's first prophetic revelation to Jeremiah set the tone for his whole ministry: God never speaks lightly or loosely, and He exercises a jealous vigilance over doing exactly what He says.

In chapter 23, Jeremiah recounts a divine oracle against false prophets (23:9-40). They fabricate their own messages and then claim to speak for the Lord (23:16-17). God is furious with those who mislead His people with their fraudulent 'dreams' and 'oracles' (23:18-22). God discharges His displeasure with three rifle cracks in quick succession (from Jer. 23:30-32):

> 'I am against the prophets ... who steal **My words** ....'

> 'I am against the prophets ... who use their tongues and say, "**He says**"'

> 'I am against those who prophesy false dreams ... and cause My people to err by their lies and by their recklessness, Yet I did not send them or command them.'

Why is God so incensed? Because they 'perverted the words of the living God, the LORD of hosts, our God' (23:36). The reason God treats prophetic misrepresentation so gravely (His final pronouncement on these false prophets is merciless, 23:39-40) is because He takes His words, and their testimony to His trustworthiness, so seriously.

In chapter 44, God confronts a contingent of Jews who fled to Egypt to escape the Babylonian invasion. But they are determined to cling to the idolatrous worship for which they were banished from the land in the first place (Jer. 44:20-25). So God swears to 'watch over them for adversity and not for good' ... until they are 'consumed by the sword and by famine, until there is an end to them' (44:27). But He will secure a remnant who will return to Judah from Egypt (44:28). What is God's goal in all of this? To vent His righteous indignation? To validate His abhorrence of idolatry? Here's how God expresses His objective:

> '... all the remnant of Judah, who have gone to the land of Egypt to dwell there, shall know **whose word will stand, Mine or theirs**. And this shall be a sign to you,' says the LORD, 'that I will punish you in this place, that you may know that **My words will surely stand** against you for adversity' (Jer. 44:28-29).

Would you say God is passionate about protecting and vindicating the integrity of His words?

Ezekiel

Nowhere does God express more resolutely or repeatedly His intention to magnify Himself before the nations than in Ezekiel. Any reader who wends his way through this prophetic Grand Canyon keeps hearing the haunting echo of the divine purpose: 'that they may know that I am the Lord'. That phrase (or some variation) surfaces seventy-eight times in the book (Bell 2010, pp. 338-40).

That thematic purpose statement was not arbitrary. Judah had displayed an incorrigible disposition to disbelieve divine warnings (Jer. 5:12) and to misinterpret providential punishments (Jer. 8:7).[12] You can draw a direct line from verses such as these to this dominating theme in Ezekiel (which begins in Ezek. 5:13).

Many of these purpose statements, though prophetic when Ezekiel uttered them, have already been historically fulfilled, mostly through Babylon's domination under Nebuchadnezzar.[13] What happened to

---

12. The Jeremiah passages predate Ezekiel by a decade or more (cf. Jer 1:2; 25:1-3).

13. Compare, for example, Ezek. 12:1-15 with 2 Kings 25:1-7, including such details as the scattering of Zedekiah's troops (Ezek. 12:14; 2 Kings 25:5) and the blinding of Zedekiah himself (Ezek. 12:13; 2 Kings 25:7).

Judah, to Jerusalem, and to the temple at the hands of Babylon was incontestable testimony to the direct judgment of God, precisely because God foretold exactly what would happen (and why) before it happened.

Objection: 'If it was so incontestable, why have so many people since that time contested the divine origin of those events? Doesn't that mean that God's whole predictive intent has failed?' Not at all. To the generation God was addressing, it *was* incontestable. God declared that 'they shall know that I am the LORD, and that I have not said in vain that I would do this evil unto them' (Ezek. 6:10 KJV)—and they *knew*. People today may scoff at God's as-yet future predictions. But when future-tense prophecy becomes present-tense reality, the generation living then will also *know*.

One striking variation on this theme appears twice. Ezekiel's ministry will convince people 'that a prophet has been among them' (Ezek. 2:5). Ezekiel's role throughout the book is to announce, 'This is what the Lord GOD says' (2:4 HCSB). And 'when this comes [whatever the Lord God says]—and come it will!—then they will know that a prophet has been among them' (Ezek. 33:33 ESV).

Ezekiel's was a solitary voice amid a clamor of phonies pretending to speak for God while dispensing verbal 'happy meals' to please an audience that had no stomach for negativity (see 13:1-23). God's purpose was not to lionize Ezekiel personally, but to validate him as a true prophet who faithfully echoed what God said. By identifying Ezekiel as the genuine article, God was clarifying that a true prophet is not a substitute for a distant God; a true prophet signals the nearness of God (Zimmerli 1979, p. 39). God Himself is present in the presence of His prophet, and the voice of a true prophet is nothing more or less than the echo of God. God's pledge in 33:33 ('when this comes—and come it will!' ESV) is a terse declaration of the utter trustworthiness of His words through His prophets.[14]

---

14. That is why Jehoshaphat could exhort the people of Judah that to trust God's prophets was to trust God Himself: 'Put your trust in the LORD your God and you will be established. Put your trust in his prophets and succeed' (2 Chron. 20:20 NASB).

The 'you/they shall know' theme is punctuated along the way with additional reminders that a word from God is as good as done:

- 'For I am the LORD. I speak, and the word which I speak will come to pass .... I will say the word and perform it,' says the Lord GOD (Ezek. 12:25).

- 'The word which I speak will be done,' says the Lord GOD (12:28)

- 'I the LORD have spoken, and I will perform it' (17:24)

- 'I, the LORD, have spoken, and I will do it!' (22:14 NET)

- 'I the LORD I have spoken it; it shall come to pass, and I will do it' (24:14)

- 'I, the LORD, have spoken it, and I will do it.' (36:36)

- 'Then you shall know that I, the LORD, have spoken it and I performed it, says the LORD' (37:14)

The chart in Appendix 1 will help you examine this 'you/they shall know' theme in more detail on your own, if you wish. It documents and broadly categorizes each occurrence of this divine emphasis throughout Ezekiel. The main emphases can be summarized as follows:

(1) The fulfillment of pronounced judgment on Israel will be the means by which they will know that 'I am the LORD; I will speak the word that I will speak, and it will be performed' (12:25 ESV).

(2) The fulfillment of pronounced judgment on the surrounding kingdoms will be the means by which those nations will 'know that I am the LORD.'

(3) The fulfillment of undeserved-but-promised blessing and restoration for Israel will be

   a) the means by which *Israel* 'shall know that I the LORD have spoken it and performed it' (37:14), and, even more remarkably,

b) the means by which the *nations* will know that 'I the LORD, have spoken, and have done it' (17:24).

How does this theme contribute to our focus on the trustworthiness of God's words? The impact of God's future actions is compounded by His *foretelling* those future actions. If God's intent was merely to amaze the nations with His omniscience, He could have limited prophecy to pure prediction—a sterile but accurate recitation of who will do what in the future, with no statement of His involvement in those events. If God just wanted to wow the nations with His power, He could simply do all these things without any prediction. But that leaves the interpretation and origin of such events open to question. Witness the debate that inevitably ensues after any disaster, whether man-made (like 9/11) or natural (like Hurricane Katrina). People argue vociferously over whether or not God has anything to do with such events. But events are coming that will quash all debate, because their explicit prediction will be eloquent, unequivocal, and universal testimony that God does what He says—*and they shall know.*

God is passionate about proving the trustworthiness of His words. If there is a hair's breadth between God's words and God's actions, between what He says and what He does, God forfeits His integrity. 'He does not utter vain promises; for him to speak is for him to execute' (Block 1997, 2:364). This is so much the case that after the Lord spells out in detail some future event, He frequently punctuates it with the phrase 'I, the LORD, have spoken it'—which is essentially longhand for a concluding exclamation mark.[15]

God's words 'are the index of reality' (Packer 1973, p. 113). A word from God is, in essence, a promise of reality—whether past (historical reality), present (contemporary reality), or future (prophetic reality). And promises have consequences.

> A promise entails an obligation. When somebody makes a promise, they're not just stating something, they are doing something. They are forming a relationship and creating an

---

15. See 5:15, 17; 21:17, 32; 23:34; 26:5, 14; 28:10; 30:12; 34:24.

> expectation that carries moral obligation. Failure to complete
> a promise is a violation of one's word. It is a serious matter.
> Certainly we can make promises with conditions. The language
> of promise will make that clear. But once the promise has been
> made, a relationship has been enacted and an expectation has
> been grounded in personal integrity (Blaising 2014, p. 160).

Prophecy verifies not merely God's omnipotence and omniscience, but the integrity and reliability of every word that proceeds from His mouth. 'God is going to make man know that he is Yahweh,' not through anonymous sovereign actions that have no definitive explanation, nor through pure prediction devoid of divine involvement, 'but by prophesying what he plans to do and then doing it!' (Bell 2010, p. 335).

'It is in the narrative of history that [God's] character is proclaimed' (Block 1997, 1:39.)[16] It's possible to read that statement as though history were another 'book' that reveals God—He is revealed in the 'book' of creation (by looking at His creative works), in the 'book' of history (by looking at His historical acts), and so forth. There is some truth to that. But Ezekiel's point is much more explicit. In Ezekiel, God not only acts in history, He *narrates* it ahead of time. And it is in His prophetic narrative of (future) history that the reliability of His words is displayed.

Zechariah

Ezekiel ministered to Judah at the beginning of their captivity in Babylon (about 590 B.C.). When you turn from Ezekiel to Zechariah, you are turning seventy years into the future to post-captivity Judah (about 520 B.C.). A remnant had returned to Judah, but persecution quickly dampened their enthusiasm for rebuilding the temple. Eventually God raised up two prophets to prod the people to finish the job (Ezra 5:1-2). One of them was Zechariah.

God introduces His oracle to Zechariah with a reminder of the reliability of His words. The previous generations of Israelites had ignored God's warnings through the prophets (Zech. 1:2-4). Prophet

---

16. Block adds that 'this formula [*you/they shall know*] transforms Yahweh's oracles from mere announcements into announcements of Yahweh's self-manifestation.'

and patriarch have passed off the scene (1:5), 'but did not my words ... overtake your fathers?' (1:6). Everything He said happened just as He said it. For our present purpose, however, I'm particularly interested in chapter 8.

Zechariah 8 functions remarkably like a movie trailer. A series of sounds and scenes flashes by in quick succession with little elaboration: God declares His eager zeal to bless Zion (8:2), then promises to return to Jerusalem Himself and make it glorious (8:3); this is followed by a scene of Jerusalem's streets teeming with healthy elderly people surrounded by the happy chatter of children playing in the city square (8:4-5). Then God pauses and in so many words says, 'You find this hard to believe? Does this amaze you?' (see 8:6). Why would it?

Well, slip into Zechariah's sandals and look around you.[17] You're struggling to make ends meet and put food on the table after a succession of bad harvests from the chastening hand of God. The temple stands embarrassingly half-finished, and everyone already knows it's going to be only a pathetic shadow of the Solomonic sanctuary that it's replacing. Jerusalem is something of a ghost town. The walls and gates are in shambles. The roads are still clogged with charred rubble from Nebuchadnezzar's demolition of the city seventy years before. On top of all that, you're surrounded by people who don't want you there.

So it's not surprising that when God describes these promises in Zechariah 8:2-5, the average Jew would blink widely once or twice, look around, cock his head and think, 'Seriously? That's incredible! Here? Unimaginable!'

The Lord anticipates that reaction: 'If it is marvelous[18] in the eyes of the remnant of this people in these days, will it also be marvelous in My eyes?' (8:6). God is never shocked by anything He promises. He never covers His mouth and thinks, 'I can't believe I just said that!' He never looks back and thinks, 'How am I ever going to manage what I just predicted?' Nothing He could say would surprise Him. He's been

---

17. The description that follows is a composite sketch drawn from passages such as 2 Kings 25, Ezra and Nehemiah, and Haggai 1.

18. The word *marvelous* (*pālā'*) is the same word that shows up in two important passages treated in Chapter 9—Genesis 18 and Jeremiah 32.

promising and doing things like this ever since He created the world—by His *words* incidentally (more on that in Chapter 7).

God emphasizes the dependability of what He promises with an expression of irrevocable guarantee. Fourteen times over, He certifies and recertifies every prophetic promise with a solemn assertion: *This is what the LORD of hosts says.*[19] Don't skim over those words when you read Zechariah 8. They are not pious padding between prophetic statements; they are the bone and marrow of everything God promises in the chapter. It is God's way of publicly and repeatedly staking His holy reputation on bringing these events to pass. This repetitious reminder that these prophetic promises are 'the word of the LORD' is intended

> to assure us at the very outset that, however incredible … these things may be, they will most *certainly* come to pass, because the Name of the infinite, eternal, and faithful Jehovah, with whom nothing is too hard … stands pledged to their accomplishment (Baron 1988, p. 230).[20]

The written words of God are as sacred and certain as the character and being of God Himself. That thought is tested and developed more fully in the next chapter.

We'll return to the subject of God's prophetic words later. One thing this means in the short term, however, is that our faithful representation of God's character rests in the balance when we handle the prophetic words of God. That ought to sober every interpreter and prompt us to 'tremble at his words' (Isa. 66:2).

A Final Thought

In perhaps his most theologically sweeping essay, Jonathan Edwards argued that the ultimate end for which God created the world is to display His glory. The glory of God is everything that makes Him

---

19. See Appendix 2 for a brief but detailed discussion of the significance of this important phrase.

20. Baron cites a similar remark from Jerome and roughly translates a statement by Lange as follows: 'By making the name of Jehovah of hosts surety for their accomplishment, a whole series of apparent impossibilities are thus turned into certainties.'

unique and uniquely excellent; it encompasses all that He is (His being and attributes) and all He does (His works). But God is beyond the access, experience, and invention of man. How can we know Him? Only if He reveals Himself to us. That means that for us to have a true and accurate understanding of God, that self-revelation must be trustworthy. That's why God goes to such lengths to insist and demonstrate that what He says is exactly what He is and what He does.

Review & Reflect

1. What other passages can you think of (or locate in your marginal references) where God communicates His jealousy for His integrity?

2. We saw several examples in Exodus of God sovereignly saying what He would do and then doing it. But in the first example (Exod. 8:10), God actually lets Pharaoh name what day He should remove the frogs. Why do you suppose He might have done that?

3. What miracles can you think of that Moses had seen prior to Numbers 11? How is it that he still balked at God's announcement in Numbers 11?

4. How do the reactions, assumptions, and decisions of Israel in Numbers 13:31–14:4 display a distrust in God's words to them in Exodus 23:27-31, 33:2?

5. We stopped our consideration of Zechariah 8 with verse 6. What else does God say He will do in the rest of the chapter?

4
The Indivisibility of God and His Words

*You have exalted above all things Your
name and Your word*

Psalm 138:2 (ESV)

'You have my word.' 'He is as good as his word.' Such expressions used to mean something. In an era and culture that prized reputation and reliability, it was an absolute pledge that whatever was promised would be performed. Why? Because one's 'word' was an indivisible extension of one's character and person.

People are profoundly communicative beings (though it may surprise my wife to hear this coming from her rather introverted husband). What I mean is that we have the capacity and the need for levels and complexities of self-expression and inter-communication that far exceed any other creature.

This is so much the case that people are ultimately *unknowable* apart from their words, whether spoken or written (or in the case of verbally-challenged people, some other understandable form of self-expression). You may be able to deduce certain things about people by observing only their actions—they are hard-working, or discourteous, or depressed. But you will not know the reasons for those actions, or whether those behaviors are actually out of character, unless the person communicates with you. Actions need context and interpretation, and interpretation requires words. God, too, is unknowable apart from His words.

People are also *inseparable* from their words. That doesn't mean, of course, that a person's words always accurately represent what he truly is. People can misrepresent themselves and their intentions. When Nazi SS-*Obersturmbannführer* Adolf Eichmann arrived in Hungary to facilitate the shipment of Jews to extermination camps, he warmly assured them, 'You have nothing to worry about. We want only the best for you. You'll leave here shortly and be sent to very fine places indeed. ... You will have wonderful lives.'[1] But even a deceptive use of language confirms the inseparableness of a person from their words. If you cannot trust a person's words, you cannot trust the person. If you trust a person, you will believe what that person says.

> It is of the essence of personal trustworthiness that people are who they claim to be; that, if you like, there is an intimate connection between their words and who they are, between what they say about themselves and the actions they can and do perform (Helm and Trueman 2002, p. ix).

Likewise, God is inseparable from His words. It is nonsense to speak of 'trusting God' in some warm and fuzzy way when you do not really believe His words. 'Faith in God' without faith in God's words (whether about His character, His expectations, or His actions) is nothing more or less than faith in your own imagination of what you think God is or should be. If that is the case, your faith is not in God at all but in an idol fashioned in your own mind. 'Faith is therefore not a self-sufficient entity,' in Scripture; 'it is always faith *placed by the individual in God's word*' (Trueman 2002, p. 176, original emphasis). Biblically, to trust God is to trust His words, and to trust God's words is to trust God Himself.

The interface between the words of God and the very being and character of God

> is a central theme of the Bible itself. That God is, in a sense, the words he speaks or, perhaps better, that God is towards his people the same as the words he speaks to them, is a recurring theme (Helm and Trueman 2002, p. x).

---

1. Bascomb 2002, p. 6. See also Kershaw 2002, p. 26.

How, and where, does the Bible teach that God and His words are indivisible?

God's Exaltation of His Words

'I will worship toward Your holy temple, and praise Your name for Your lovingkindness and Your truth; **for You have magnified Your word above all Your name**' (Ps. 138:2). That final phrase is a stunning statement. Versions differ on exactly how to translate David's meaning. Besides the NKJV just above which echoes the KJV, it is also rendered:

- 'You have made Your word great according to all Your name' (NASB)

- 'You have made your word [even] greater than the whole of your reputation' (CJB)

- 'You have exalted Your name and Your promise [word] above everything else' (HCSB)

- 'you have exalted your promise [word] above the entire sky' (NET)[2]

At the very least, the verse teaches that God intends His word, along with His name, to receive the highest possible esteem over all else in creation. At the most, it asserts that as far as His own reputation and attributes are concerned, God Himself places *supreme* value on His word. As enthusiastic as I am in this book about magnifying the trustworthiness of God's words, I would never presume to make either of those claims. But God has.

What is the significance of comparing the word of God to the name of God? Sometimes the 'name of God' simply refers to the appellation(s) by which God is called and makes Himself known (Ps. 74:10, 18). But names in the ancient culture of biblical times were not mere labels; names often memorialized some detail of a person's background or embodied some aspect of their personality. God revealed Himself

---

2. The NET suggests emending 'your name' to 'your heavens' to imply that God's faithfulness to His promise is universally apparent. The emendation is unnecessary, but the result is still an exalted statement about God's Word.

by many names and all of them are freighted with meaning that communicates truth about His person.[3] Often, however, a reference to the 'name of God' is a metaphor for the power of God (Ps. 44:5; 54:1), or the reputation of God (Ps. 8:1, 9; 135:13), or the presence of God (Ps. 52:9; 75:1), or even the very being of God (Ps. 18:49; 61:5; 83:16).

David's statement in Psalm 138:2 invites several observations. First, the 'name of God' is theological shorthand for God's self-revelation.[4] His words are an extension and expression of Himself. So for God to exalt His word 'above all his name'—or even along with His name—means that He places the highest possible premium on His words. And if He does, we should.

Second, for God to make His word more important than His very name—or even to make it of equal importance with His name—implies a coordination of all His attributes toward a common goal. Every other attribute of God works in harmony to fulfill what He has verbally committed Himself to do and communicated Himself to be. Just as a trustworthy man will bend all his efforts and qualities in order to keep his word, so

> the Lord lays all the rest of his name under tribute to his word:
> his wisdom, power, love, and all his other attributes combine
> to carry out his word (Spurgeon n.d., 6:244).

Third, and more specifically, it highlights God's holy preoccupation with what this book is all about: the trustworthiness of His words. That preoccupation focuses on a particular spectrum of God's character—qualities captured in some of the Old Testament's most important words used to describe God's relationship to His people.

God's Faithfulness and Lovingkindness are Measured by His Words

One of the Old Testament's major words to describe God's relationship to His people is *faithfulness*. It is also one of the Old Testament's most important words describing God's relationship to His words.

---

3. See Waltke 2007, pp. 359-75; Walker 1982, 2:504-08.

4. Cf. Payne 1962, p. 144; Oehler 1978, pp. 124-25.

> The name of God includes all the perfections of God;
> everything that God is, and which God has revealed himself
> as having—his justice, majesty, holiness, greatness, and glory,
> and whatever he is in himself, that is God's name. And yet
> he has magnified something above his name—his word—his
> truth. ... God's faithfulness being so dear to him, he has exalted
> his faithfulness above all his other perfections. ... [They] would
> all sooner fail than his faithfulness—the word of his mouth
> and what he has revealed in Scripture. ... [I]f God has revealed
> his truth to your soul and given you faith to anchor in the word
> of promise, sooner than that should fail, he would suffer the
> loss of all.[5]

Another key Old Testament word to describe God's relationship to His people is *lovingkindness*. These two qualities, lovingkindness and faithfulness, are so tightly intertwined that they are frequently paired up in the same verse, married together with the word 'and,' and treated as though they are one flesh.[6] And both terms are indivisibly wedded to the words of God. God's faithfulness (truth) and lovingkindness (loyalty) have no meaning or expression apart from His words; both are measured by the degree to which God's actions match His words. Both of these qualities surface in Psalm 138:2. David is praising the Lord (138:1-2a), but for what? 'For Your *lovingkindness* and Your *truth*.'

'Lovingkindness' (ESV, 'steadfast love'; NET, 'loyal love') is the Hebrew word *chesed* and has reference in this context to God's loyalty to His covenant words. Covenants are based on words—words of promise and warning, obligation and expectation. God's 'covenant promises are to be relied upon forever because he himself is irrevocably committed to the promises he has made' (Merrill 2006, p. 67). But this is no aloof, impersonal duty; the term often carries a strong undercurrent of love that motivates acts of kindness (hence 'lovingkindness') displayed

---

5. John C. Philpot, quoted in Spurgeon n.d., 6:251. Philpot separated from the Church of England in 1835 during one of its pendulum swings back toward Romanism, and pastored as a Particular Baptist for the rest of his life.

6. 2 Sam. 15:20; Pss. 25:10; 26:3; 40:10, 11; 57:10; 61:7; 69:13; 85:10; 86:15; 89:14; 108:4; 115:1; Prov. 3:3; 14:22; 16:6; 20:28. Cf. also *chesed* and *'emunah* in Pss. 36:5; 40:10; 88:11; 89:2, 24, 33, 49; 92:2; 98:3; 100:5.

toward those with whom He is in a covenant relationship.[7] You can see the kinship between covenant and *chesed* when God is described as the one 'who keeps covenant and mercy [*chesed*]' (Deut. 7:9; 1 Kings 8:23; 2 Chron. 6:14; Neh. 1:5, 9:32; Dan. 9:4). God's words are the very basis and content of His *chesed*, and 'his immutable character ensures the complete reliability of the promises that stem from his loving loyalty' (Jaeggli 2004, p. 209).

'Truth' is the Hebrew word *'ĕmet*, though the same idea often shows up in the closely related word *'ĕmûnâ*. Both words link back to the root *'āman* (discussed in Chapter 2, and the source of our word 'amen'), which can mean both to have faith (believe) and to be faithful. The core idea shared by all these words is *certainty, assurance, reliability, dependability* (Merrill 2006, pp. 69-70). Like 'lovingkindness,' this concept has virtually no meaning apart from words. How do you judge someone's faithfulness apart from whether they are and do what they say?

Because Psalm 138 is a psalm of David, two other passages relating closely to David help cement all this together: 2 Samuel 7 and Psalm 89.

2 Samuel 7

The Davidic covenant laid out in 2 Samuel 7 is 'a mountain peak in redemptive history' (McComiskey 1985, p. 25). God vows to set apart David's family as the royal line of Israel forever. Some think Psalm 138 is David's expression of gratitude specifically in response to God's covenant in 2 Samuel 7.[8] Whether or not David had this passage in view when he penned Psalm 138, the links between these passages are strong.

In his praise for the privileges of grace heaped upon him and his descendants in the Davidic covenant, David calls repeated attention to what God Himself had just said. Every bolded word represents the same term in Hebrew (the noun *dābār* or the verb *dābar*):

---

7. This is a generalization, but only a slight one. The word *chesed* occurs nearly 250 times in the OT, and in a few passages no clear relationship is in sight, covenant or otherwise; but those are rare and exceptional occurrences that occupy the shadows of its predominant relational orientation. See Merrill 2006, pp. 67-69.

8. Leupold 1969, pp. 937-38. Cf. Alexander 1991, p. 544, who sees God's 'word' in Psalm 138:2 as a direct reference to the Davidic covenant in 2 Samuel 7.

Now, O LORD God, the **word** which You have **spoken** concerning Your servant and concerning his house, establish it forever, and do as You have **said**. So let Your name be magnified forever … And now, O Lord GOD, You are God, and Your **words** are true, and You have **promised** this goodness to Your servant. Now therefore, let it please You to bless the house of Your servant, that it may continue before You forever; for You, O Lord GOD, have **spoken** it … (2 Sam. 7:25-29).

Psalm 138 also echoes this passage when David prays, 'Let Your name be magnified forever' (see 2 Sam. 7:26). So indivisible are the words and the name of God that to perform the one is to exalt the other. It would reconfirm the yoke between God's *lovingkindness* and *faithfulness*, and the connection of both of those qualities to His words, if these terms showed up in this passage. And they do.

God affirms His *lovingkindness* to David and to these promises in 2 Samuel 7:14-15. What if some of his descendants wander from God and forsake the faith of their father David? God promises to chasten those individuals, 'but my **mercy** (*chesed*) shall not depart from him, as I took it from Saul' (see 2 Sam. 7:15).[9] And in the passage already quoted above, David exults in the *faithfulness* of God by affirming, 'Your **words** are **true** [*'ĕmet*; NIV *trustworthy*]' (2 Sam. 7:28).

I will venture out on a limb for one final observation. It's a limb because very few seem to be curious enough about it to comment, except a few of the older commentators. Early in his prayer, David makes an intriguing statement: 'For Your word's sake, and according to Your own heart, You have done all these great things, to make Your servant know them' (See 2 Sam. 7:21). The 'according to Your own heart' is clear enough; it means that God did it because He wanted to and it was entirely His own idea. But what does David mean when he says that God made this great and gracious covenant with him

---

9. If God took away His loyalty from Saul, why should He not do so with David? The answer lies in the type of covenant. The Saulide covenant was a conditional covenant in which Saul's failure to abide by the conditions meant he would forfeit God's promises (1 Sam. 12:13-25; 13:13-14). The Davidic covenant is a unilateral covenant that God undertakes to fulfill unconditionally.

'for Your word's sake' or (it may also be translated) 'on account of Your word'?

The phrase can face in one of two directions. (1) It can be looking backward: *on account of* or *for the sake of something He said earlier*, God is now establishing this covenant with David in fulfillment of that word. If this is the intent, it implies that this covenant is the means by which God is bringing the promises of the Abrahamic covenant to fruition and, even more specifically, the promise that the scepter of royalty within Israel would reside in the house of Judah (Gen. 49:10).[10] Or, (2) it can be looking forward: this Davidic covenant was made *on account of His word* or *for the sake of His word* in the sense of God's desire (in keeping with Psalm 138:2) to magnify His word and, consequently, His trustworthiness by faithfully fulfilling every word of this covenant.[11]

Either way, for God to do all this *on account of His word* or *for the sake of His word* is a testimony to the total dependability and trustworthiness of God's words.

Psalm 89

Psalm 89 is both a celebratory (vv. 1-37) and poignantly prayerful (vv. 38-52) reminder to God of the eternal promises of the Davidic covenant, 'which the turn of events seemed to have flatly contradicted' (Kidner 1973, p. 319). The psalmist celebrates God's covenant loyalty (*chesed*) seven times in the psalm,[12] and God's faithfulness (*'āman* and all root-related forms) twelve times.[13]

The traditional author of the psalm was Ethan the Ezrahite,[14] a contemporary of David. Therein lies the problem. How could the second half of the psalm, lamenting the loss of the Davidic throne, reflect Davidic times? Perhaps Ethan penned it under the duress of David's exile during the rebellion of Absalom (2 Sam. 15-19), when the consternation and uncertainty of the sudden dominance of one's

---

10. Cf. Keil and Delitzsch 1982, 2:351; Lange 1980, 3:435.
11. Cf. Henry n.d., 2:483.
12. Ps. 89:1, 2, 14, 24, 28, 33, 49.
13. Ps. 89:1, 2, 5, 8, 14, 24, 28, 33, 37, 49, 52.
14. See 1 Chron. 2:6, 15:19; aka Jeduthan in 2 Chron. 5:12.

antagonists make every day feel like a month. On the other hand, it's not impossible that Ethan's original composition was later appended, perhaps in the post-captivity time of Ezra when the Davidic dynasty was in total eclipse (Kidner, 1973, p. 320). In either case, even amid circumstances suggesting that God had renounced the eternal covenant He had made with David (Ps. 89:39), the psalmist maintains a bulldog grip on the impossibility that God could ever abandon His promises, however much it may look like He has at present.

That's why the psalmist grounds his confidence in God's own words and His loyalty and faithfulness to those words. He quotes God as having made a *covenant* with David and having *sworn* to His servant (89:3, 28). He reminds God, 'You **said** (89:19), "My covenant I will not break, nor alter the word that has gone out of My lips. Once I have sworn by my holiness; I will not lie to David"' (89:34-35).

In fact, twenty-one verses of the psalm (89:3-4, 19-37) are direct quotation from God, the psalmist's reverent reminder of what the Lord had promised. In light of where this psalm is headed (89:38-51), he is respectfully putting God's trustworthiness on the line in a mighty public way. It is a classic example of praying God's words back to Him. God relishes such prayers, because they reveal a life-or-death reliance on His words and give Him the opportunity to display afresh that He does what He says.

Let's pause to regroup and sum up where we've been before we plunge ahead. One way God asserts His indivisibility from His words is by exalting His word (Ps. 138:2) and by highlighting the attributes (*lovingkindness* and *faithfulness*) that especially underscore His relationship to His words. But the Bible also has other ways of making the point that God is inseparable from His words.

Attributes of God's Words

God alone is spirit and life, eternal, pure, perfect, and righteous. Yet many of the attributes of God are also attributed directly to the words of God.[15]

---

15. References in the chart are representative, not exhaustive.

God's Person	Attribute	God's Words
Hab. 1:13	*pure*	Pss. 12:6; 19:9
Matt. 5:48[16]	*perfect*	Ps. 19:7
Deut. 7:9	*reliable*	Ps. 19:7
Deut. 32:4; Ps 25:8	*upright*	Pss 19:8; 33:4
Exod. 34:6	*true*	Ps. 19:9
Deut. 32:4	*righteous*	Ps. 19:9
Deut. 33:27	*eternal*	Ps. 119:89; Isa. 40:8; 1 Pet. 1:25; Matt. 24:35
Isa. 28:16[17]	*proven*	Pss. 12:6; 18:30; 119:140; Prov. 30:5
Pss. 62:11; 66:3; 68:35	*powerful*	Jer. 23:29
John 4:24	*spirit*	John 6:63
Heb. 3:12	*living*	Heb. 4:12
Phil. 2:13; Col. 1:29	*active*	Heb. 4:12
Acts 1:24; 15:8	*omniscient*	Heb. 4:12

Most of the passages in the right-hand column apply divine attributes in the form of adjectival descriptions (Pss. 12, 19). Some apply similes— God's word is like a fire and a rock-crushing hammer (Jer. 23:29). Hebrews 4:12 attributes to God's words not just divine qualities but personal *actions*—living, working, penetrating, discerning. Such actions are the extension of the person who speaks those words.

The fact that the Bible ascribes the same divine attributes to both the person of God and the words of God does not, of course, mean that the Bible is God or is equal to God. But it is one more way in which the Bible underscores the inextricable connection between God and His words. If Scripture teaches that God's words share the same attributes as God Himself, does that mean that we owe to God's words the same responses that we owe to God Himself? Let's explore that question.

---

16. Matthew 5:48 uses the Greek equivalent of the Hebrew word in Psalm 19:7.

17. The Hebrew word is different but essentially synonymous. The description is a metaphorical reference to the Messiah as a 'tested stone' laid in Zion.

Scriptural Responses to God's Words

In a series on gathered church worship, my pastor posed the question: What are the human responses to God of which He alone is worthy? God alone is to be supremely loved, valued, and praised. He alone is worthy to evoke reverence, fear, and trembling. *Yet Scripture teaches that we owe all these same responses not just to God's person but to God's words.*

His *words* are to be supremely loved (Ps. 119:97, 113, 165) and desired above all else (Ps. 19:10). His *words* are to be praised (Ps. 56:4, 10), believed (Ps. 106:12), rejoiced in (Ps. 119:162), and revered (Ps. 119:161). Indeed, God looks with favor and tender regard on those who tremble at His *word* (Isa. 66:2). In other words, the Scripture writers

> view the words of God with religious reverence and awe, attitudes appropriate only to an encounter with God himself.... This is extraordinary, since Scripture uniformly considers it idolatrous to worship anything other than God. But to praise or fear God's word is not idolatrous. To praise God's word is to praise God himself (Frame 2010, p. 67).

This seems self-evident, because it is only in and through God's words (Scripture) that we come to know God Himself most fully as He is. Communication is the irreplaceable medium of personal, relational knowledge. But this language of responding to the Bible the same ways we respond to God Himself may disturb some people. Frame himself raises the question, 'Does this worship justify "bibliolatry"?' (ibid.).

Is This Bibliolatry?

Do these responses to Scripture constitute bibliolatry? On the face of it, the charge sounds bogus since it is God Himself in the Scripture that commands and commends these responses to His words. A kind of bibliolatry is possible, however, when we sever the Bible from God Himself, and 'worship and serve' the book rather than its Speaker.

Bibliolatry— making the Bible into a sacred object that replaces God.

In a transparent personal testimony, New Testament Greek scholar Daniel Wallace admits that he fell into this very trap. I mentioned his story briefly in Chapter 2, but I return to it now because he specifically discusses the problem of bibliolatry. As he progressed in his advanced academic training in biblical studies and exegesis, he says, 'I began to slip away from my early, vibrant contact with God. My understanding of Scripture was heightened, but my walk with God slowed down to a crawl' (Wallace 2005, p. 5). It was not until God, in His grace, allowed a very painful family experience to invade his life that he became acutely aware of his true spiritual condition.

When a school bully savagely kicked his eight-year-old son in the stomach, a subsequent biopsy inadvertently revealed the presence of renal cell carcinoma. Months of painful medical tests and chemotherapy followed. As a father, watching his son go through these excruciating circumstances, Wallace needed God in a way he never had before. But, New Testament Greek scholar though he was, he didn't know how to find Him.

> I needed God in a personal way—not as an object of my study, but as friend, guide, comforter. I needed an existential experience of the Holy One. Quite frankly, I found that the Bible was not the answer. I found the scriptures to be helpful— even authoritatively helpful—as a guide. But without *feeling* God, the Bible gave me little solace. ... I began to examine what had become of my faith. I found a longing to get closer to God, but found myself unable to do so through my normal means: exegesis, scripture reading, more exegesis. *I believe that I had depersonalized God so much that when I really needed him I didn't know how to relate* (Wallace 2005, p. 7 emphasis added).

The very gift God gave as the primary means through which we can know Him became the primary obstacle to knowing Him—not because of the Bible, but because of the God-less approach to the Bible that Wallace had cultivated over years of seeking to understand the Bible without seeking to understand God Himself through it. The problem is not preoccupation with the Bible—just start reading Psalm 119 and witness the psalmist's passionate preoccupation with God's words that permeates that psalm. The problem is a preoccupation with the Bible that is not motivated and fed by a preoccupation with God.

If I am reading his experience correctly, I would suggest that the problem was not merely that he 'depersonalized God' but that he depersonalized the Bible. We must not sever our pursuit of the Bible from a pursuit of God Himself, or compartmentalize our knowledge of the Bible from our knowledge of God, or isolate the words of God from the God who speaks those words. What happens when we do that? 'Eventually, we no longer relate to him. God becomes the object of our investigation rather than the Lord to whom we are subject' (Wallace 2005, p. 9). The 'living' words of God (Heb. 4:12; 1 Pet. 1:23) become a lifeless text. Precise and expert exegetical operations become the scholarly equivalent of an autopsy.

It is at that point that such a person is ripe for bibliolatry. Wallace himself says as much:

> This emphasis on knowledge over relationship can produce in us a bibliolatry. For me, as a New Testament professor, the text is my task—but I made it my God. The text became my idol. Let me state this bluntly: *The Bible is not a member of the Trinity* (Wallace 2005, p. 8 emphasis original).

And yet the Bible is the speech of the Trinity, and the only place on earth where we have access to the words of the Trinity. Wallace is not denying that. Communication is the indispensable means to personal knowledge. No one can know God as He is apart from His self-revelatory words in the Bible.

It's not just scholars like Daniel Wallace who are susceptible to bibliolatry. All of us, any of us, can cultivate a fierce allegiance to the text that is devoid of a felt adoration for the God who speaks it. There lie the beginnings of Pharisaism, which is just another species of bibliolatry.

Judah took an ancient, revered, redemptive gift from God—the bronze serpent (Num. 21:8-9)—and made it into an object of worship as a substitute for the right worship of Yahweh Himself. The result was idolatry (2 Kings 18:4). Hezekiah's solution was to pulverize what Judah had idolized, so that it could no longer be a stumbling block to them. Question: Did that cure Judah of idolatry? Hardly. The problem wasn't in the bronze serpent; the problem was in the people. Hezekiah's action was appropriate and necessary, but that's where the analogy begins to break down. By demolishing the bronze serpent, Hezekiah was not removing the very means of God's communication with His people.

The solution to bibliolatry is never to do away with the Bible; you will never find God apart from it. The Bible is not the problem. *We are.* Even the desire for an accurate and technically precise understanding of the Bible is not the problem; God's words deserve all the precision and accuracy we can bring to the task of studying the Scriptures. The problem is parsing the speech while ignoring the Speaker. The solution to bibliolatry is repentance for loving to be right without loving the Righteous One (Rev. 2:2-4).

John Frame answers the charge of bibliolatry on a more physical level. 'The Bible is God's word in a finite medium.' Just as Judah was guilty of idolatry for worshipping the bronze serpent, 'We should not worship the created medium; that would be idolatry.' Yet as I pointed out earlier, there's a critical difference between the Bible and the bronze serpent. Because

> through the created medium [of the Bible] we receive the authentic word of God, and that word of God should be treasured as if God were speaking it with his own lips. It should be received with absolute trust, obedience, and, yes, worship. Opponents of evangelicalism commonly say that it is idolatrous to accept any human word as having divine authority. Scripture, however, teaches that we should accept [and respond to] the divine-human words on its pages precisely as God's own (Frame 2010, pp. 67-68).[18]

When my children would respond promptly and properly to a command, or a request, or a promise that I communicated—whether spoken or written—were they somehow substituting my *speech* for *me*? Would it ever occur to any normal father to rebuke such children for

---

18. Because he is thinking primarily of critics of the inspiration and authority of the Bible, Frame goes on to add, 'Evangelicals are often too sensitive to the charge of bibliolatry. That charge is illegitimate, and it should not motivate evangelicals to water down their view of Scripture' (ibid.).

'worshipping' his words by paying close attention to them? My speech is an indivisible extension of me, just as God's speech is an indivisible extension of Him—His will, His person, His presence, and His purposes.

Because they are from God, and God is inseparable from His words, we owe the same response to His words that we owe to God Himself. This notion is not strange to a lover who has exchanged letters with a fiancé, or a mother corresponding with her son on a distant military post. The notes are treasured because the words embody the presence of the one who is loved but absent.[19]

Finally, one negative response to God's words is worth pondering, because it potently reasserts the indivisibility of God and His words. Any believer should recoil from the idea of being ashamed of God or of Christ. But Jesus takes that a step further when He says that 'whoever is ashamed of Me **and of my words** in this adulterous and sinful generation, of him will the Son of Man also be ashamed when He comes in the glory of His Father with the holy angels' (Mark 8:38). We may not understand everything God says, but we should never be ashamed of anything He says. To do so is to be ashamed of Him, because God and His words are inseparable. We should be so convinced of His trustworthiness that we are confident that whatever He says, when rightly understood, is not only reliable but right.

'Word of God' as a Name of God

'In the beginning...' You know those words. But what follows? Moses says 'God' (Gen. 1:1). John says 'the Word' (John 1:1). Moses and John are not disagreeing. John goes on to clarify that he and Moses are saying the same thing: 'the Word was God.' That's an astonishing juxtaposition: *Word* and *God*. And God Himself is the one who merges them.

'The Word,' a title applied specifically to Christ as the second person of the Godhead (John 1:17), is rare and revealed only through John.[20]

---

19. I know this is hard for younger readers to relate to. If you don't remember life without email or skype, or free long-distance phone calls, you have to realize that for 98 per cent of human history, letters were the only means of being together and sharing each other's presence in times of physical absence from one another. In those circumstances, the words are the person.

20. John 1:1, 14; 1 John 1:1; Revelation 19:13.

Of the passages that use it, John 1 is the most theologically fertile. But the most arresting, for our purposes, is in Revelation.

> Now I saw heaven opened, and behold, a white horse. And **He who sat on him was called Faithful and True**, and in righteousness He judges and makes war. His eyes were like a flame of fire, and on His head were many crowns. He had a name written that no one knew except Himself. He was clothed with a robe dipped in blood, and **His name is called The Word of God** (Rev. 19:11-13).

This title is not merely a passing theological description connected only with Christ's incarnation. The name by which He is known and identified at His glorious and victorious return is 'The Word of God.' And the descriptors that accompany His appearance as 'The Word of God' are *faithful* and *genuine*, *reliable* and *real*, *trustworthy* and *true*.[21]

Perhaps this is what David was unwittingly communicating in Psalm 138:2—that God has supremely magnified His word alongside His very name, by merging them![22] What more eternal or emphatic way could God assert that He and His words are indivisible than by memorializing that truth in one of His names?

Last Words

Whatever is true of God is true of the words of God, or else God Himself is a deceiver and a fraud. His words proceed from His character. So the qualities of His character extend to His words. God is trustworthy only if His words are also trustworthy.

> There is a permanent relationship between faith and the Word ...; if it turns away from the Word, it falls.... [God] always represents himself through his Word.... It is not even enough

---

21. These are all legitimate translations of the respective Greek words in 19:11, *pistos* and *alēthinos*. This couplet appears several times in Revelation (3:14, 19:11; 21:5; 22:6).

22. Peter makes it clear that the OT prophets did not fully comprehend everything they were revealing (1 Pet. 1:10-12).

> to believe that God is trustworthy ... unless you hold that
> whatever proceeds from him is sacred and inviolable truth
> (Calvin 1960, pp. 548-49 [3.2.6]).

There is a mentality that wants to embrace the 'truths' of the Bible but not necessarily the 'facts' of the Bible. Some view the biblical account of the virgin birth and deity of Immanuel as a legend intended only to teach the 'truth' that 'God is with us.' Others affirm the 'truth' that God can overcome even death, but deny the factuality of the literal resurrection of Christ from the dead that proves it. Still others, including an increasing number of evangelicals, believe that man evolved naturally; the Bible's creation account is a myth designed to teach us the 'truth' of the reality of a Being bigger than us. As we'll discover in Chapter 7, God has staked His integrity on His account of creation.

There is no truth without fact. 'The apostle Paul famously remarked to the Corinthian Christians' (1 Cor. 15:17) 'that if Christ had not in fact been raised from the dead, then their faith was futile and they were still as lost [as] they had ever been' (Thompson 2006, p. 125). And there is no true faith in God without confidence in His words.

> When we encounter the word of God, we encounter God. When
> we encounter God, we encounter his word. We cannot encounter
> God without the word, or the word without God. God's word
> and his personal presence are inseparable. His word, indeed, is
> his personal presence. Whenever God's Word is spoken, read,
> or heard, God himself is there (Frame 2010, p. 68).

Nothing on earth is closer, or gets you closer, to God Himself than His words.

Review & Reflect

1. Since there has been no Davidic king over Israel ever since the Babylonian captivity, how has God's promise to David not failed? How does Psalm 89:36-37 help address that question?

2. Choose two or three of the attributes in the chart in this chapter and reflect on how that attribute of God's words might change your view and use of Scripture.

3. Can you think of Bible characters who questioned whether God truly was as good as His word, or would make good on His word?

4. What attributes or characteristics of God are necessary in order for all of God's words to be entirely trustworthy?

5
The Theological Foundations of God's Trustworthiness

God, who cannot lie, promised
Titus 1:2

In Chapter 3, I proposed that God's trustworthiness is foundational to our knowledge of all His other attributes, because we are dependent on His self-revelation to know what He is like. If He's not trustworthy, then neither is His self-revelation. The objection that we could still know God through His actions fails because actions alone are much more ambiguous than words, subject to different (and often opposing) interpretations. The only way we can reliably interpret His acts is if we have an authoritative guide to His character. If God, and therefore His word, is not trustworthy, then we cannot know anything about who God really is or what He is really like. But it's equally true that God's trustworthiness is, itself, rooted in other attributes. That's what this chapter investigates.

In Chapter 4 we noted that at the core of trustworthiness is being and doing what one claims. That begins with simple honesty. A parent who repeatedly promises a trip to the zoo, or who continually warns that consequences will follow 'if you do that one more time' and habitually fails to follow through, forfeits the expectation to be trusted. Worse, the adult who *knowingly* deceives a child—whether through promise or threat—in order to secure short-term cooperation or compliance, might be called many things, but trustworthy is not one of them.

We value good and honest intentions. But, in the end, that alone is not enough to warrant confidence. Something about being a youngest child makes one relish the opportunity to be the first to update the family on some latest piece of news. I was like that. My youngest son, likewise, was affectionately dubbed the family 'informer.' It's frustrating when you always feel like the last person to find out what's going on. So to a youngest child, a scoop is irresistible. You can't wait to surprise others with some bit of news that you picked up. You wander from room to room, updating each sibling individually of what just happened outside, or what was just said in the kitchen, or what you heard from someone at church. I'm not talking about tattling or gossiping, just news-ing. The glory of a youngest child is to give someone older a fact of which they were previously ignorant. The problem is, a youngest child's generally limited scope of experience and context means that he may not always get it quite right. The last thing in the world he wants to do is misinform, but sometimes that's what happens. Once his 'credibility' is tarnished, later bits of news are often met with a skepticism that he finds profoundly frustrating.

The point? Sometimes trustworthiness is compromised not by dishonesty but by honest error. Someone gives information in good faith because he believes it's good information; he just happens to be earnestly and sincerely mistaken.

Then again, sometimes trustworthiness can be compromised not by outright dishonesty or even honest error, but when one's good will exceeds one's capacity to deliver.

> The woman who promises her friend that she will give her £1000 yet does not have two pennies to rub together may have the best intentions in the world; but her inability to honor the promise indicates that she is, however reluctantly, untrustworthy (Helm and Trueman 2002, p. ix).

Trustworthiness demands integrity. But integrity is a complex of several factors. In his presentation of God's attributes, theologian Millard Erickson divides God's integrity into three components: '(1) genuineness—being true; (2) veracity—telling the truth; and (3) faithfulness—proving true' (Erickson 2013, pp. 260-62). Those are valid and helpful distinctions. For my purposes, however, I want to develop the components of integrity in a slightly different direction.

This book is largely focused on that third component—the faithfulness of God and, more specifically, the trustworthiness of His words. Certainly that starts with the first component, the genuineness of God as the one true God in contrast to all imposter deities (Jer. 10:1-10). But how do we know that? Because He has told us.

Again, we're back to the trustworthiness of His words, which require certain things to be true of Him, namely (1) veracity—He always tells the truth and is never deceptive; (2) omniscience—He always knows the truth and is never deceived; and (3) omnipotence—He always has the capacity to deliver anything He predicts or promises.[1] So it will be worth briefly establishing these three attributes of God.[2] After that, however, we'll investigate one more component that often goes unnoticed but is essential for trustworthiness to be meaningful.

Truthfulness: The Veracity of God

The veracity of God simply means that God tells the truth. Always. He does not and cannot deceive in what He says. 'God is not a man, that He should lie' (Num. 23:19). That statement says as much about us as it says about God. The psalmist complains that he is surrounded by people to whom lying is as natural as breathing (Ps. 12:1-4). By contrast, 'the words of the LORD are pure words' (Ps. 12:6). Likewise, Numbers 23:19 concludes, 'Does He speak and not act, or promise and not fulfill?' (HCSB). Or to turn the rhetorical question into a declaration: 'When he says something, he will do it; when he makes a promise, he will fulfill it' (CJB).

God is incapable of deception (Titus 1:2; Heb. 6:18) because He is the God of truth (Deut. 32:4; Ps. 31:5; Isa. 65:16). Consequently, all His words are factually accurate (2 Sam. 7:28; Ps. 119:160), which means that all He says—history, testimony, promise, prophecy—is reliable. Jesus Himself affirmed this when He said to the Father, 'Your word

---

1. Paul Helm, likewise, argues that 'divine trustworthiness presupposes' these same three attributes of knowledge, power, and veracity (Helm 2002, p. 240).

2. What follows are hardly exhaustive definitions or defenses of these divine attributes. For fuller treatment see the systematic theologies of Frame (2013), Erickson (1998), Grudem (1994), and others.

is truth' (John 17:17). It is useless to try to limit that quality to God's *person* and not to God's *statements*. Veracity is meaningless if it does not extend to a person's words. 'God's Word is inherently trustworthy because his character is completely reliable' (Jaeggli 2004, p. 244).

So, 'it is impossible for God to lie' (Heb. 6:18). But what if He is mistaken and unintentionally misinforms us? 'Does veracity mean that what God says can also be trusted?' Erickson queries. 'Or does it mean simply that he does not knowingly tell an untruth?' That brings up another divine attribute that is necessary to trustworthiness. God's omniscience 'combines with his veracity to guarantee the truth of everything he tells us' (Erickson 2013, p. 261).

Omniscience: The Accuracy of God

Omniscience means 'all-knowing.' To fill that out a bit more, 'God knows all things actual and possible in one simple and eternal act' (Grudem 1994, p. 190). God's omniscience certifies the accuracy of God's veracity. God cannot deceive; but beyond that, God cannot be deceived, mistaken, or misinformed because He knows everything.

He is 'perfect in knowledge' (Job 37:16), meaning that His knowledge is complete and all-inclusive—nothing omitted, no missing pieces. His knowledge encompasses things as mundane as a single sparrow's fall and as minute as how many hairs you have (Matt. 10:29-30). As in Job 39:1, he is even 'aware whenever wild mountain goats labor to give birth and whenever a deer calves' (Talbert 2007, p. 205).

His knowledge embraces every detail of your life. David infuses Psalm 139 with a multiplicity of divine actions —God *searches, knows, understands, comprehends, is acquainted, encloses, sees, writes*—all expressing God's omniscience. He knows not only my actions but even my plans (v. 2). He sifts[3] my ways (v. 3) and detects my words even before I speak them (v. 4). His awareness surrounds and envelopes me (v. 5). Darkness conceals nothing from Him (vv. 11-12). God's knowledge even ultrasounds the womb, where He observed your embryo (v. 16) and saw all 206 bones in your skeletal frame before

---

3. The first verb in Psalm 139:3 is the word for winnowing.

you were born (v. 15). Such intimate and inclusive knowledge should both excite and awe us (v. 6). God's knowledge is both individual and universal (Ps. 33:13-15; Heb. 4:13).

God's knowledge extends not only to actualities but even possibilities. This fact is not so much stated in Scripture as demonstrated. While David was hiding in the city of Keilah, news reached him that Saul had discovered his whereabouts (1 Sam. 23). So David asked the Lord (a) if Saul would come to Keilah, and (b) if the men of Keilah would betray him into Saul's hands. The answer to both, God said, was yes. As a result, the first happened (Saul came to Keilah) but the second never did, because David and his men—acting on God's knowledge of what would happen—abandoned Keilah before Saul arrived. In other words, God knows not only what will happen and does, but what would happen but doesn't.[4]

Finally, His knowledge covers all of reality from beginning to end. 'His understanding is infinite' (Ps. 147:5; Isa. 40:28). So all-inclusive is God's knowledge that He 'announces the end from the beginning and reveals beforehand what has not yet occurred' (Isa. 46:10, NET). Fulfilled prophecy furnishes abundant evidence of God's omniscience.

So God can never be mistaken or misinformed in what He says. But suppose He predicts or promises something that He fully intends to do and tries His best to accomplish, but cannot quite pull off? One more divine attribute works with these others to seal the rock-solid reliability of every word He utters.

Omnipotence: The Ability of God

Divine omnipotence refers to God's 'ability to do all things that are proper objects of his power' (Erickson 2013, p. 384).[5] God cannot be thwarted in performing what He says.

We've already heard the testimony of Isaiah 46:10 to God's omniscience, but listen to the rest of the verse: 'I declare the end from

---

4. Other examples of God's knowledge of all things actual and possible are 2 Kings 13:19 and Matthew 11:21, 23.

5. Alleged challenges to God's omnipotence ('Can God do so-and-so?') often confuse the issue of power with the issue of nature.

the beginning, and from long ago what is not yet done, saying, My plan will take place and I will do all My will' (Isa. 46:10, HCSB). 'Many are the plans in the mind of a man,' observes Solomon, 'but it is the purpose of the LORD that will stand' (Prov. 19:21 ESV).

What if the plans of great and powerful nations conflict with God's plan? 'The LORD brings the counsel of the nations to nothing; He makes the plans of the peoples of no effect. The counsel of the LORD stands forever, the plans of His heart to all generations' (Ps. 33:10-11). Why? Because God's 'dominion is an everlasting dominion, and His kingdom is from generation to generation. All the inhabitants of the earth are reputed as nothing; He does according to His will in the army of heaven and among the inhabitants of the earth. No one can restrain His hand or say to Him, "What have You done?"' (Dan. 4:34-35).

Job's final repentance (for sins of attitude and speech that resulted from his suffering) begins with a confession of faith that God has the right to do anything He chooses, and that 'no plan of Yours can be thwarted' (Job 42:2, HCSB). 'Our God is in heaven,' the psalmist echoes, 'He does whatever He pleases' (Ps. 115:3).

Reliability, then, requires honesty, accuracy, and ability. These are not just possessions of God, they are infinite perfections of God. That makes God infinitely, perfectly reliable in His person and every word from His lips intrinsically trustworthy.

But what if He chooses not to speak? Or what if His words are vague, mystical, or in some strange language that only a select few, a priestly hierarchy, have the gift to understand them? That's exactly what many false religions believe. Or suppose God's words are so esoteric or ambiguous that only a scholarly hierarchy has the wit to interpret them correctly—which is only a more sophisticated version of the same thing.

> Having escaped the clutches of the priests, to some it seems as if today the Bible is being sequestered by the academic guild under the guise of hermeneutical sophistication (Thompson 2006, p. 132).

To be meaningful, trustworthiness requires one last component.

Communicativeness: The Clarity of God's Words

A man shipwrecked alone for life on a deserted island may cultivate many admirable qualities. He may develop great knowledge by learning all there is to know about the island's flora and fauna. He may be industrious and creative. But you'd be hard-pressed to have any demonstrable or justifiable reason for calling him trustworthy. He's simply not in a position to develop or display that quality. 'Trustworthiness is a relational expression' (Helm 2002, pp. 239-40). That is, it must be demonstrated *to* someone, and can therefore be displayed only in the context of a relationship.

So trustworthiness requires relationship, and relationship requires communication. Trustworthiness necessarily describes both a person and his words, or neither. And one's speech is the chief means of demonstrating and measuring one's trustworthiness. That means that trustworthiness is both relational and communicational.

Those two qualifications lead to a fourth component that is necessary for trustworthiness to be meaningful: one's speech must be not only honest but also comprehensible. In the end, God's trustworthiness doesn't mean anything if we routinely can't really understand what He means. How else are we to gauge His trustworthiness than by the correlation between what He says—and the expectations that creates—and what He does?[6]

Permit me a facetious illustration. We don't do a lot of hockey down south where I grew up, so I don't know much about it. Suppose I visit Chicago to watch the Blackhawks; but all the Zamboni[7] drivers are on strike, so they're looking for a substitute and I volunteer: 'Sure, I'll drive the Zamboni during halftime!' Halftime comes and I drive the Zamboni to the Arby's drive-through for a beef-and-cheddar sandwich (heavy on the horsey sauce) and a mocha shake. (The scenario is

---

6. It is not my intention to oversimplify the matter of the perspicuity (clarity) of Scripture, nor to bog down the reader here with an extended foray into the complexities of the issue. For a comprehensive discussion see Thompson 2006.

7. Named after American inventor and engineer Frank Zamboni, this ice-resurfacing vehicle is designed to mechanically clean and smooth the surface of an ice-skating rink.

admittedly ridiculous, but not impossible.[8]) I did what I said I would do: I drove the Zamboni at halftime. I knew what I meant when I volunteered, so I was not being deceptive. My trustworthiness to do what I said was compromised, however, not by dishonesty or lack of intentionality but by a breakdown in clear communication and mutual understanding.

That bit of absurdity was just for fun and to make the point. Let me try to translate the issue into more biblical terms. What expectations are created when God speaks of a six-day creation and the formation of a man and a woman from the dust of the ground (Gen. 1-2)? What does the promise to Abraham's seed of a land that they will possess forever lead them—and us—to anticipate (Gen. 17)? What does a solemn oath that Israel will never cease to be a nation imply (Jer. 31)? Especially when God has established an otherwise invariable pattern of doing exactly what He says.

I bring up these examples simply to establish a point: because trustworthiness is both a relational and a communicational attribute, then essential to God's trustworthiness is the clarity and comprehensibility of God's words to those in whom He wishes to engender trust in Him. 'If Scripture is not clear, not generally accessible to faithful men and women who prayerfully read, seeking to know the mind of God, what are we then saying about God?' (Thompson 2006, p. 79).

There must be a meaningful correlation between what He says and what He does, or the basis for trustworthiness dissolves. If God routinely speaks in riddles, if God chooses language and expressions that He knows His audience will naturally interpret differently than He intends,[9] then God is purposely creating expectations that He knows He will not fulfill. If that's the case, it's difficult to escape the conclusion

---

8. After I wrote this paragraph, I discovered a story about two employees of Idaho IceWorld who were fired after driving a pair of Zambonis to a Boise Burger King drive-through after midnight on November 10, 2006.

9. The word 'naturally' is an important qualifier. Jesus often used language that He knew some in His audience would stumble over (e.g., John 6:51-52). But they misconstrued Him out of stubborn rejection despite clarifications Jesus made in the context (e.g., John 6:35).

that His trustworthiness (and potentially even His truthfulness) is compromised.

How do I trust someone if I don't know what he means because he is purposefully vague? What does it mean to trust God if my hermeneutic teaches me that I can't know for sure what He means because He always speaks symbolically or allegorically? Faith cannot meaningfully 'be sustained without promises that are direct and univocal' (Thompson 2006, p. 69).[10]

God is a flawless communicator. He does not always reveal all, but neither does He purposely mislead His people. 'God has something to say and he is very good at saying it' (Thompson 2006, p. 170). God means exactly what He says; that's veracity, backed up by omniscience and omnipotence. But God also says exactly what He means; that's clarity.[11] Both are necessary for trustworthiness to be a fully functional attribute.

Final Snapshot

Let me leave a picture with you. When the disciples faced a fearful storm on the Sea of Galilee, Jesus came to them walking on the water (Matt. 14). Each flash of lightning revealed a figure moving closer and closer to them over the surface of the storm-tossed whitecaps. They were terrified, certain it was a spirit. What else *could* it be? Jesus sought to calm and encourage them with the assurance that it was Him. Peter wanted confirmation: 'Lord, if it is you, command me to come to You on the water' (v. 28). Jesus replied in one word: 'Come.' And Peter came. He 'walked on the water to go to Jesus' (v. 29). But when he focused on the bizarre clash between his circumstances and his actions (instead of the word from Jesus), he faltered. Jesus was there both to rescue and to rebuke: 'Why did you doubt?' (v. 31). Doubt what? Peter stepped out

---

10. This does not mean that God never uses symbolism or allegory; He does (e.g., Isa. 5:1-6; Ezek. 17:1-8; Rev. 12:1ff.). When He does, however, He routinely either identifies it as a symbol (Rev. 12:1) or explains the allegory (Isa. 5:7ff; Ezek. 17:11ff.). Cf. Thompson 2006, p. 125.

11. 'When [God] intends to communicate with a human being, he is always able to do it successfully. But another name for successful communication is *clarity*' (Frame 2010, p. 204, original emphasis).

into a storm at a word from Christ, and what held him up was not the sea but a single word from the Son of God. When he looked at the sea, he doubted Christ's word.

God is always utterly honest, infallibly informed, eminently able, candidly communicative, and therefore unworthy of any shadow of doubt, whether He is relating past history, prophesying future events, promising present provision, or even calling you to do what seems to you impossible.

Review & Reflect

1. Summarize how the attributes of God discussed in this chapter work together to guarantee the trustworthiness of His words.

2. What kinds of life experiences have made you wonder about God's veracity, omniscience, or omnipotence?

3. How does the argument for the essential clarity of God's words relate to the Bible's use of parables, allegories (Judg. 9:7-15; Isa. 5:1-6; Ezek. 17:1-8), symbolism (the tabernacle; Revelation 12), etc.?

6

Jesus on the Trustworthiness of God's Words

Scripture cannot be broken
John 10:35

This chapter actually bridges Parts 1 and 2 of this book. What Jesus has to say about the trustworthiness of God's words is clearly part of the theological foundation of this subject; there is no more astute theologian than the Son of God, and anything He has to say about God's words must be considered foundational to the doctrine we're investigating. At the same time, what He does with Scripture models for us how to apply God's words in a variety of practical areas.

Much has been written elsewhere about Jesus' testimony, both directly and indirectly, to the authority and reliability of the Old Testament.[1] It is a standard topic in works on apologetics, and rightly so. What Jesus said about the Old Testament demonstrates what He believed about it, and what Jesus believed about the Old Testament has to matter to believers.

The goal of this chapter is not (like most other treatments of this topic) to prove that Jesus believed the Old Testament to be God's authoritative word. This chapter aims to demonstrate Jesus' utter confidence in the trustworthiness of God's words in all His teaching and all His living. Whether He was interpreting events or instructing people, confronting sin or correcting error, facing temptation or

---

1. See, for example, Wenham 1994, pp. 16-90 and, more recently, DeYoung 2014, pp. 95-110 or Piper 2016, pp. 99-113.

enduring suffering, Jesus' confidence in God's words has profound relevance for our confidence in God's words.

Every time Jesus said 'as it is written'[2] He was affirming the trustworthy authority of God's Old Testament words. Every time He asked His learned detractors, 'Have you never read?'[3] it was an implicit assertion of the reliability of God's words to settle whatever challenge they had thrust at Him.

We'll survey three major areas of Jesus' relationship to God's words: His assumptions about God's words, His teachings about God's words, and His use of God's words. Jesus' exemplary attitude toward Scripture should encourage believers to lean all their confidence on the trustworthiness of God's words in every circumstance, just like Jesus did.

Jesus' Assumptions About God's Old Testament Words

No one who thinks highly of Jesus can dismiss His view of God's words in the Old Testament. And anyone who is unwilling to take the statements of the Old Testament at face value—about prophecy, or creation, or whatever else it records or affirms—has to explain why Jesus so clearly did. It's an uncomfortable position for someone to be in, since it unavoidably says something either about Jesus or about himself. One of them has to be mistaken.

The Historical Reliability of Scripture as God's Words

The list is impressive. Jesus made passing remarks—comments that assert His assumption of complete factuality— about Abel, Abraham, Adam and Eve, David, Daniel, Elijah, Elisha, Isaac, Isaiah, Jacob, Jonah, Lot, Moses, Naaman, Nineveh, Noah, the Queen of Sheba, Sodom and Gomorrah, Solomon, Zechariah, and the widow of Zarephath. In many cases, Jesus specifically mentioned the extraordinary or even miraculous events connected with some of these people and places. He also matter-of-factly references the stories of the creation, the flood, the burning bush, the miraculous manna, the serpent in the

---

2. E.g., Mark 7:6; 9:13; 14:21.
3. Matt. 12:3, 5; 19:4; 21:16, 42; 22:31.

wilderness, and even (blush) the great fish that swallowed Jonah. It's almost as if Christ purposefully chose to validate many of the stories later deemed most objectionable to the scholarly mind (Wenham 1994, p. 18).

But just because Jesus referenced certain stories or names, does that necessarily mean that He condoned their historicity? After all, I might allude to Prospero, Aslan, hobbits, or Marley's ghost without implying that I believe any of them to be historical realities. We use fictional literary allusions for illustration all the time. Why may we not assume Jesus did the same?

Yet something very different is going on, for instance, when Christ said that the contemporary population of Capernaum and the ancient population of Sodom would both appear at the final judgment—and even the Sodomites would fare better than the Capernaumites (Matt. 11:23-24). The comparison is meaningless apart from the historical reputation of Sodom. Or consider when He paralleled His own burial in the heart of the earth with Jonah's three-day entombment in the belly of the fish (Matt. 12:39-40). In the same breath He then extended the Jonah narrative by warning that 'the men of Nineveh will rise up in the judgment with this generation and condemn it, because they repented at the preaching of Jonah' (12:41). If Jesus was merely citing literary, non-historical events, then His whole argument evaporates in a puff of absurdity. Probably no one has expressed this more effectively than the oft-quoted T. T. Perowne did long ago.

> The future Judge is speaking words of solemn warning to those who shall hereafter stand convicted at His bar.... And yet we are to suppose Him to say that imaginary persons who at the imaginary preaching of an imaginary prophet repented in imagination, shall rise up in that day and condemn the actual impenitence of those His actual hearers, that the fictitious characters of a parable shall be arraigned at the same bar with the living men of that generation (Perowne 1878, p. 15).[4]

---

4. Put more modernly, 'It would be like ... issuing a very serious warning to your audience that the orcs of Mordor will rise up to judge and condemn them' (DeYoung 2014, p. 103).

If the historicity of Jonah falls, so does the credibility of Jesus. But if the credibility of Jesus stands, and the story of Jonah happened, then anything can happen and there's no valid reason to doubt anything else Jesus affirmed from God's words, directly or indirectly.

For Jesus, in order to validate His teaching, to cite the miraculous provision of manna (John 6:49), or Elijah's ministry to the widow of Zarephath (Luke 4:25-26), or Elisha's miraculous healing of Naaman's leprosy (Luke 4:27), or Noah's ark and the flood (Luke 17:25-26), or the divine destruction of Sodom (Luke 17:28-29), would be meaningless if these events were fictional. Jesus regarded God's Old Testament words to be utterly reliable in their depiction of historical realities, and trustworthy enough to validate His soberest teachings and sternest warnings.

The Identification of Scripture as God's Words

Another assumption that underlies Jesus' use of the Old Testament is 'the remarkable interchangeability of the terms 'God' and 'scripture' (Wenham 1994, 34).[5] For example, in Mark 7 the very words Jesus first attributed to Moses ('Moses said,' 7:10) He also attributed directly to God ('the word of God,' 7:13). To Jesus, the two are synonymous. Scripture's words are God's words and, therefore, entirely trustworthy.

When Jesus was questioned about marriage and divorce in Matthew 19 (a passage we'll consider in more detail later in the chapter), He cites two passages from Genesis as decisive for His argument:

> He who made them at the beginning 'made them male and female' [Gen. 5:2] and said, 'For this reason a man shall leave his father and mother and be joined to his wife, and the two shall become one flesh' [Gen. 2:24] (Matt. 19:4-5).

Look closely, however, and you discover that God is not directly speaking in Genesis 2:24; there is no quotation, no 'Then God said ....' The statement is simply a narrative remark inserted by Moses at the direction of the Spirit of God; so ultimately it is God's speech. In other words, the statement that Jesus here attributed to God 'can be treated

---

5. This observation is not a new one. See Warfield 1948, p. 299ff.

as a declaration of God's only on the hypothesis that all Scripture is a declaration of God's' (Warfield 1948, p. 143). To Jesus, Scripture said equals Moses said equals God said.[6]

Jesus' Teaching about God's Old Testament Words

We've examined the assumptions that underlie Jesus' view of God's words. But He also made explicit claims concerning God's words that speak directly to their trustworthiness.

God Will Do Exactly Everything He Has Said (Matt. 5:18)

Near the beginning of His ministry Jesus assured His hearers that His relationship to God's Old Testament words was purely corroborative and confirmatory. He came, in fact, to fulfill them.

> For I assure you: Until heaven and earth pass away, not the smallest letter or one stroke of a letter will pass from the law until all things are accomplished (Matt. 5:18 HCSB).

This is the famous jot-and-tittle passage, which the HCSB translates so helpfully and accurately here that I don't need to explain what a 'jot' or a 'tittle' is. Jesus' statement cannot be dismissed as hyperbolic; it was purposeful, measured, and solemnly certified ('I assure you'). And it is staggering, because it is so extreme, so excessively specific, and so utterly unnecessary—unless He actually meant it.

He could have simply said, 'God will do all He has said.' Or, 'No statement will fail.' Or even, 'No word will be left unperformed.' Any of those would be arresting claims. But Jesus is so convinced of the inviolable reliability of every word of God that He unhesitatingly hangs all His weight from the tip of the slenderest branch: *not a letter or penstroke* will be left dangling and unfulfilled.

This is as unblinking and unambiguous an assertion of verbal inspiration ('syllabic inspiration' would not overstate it) as can be

---

6. The NT also equates the words of Jesus with the words of God (Luke 5:1; 8:21; John 3:34).

found anywhere. It emerges not from the mouth of some antiquated fundamentalist fogy, but from the lips of the Son of God Himself. And according to Him, God is committed to doing everything He has said exactly as He has said it.

God's Words Are Irrefutable (John 10:35)

Near the end of His ministry Jesus made another telling statement about God's words. So much has been written elsewhere about John 10:35—'the Scripture cannot be broken'—that there is little to be added. Jesus' words 'mean that the Scripture cannot be annulled, or set aside, or proved false' (Carson 1991, p. 399; cf. Warfield 1948, p. 139). 'It means that Scripture cannot be emptied of its force by being shown to be erroneous' (Morris 1971, p. 527).

> It's Jesus' way of affirming that no word of Scripture can be falsified. No promise or threat can fall short of fulfillment. No statement can be found erroneous (DeYoung 2014, p. 98).

Reduced to its simplest terms: in Jesus' estimation, whatever Scripture says is so. Period.

The potency of Jesus' statement in John 10:35 lies in three facts. First, it was *an offhand remark*. It was not Jesus' main point, just a passing footnote. He did not go out of His way to argue for it. He interjected it matter-of-factly as a passing comment; 'and it is often in such passing comments that our real convictions come to the surface' (Ferguson 2014, p. 39).

Second, it was an offhand remark about *an obscure passage*. He drew this footnote affirmation about the inviolability of Scripture not from some major doctrinal or prophetic section, but from one of the most out-of-the-way texts He ever cited to prove anything—Psalm 82:6.[7] If even the most obscure passages qualify as reliable and certain, what does that say about the rest of Scripture?

Third, it was an *all-inclusive* offhand remark about an obscure passage.[8] The statement Jesus cited from Psalm 82:6 is unarguable not because it was spoken by David or a rabbi or any other revered

---

7. Morris 1971, p. 526; Warfield 1948, p. 140.

8. Carson 1991, p. 397; Warfield 1948, p. 139.

authority, nor because its logic is inherently indisputable, but simply because it is 'the Scripture.'

Jesus' Use of God's Words

No one modeled how to 'live by every word that proceeds from the mouth of God' better than Jesus. Jesus not only taught about God's words. A whole raft of passages demonstrate how Jesus used God's words in every circumstance of life.

In Temptation

Jesus leaned on God's words in combatting temptation

The strategy of the Son of God in the face of Satanic suggestion is astonishing (Matt. 4). He might have offered any number of counterarguments or rationales to these temptations, or attacked the absurdity of Satan's challenges, or appealed to larger spiritual realities of which they were both well aware. He could have said, 'It's been forty days already; I can wait a little longer.' Or, 'I do not need theatrics to prove who I am; I will do greater works than this.' Or, 'I created you! You will bow down to me!' He even could have articulated a brilliant and flawless theological rationale in His own words. What He did instead was revolutionary in its simplicity, and profoundly encouraging for ordinary people like us. He did only what you and I can do in temptation, and He did it as our example: He quoted God's words and leaned all His weight on them.

There was no desperation in Christ's quotation of Scripture; the strength to stand against temptation does not lie in feverish self-reminders amid the heat of battle. Nor was He engaging the devil in argumentation. He was simply countering Satan's suggestion of a possibility with an authoritative statement of reality, because reality is always defined by Gods words.

> Jesus defined, in the hearing of the enemy, His own position.... 'It is written' is a declaration of the fact that He stood within the circle of the will of God, and what that will permitted, He willed to do; and what that will made no provision for, He willed to do without (Morgan 1936, pp. 169-70).

By hanging His response on a word from God in every case, Jesus modeled a settled commitment to God's words as expressing reality,

Our best defense in temptation is offense.

and therefore as the basis on which we must stake out our position in temptation. Often, our best defense in temptation is offense, defining our position positively in terms of God's words, staking out our territory by siding with what God says about who He is and who we are, and about what He requires of us and promises to us.

How about applying Jesus' example to using statements like these when we are tempted? It is written:

- 'present your bodies a living sacrifice, holy, acceptable to God, which is your reasonable service' (Rom. 12:1)

- 'whether, therefore, you eat, or drink, or whatever you do, do all to the glory of God' (1 Cor. 10:31)

- 'Satan himself transforms himself into an angel of light' (2 Cor. 11:14)

- 'I have been crucified with Christ; it is no longer I who live, but Christ lives in me ... who loved me and gave Himself for me' (Gal. 2:20)

- 'we are His workmanship, created in Christ Jesus for good works, which God prepared beforehand, that we should walk in them' (Eph. 2:10)

- 'for to you it has been granted on behalf of Christ, not only to believe in Him, but also to suffer for His sake' (Phil. 1:29)

- 'if, then, you were raised with Christ, seek those things which are above, where Christ is sitting on the right hand of God; set your mind on things above, not on things on the earth; for you died, and your life is hidden with Christ in God' (Col. 3:1-3)

These are more than shields to parry temptation's thrusts; they are short swords with which to counterattack sinful suggestions, whatever their source. And there are hundreds more. Jesus could unsheathe just the right dagger for each temptation because He learned God's words so well.[9] The better we know God's words, the more skillful swordsmen we will be as well.

The Bible's record of this event could hardly be more significant. The first Adam collapsed under temptation, largely because he failed to counter Satan's words with God's words (see Chapter 7). The second Adam (1 Cor. 15:45) overcame temptation by countering Satan's words with God's. His example in relying on God's words should not be lost on us.

In Teaching

If Jesus was God, couldn't He just ground His teaching in the independent authority of His own pronouncements? Yet Christ repeatedly made God's words in the Old Testament the ground and authority of His teaching, both to establish His own doctrine and to correct the errors of others.[10] That, too, says something about the trustworthiness of God's words.

Jesus relied on God's words for a right view of marriage

The Pharisees posed a question to Jesus about divorce in order to test Him: 'Is it lawful to divorce a wife for any cause?' (Matt. 19:3 NET). What they may have hoped He might say on this issue is not clear. Perhaps they just wanted to get Him to commit one way or the other on a controversial issue in hopes of alienating at least some of His followers.[11]

---

9. There is a great deal we don't know about the 'mechanics' of the incarnation, but it is almost certainly a mistake to think that Jesus carried into His humanity an omniscient knowledge of Scripture on which He could draw effortlessly. He was made just like us so He could help us when we are tempted (Heb. 2:17-18), was tempted just like we are (Heb. 4:15), learned obedience through suffering (Heb. 5:8), and relied on the Father's instruction day by day (Isa. 50:4-5). He learned the holy Scriptures just like we have to.

10. Even in the Sermon on the Mount, when He issued His six-fold 'You have heard it said,' each 'but I say to you' was not some revolutionary new assertion, but a clarification and application of the divine intention underlying God's original words.

11. Some have argued that because Jesus was, at this time, in the region ruled by Herod Antipas, the Pharisees hoped He would denounce divorce just as John the Baptist had denounced Herod's divorce and remarriage and, like John, lose

Jesus' reaction is noteworthy. Rather than wading into the rabbinic wars over this issue, He appealed directly to God's words and seemed to assume that they are both clear and authoritative. There is a delicious irony in the words that Jesus matter-of-factly leveled at those who were supposed to be experts in the Law: 'Have you not read?' Sometimes all the theological debate generated by assumptions and extrapolations evaporate if we will simply go back and ask what God's first words indicate to be His original intent from the beginning. What should they have read?

> ... that He who made them at the beginning 'made them male and female,' and said, 'For this reason a man shall leave his father and mother and be joined to his wife, and the two shall become one flesh'? So then, they are no longer two but one flesh. Therefore what God has joined together, let not man separate (Matt. 19:4-6).

Jesus spoke as if that settled the issue. If we follow His example of assuming the trustworthiness of God's words and drawing simple, obvious conclusions from them, the words He cited still address a number of contemporary issues: the divine origin of man (God made them at the beginning), the divine intention of gender distinctions (God made them male and female), the definition of marriage (a man and his wife), the indivisibility of the marriage bond (they two shall be one flesh), the sanctity of the marriage relationship (what God joins together), and the intended permanence of marriage (let not man separate).

The Pharisees, however, were still inclined to argue: 'Why then did Moses command to give her a certificate of divorce, and to put her away?' (19:7). A fair question, since that, too, is written in God's

---

His head for it (see Matt. 14:1-12). That's a possible motive, but far from certain; despite John's denunciation, Antipas (a) was unwilling to execute John (Matt. 19:5; Mark 6:19-20), (b) was regretful when his hand was forced to do so (Matt. 16:9; Mark 6:26), and (c) was unnerved by the thought that Jesus was a reincarnation of John (Matt. 14:1-2). Under the circumstances, the likelihood that Antipas would have touched Jesus is remote; and, despite Jesus' unequivocal statement on the same subject, the fact that he did nothing is a matter of historical record.

words. But Moses (Jesus explained) did not command divorce; he merely regulated it. What he commanded was the divorce *procedure*; and that was only a concession to their hard-heartedness, 'but from the beginning it was not so' (19:8). The legislation cited by the Pharisees

> is not a command to divorce; it is not properly a permission to divorce since the divine pattern of Genesis 2:24 ... had never been modified; it is rather a disapproving recognition of the fact of divorce, with regulations to mitigate its worst evils.... The law gave civil permission, but not moral permission for divorce (Wenham 1994, pp. 40-41).

Twice Jesus appealed to how things were from 'the beginning' and what that conveys about God's obvious original intent. God may permit what He does not intend, and allow what He does not approve.

The larger point for our present purpose, however, is that the words of Genesis 1:27 and 2:24 are a reliable and sufficient basis on which to stake an understanding of God's view of marriage and God's opinion of divorce. At least Jesus thought so.

Jesus used God's words to affirm difficult doctrines, like the eternality of hell

As if the issue of divorce were not prickly enough, Jesus Himself raised the issue of hell and affirmed not only its existence but its eternality (see Mark 9:42-48). Again, He did not appeal to His personal knowledge as the Son of God, but to the certainty of God's words (Isa. 66:24). The words He cited are, in fact, the final words of Isaiah's prophecy, describing hell

> in its ceaseless corruption (*their worm will not die*) and unending holy wrath (*nor will their fire be quenched*). The cause of it all is that *they rebelled against me*; Isaiah ends where he began (1:2). They did not tremble at the word of the Lord (66:2, 5) and so they came to this endless state.... No doubt when they refused to hear they sought to give a good account of their choices, of what they expected to attain and enjoy through following their own way.... Is it fanciful to imagine that as they debated their choice they heard a voice which said,

'Did God really say …?' (Gen. 3:1). The first truth to be set at a discount by the tempter was the doctrine of the wrath of God expressing itself in the sentence of death, but in the end how wrong that voice is proved to be …. On the lips of Jesus these verses will become the vehicle of the doctrine of eternal loss (Motyer 1993, p. 544).

Isaiah counterpoints images of glorious grandeur and terms of stern warning, so 'that if the glory does not win us to the life of obedience, then maybe the unmistakably horrible rewards of disobedience will drive our wayward hearts to tremble at the word of the Lord' (Motyer, ibid.). It all comes back around again to being convinced of the trustworthiness of God's words about everything—even hard and controversial things.

In Controversy

Jesus employed God's words to rebuke sacrilegious innovations

Days before His crucifixion, Jesus came to Jerusalem and found the Temple awash in commercial activity (Matt. 21:12-13). Nothing inherently sinful about commercial activity—though by most accounts the currency exchange and monopoly on officially kosher animals was rife with exploitation and abuse. It was the raw commercialization of the Temple precincts to which Jesus objected so violently. Something may be legitimate in its own context which, when mingled with the sacred, results in a pollution and prostitution that twists something sacred into something sordid.

What was intended to furnish an atmosphere of solemnity and worship had become a circus of clamor and corruption.[12] The Bazaars of the Sons of Annas they came to be named, after the high

---

12. These abuses appear to have been new; there is no evidence for the marketing of sacrificial animals in the temple precincts before A.D. 30. This novel and enterprising desecration seems to have been instigated by Caiaphas the high priest (son-in-law of Annas the high priest, John 18:13). There were already approved markets on the Mount of Olives where kosher items could be procured for Temple sacrifice; but Caiaphas apparently 'wished to set up a market which would be in punitive competition with the traditional markets on the Mount of Olives' (Lane 1974, p. 403).

priest whose infamy is detailed not only in the New Testament but by the ancient historian Josephus as well (Edersheim 1976, 1:371-72). This market was located in the large and outermost precincts of the Temple known as the Court of the Gentiles. The volume of animals necessary to service the sacrifices was phenomenal. 'The Court of the Gentiles was a virtual stock market of animal dealers and money changers' (Edwards 2001, pp. 341-42). Even aside from the financial shenanigans, the noise and smell and commotion can only be imagined.

Jesus protested on the grounds of Isaiah 56:7, 'It is written, "My house shall be called a house of prayer"' (Matt. 21:13). In the same breath, He pulled a phrase from Jeremiah 7:11 to highlight the contrast between what God intended the Temple to be and what they had made it: 'a den of thieves.'

Jesus was not merely condemning the dodgy dealing going on in this unholy bazaar. He was accusing them—as God had accused their forefathers through Jeremiah seven centuries earlier—of turning the house of God into their lair, their own safe haven and base of operations. It was not uncommon for bands of robbers to hole up between raids in a remote cave for secrecy and security. The wicked and the unprincipled of Jesus' day were treating the Temple as their communal refuge, 'believing that participation in the formal rituals of the cult would somehow deliver them from the Judge' (Thompson 1980, p. 281)—again, just like their fathers did in Jeremiah's day (Jer. 7:1ff.). It is no accident, then, that what Jesus did ('He went into the temple and began to **drive out** those who bought and sold in it,' Luke 19:45) is what God said He would do in the Jeremiah passage—'I will **cast you out** of My sight as I have **cast out** all your brethren' (Jer. 7:15).

But there's more. Mark notes that Jesus actually cited the fuller version of Isaiah 56:7: 'Is it not written, "My house shall be called a house of prayer **for all nations**?"' (Mark 11:17). It wasn't just the Jews God cared about; His Temple was supposed to provide a welcoming refuge for anyone from the surrounding pagan nations who sought the true God (cf. 2 Chron. 6:32-33). That detail becomes significant when combined with another point that is easily overlooked.

Have you ever noticed that Jesus targeted not only the sellers but also the *buyers* (Matt. 21:12; Mark 11:15)? Many have assumed that Jesus was angry at the money-changers and merchants (the 'sellers') for taking advantage of the poor Jews who came to worship. But He seems to be just as angry with the 'poor Jews' themselves (the 'buyers'). Why?

> The use to which the forecourt was devoted entrenched the entire people in disobedience to God.... The installation of stalls for the sale of animals and of other requirements for the sacrifice ... had the effect of transforming the Court of the Gentiles into an oriental bazaar and a cattle mart. Jesus was appalled at this disregard for the sanctity of an area consecrated for the use of Gentiles (Lane 1974, pp. 404-06).

Both sellers and buyers were marginalizing, insulting, and imposing on Gentile worshippers and seekers (like those in John 12:20), turning the Court of the Gentiles into a zoo.

> By allowing the Court of the Gentiles, the only place in the temple area where Gentiles were allowed to worship God, to become a noisy, smelly, public market, the Jewish religious leaders were preventing Gentiles from exercising the spiritual privilege promised them. How could a Gentile pray amid all that noise and stench? (Wessell 1984, pp. 727-28).

> *Both the leaders and the people had turned worship into a racket.*

In more ways than one, worship had become a racket. And it seems both priests and people were to blame. There is nothing new under the sun.

By now you are probably wondering how all this relates to the trustworthiness of God's words. Think about what Jesus was doing here. He was not asserting any fulfilled prophecy. He was not even citing a breach of any specific Old Testament law. *He was taking two historic Old Testament descriptions and applying them to a contemporary situation.*[13] Jesus was neither

---

13. Both passages have historic overtones, while the Isaiah 56 passage also has eschatological undertones. But this does not unseat the larger point; it only reinforces it.

spiritualizing nor moralizing these texts. He was making authoritative modern applications and taking authoritative actions grounded in the assumption that God's words are timelessly trustworthy.[14]

> *Jesus modeled practical application based on God's timeless words.*

The last several decades have seen a growing disdain for the practical application of God's words in preaching. It is often regarded as invasive and legalistic. Jesus' applicational use of Scripture in this passage underscores the reliability of God's words to diagnose and speak to contemporary issues.[15]

Jesus applied God's words to defend others and to condemn His attackers

Jesus repeatedly clashed with the religious leaders of His day when their traditions and interpretations clashed with God's words. On several occasions, Jesus' detractors attempted to discredit Him indirectly by accusing Him of permitting others to do what was unlawful. Why, they wanted to know, did Jesus allow His disciples to break the Sabbath (Matt. 12) and the traditions of the elders (Matt. 15), and allow children to blaspheme by praising Him as the messianic Son of David (Matt. 21)? Jesus countered each accusation by citing the words of God on the assumption that they were dependable and decisive, trustworthy and timeless.

Jesus and the Sabbath

The issue in Matthew 12 appears to be what was (and was not) considered lawful activity on the Sabbath.[16] But that was just the surface issue. Jesus took the discussion to a deeper, internal level. What the disciples did in the grainfield (12:1-2) was expressly allowed by the Law (Deut. 23:24-25). But the Pharisees objected that the Sabbath

---

14. I have not chosen the word 'authoritative' lightly; this is precisely the point on which the Jews challenged Him the next day (Matt. 21:23).

15. The methodology of legitimate application is outside the scope of this book. For an excellent discussion of the subject, see Ken Casillas, *Beyond Chapter and Verse: The Theology and Practice of Biblical Application* (Wipf & Stock, 2018).

16. Matthew mentions the Sabbath 10 times; 8 of them are in this chapter (12:1-14). You can also see the emphasis on the question of 'lawfulness' in this passage (12:2, 4, 5, 10, 12).

rendered such 'work' unlawful. Jesus' rebuttal cited an example from Old Testament narrative (12:3-4), a pattern from Old Testament law (12:5), and a principle from the Old Testament prophets (12:7).

Once again, Christ prefaced His comeback with the prodding question, 'Have you never read?' (twice, Matt. 12:3, 5). It implied that the Pharisees—self-professed scriptural experts and widely acknowledged spiritual leaders though they were—had been reading God's words through defective lenses, spectacles that permitted them to see only what fit their own preconceptions and priorities. By that one simple question, Christ advertised the practical ignorance of the Scriptures on the part of those who should have known the most.

Jesus' first argument from David's example (Matt. 12:3-4) had nothing to do with the Sabbath. He merely pointed out that even though David (and his men) ate bread that was set aside exclusively for the priests, neither the Scripture nor the Pharisees condemned him for it. Why?

> *The Pharisees misunderstood Scripture because they misunderstood God.*

Jesus wasn't so much interested in answering that question as in asking it. He was not arguing that all rules have exceptions, or that personal needs trump divine law (Cranfield 1985, p. 115; Carson 1984, pp. 280-81). He was simply highlighting the fact that the Pharisees misunderstood and misapplied Scripture because they misunderstood God Himself.

> The Pharisees seem to begin with the institution of the Sabbath and view it as of utmost importance. Their oral tradition on proper Sabbath observance overrides the humanitarian concerns behind Deut. 23:25 .... Jesus, on the other hand, begins with God's concern for his people ... (Turner 2008, p. 310).

The line of argument here is a fine one, and mis-steps are easy. In the above quotation, for example, Turner concludes this way: 'Jesus, on the other hand, begins with God's concern for his people, *which takes precedence over the institution of the Sabbath on certain occasions*' (ibid., emphasis added). But that concedes too much and tilts precariously in the opposite direction toward a man-centered view of God's laws. To be sure, God's concern for people is part of Jesus' case; that's why He punctuates His argument by asserting that 'the Sabbath was made for man, and not man for the Sabbath' (Mark 2:27). God didn't create people just so there would be someone around to keep His rules; He established rules to help keep His people.

But Jesus' bottom line was that His disciples were 'guiltless' in this case and wrongly condemned by the Pharisees (Matt. 12:7). This was not about God's concern for people taking 'precedence over the institution of the Sabbath on certain occasions.' The disciples' actions were not an *exception* to Sabbath law; they did not breach legitimate Sabbath law at all, only the Pharisees' tradition of how the Sabbath law must be observed. It was the Pharisees' traditions that breached God's Sabbath laws. 'Jesus argues that the tradition of the Pharisees is unduly stringent and exceeds the intention of the Law' itself (Lane 1974, p. 117).[17]

Jesus' second argument (Matt. 12:5-6) posed an even greater problem for the Pharisees: 'Or have you not read in the law that on the Sabbath the priests in the temple profane [desecrate] the Sabbath, and [yet] are blameless?' It's one thing to appeal to an example from an Old Testament story; it's quite another to appeal to an explicit Mosaic law (the sacrificial law) that apparently compels the priests to violate another Mosaic law (the Sabbath law, at least as the Pharisees defined it). And yet before the Law they are 'blameless'? How does that work?

God who gave the Sabbath laws also gave the sacrificial laws. The Sabbath law forbade people to pursue their customary work on the Sabbath; but when it came to the priests, laboring in the temple on the Sabbath was their God-ordained work. Jesus raised the argument to prod these Pharisees

---

17. The history of the Pharisees suggests that the original intent of such specific applications was good and noble. It was called 'fencing' or 'hedging' the law and was intended to give people definitive guidelines to help them keep God's laws. Meticulous attention to keeping God's laws cannot be faulted; nor is the problem extending scriptural authority to applications of Scripture. The problem is extending scriptural authority to flawed applications that clearly conflict with other Scriptures. This was the problem addressed in Matthew 15 as well.

who reverenced Scripture to think hard about what God meant the Sabbath to be and what people should do to keep it holy. They had too easily accepted views that made the Sabbath a burden and had overlooked the fact that Scripture did not fit into their pattern (Morris 1992, pp. 302-03).

Jesus' third argument quoted God's words in Hosea (6:6), and raised the stakes considerably. 'Have you never read?' was a probing question. But Jesus introduced his final remark with a preface that really pricked: 'If you had known what this means, "I desire mercy and not sacrifice," you would not have condemned the guiltless' (Matt. 12:7; cf. 9:13).[18] Jesus apparently quoted only the first half of the verse, but there wasn't a Pharisee there who couldn't finish that saying in their mind: 'For I delight in loyalty rather than sacrifice, **and in the knowledge of God rather than burnt offerings**' (Hosea 6:6 NASB). 'Jesus claims, in effect, that the Pharisees had not really grasped the significance of the law' at all (Carson 1984, p. 282). Why? Because *they had failed to grasp the character of God.* You can know all about the Bible, and yet God is a total stranger to you. And being a total stranger with God makes you a very bad judge of people, however much you may know about the Bible.

> *You can know all about the Bible and yet God is a total stranger to you.*

Christ's complete reliance on God's words as totally sufficient to answer His detractors is one more testimony to their trustworthiness in yet another arena of life.[19] In fact, Jesus was doing much the same thing in Matthew 12 that we saw Him do above in Matthew 21:12-13—applying God's words to settle current issues, diagnose contemporary problems, and evaluate not only one's interpretations but also one's misconceptions about people and about God.

---

18. God's statement in Hosea 6:6 is not a denial that He commanded sacrifice; it is a statement of divine priority, of what God (literally) *delights* in. God values His people's being *loyal* to Him and *knowing* Him above mere external conformity to the forms of religion.

19. They had no answer to His arguments, but that's not to say they were satisfied (Matt. 12:14). God never promises that we will always convince our enemies. Even the Son of Man didn't.

Jesus and the Tradition of the Elders

On another occasion, the Pharisees faulted Jesus' disciples for eating with unwashed hands. The issue was not hygiene, but tradition. Mark gives the fullest explanation (7:1-5). To the Pharisees, this was no minor matter; it came to be regarded as a distinguishing mark of one's very Jewishness.[20]

In the Sabbath controversy above, Jesus met their accusation with scriptural reasoning; here He deploys a scriptural 'counterattack' (Carson 1984, p. 348). The contrast between the accusations is startling. The Pharisees asked, 'Why do your disciples break the tradition of the elders?' (Matt. 15:2 ESV). Jesus asked, 'And why do **you** break the **commandment of God** for the sake of **your tradition?**' (Matt 15:3 ESV). He filled out His accusation with a specific case in point; despite two direct commands from God to honor one's parents on pain of death (Exod. 20:12; 21:17), the Pharisees managed to devise a way to officially sanction behavior that amounted to grave parental disrespect.

Jesus' contrast between God and the Pharisees was equally shocking: 'God says .... But **you** say ....' The result? 'So for the sake of your tradition you have made void the word of God' (Matt. 15:6 ESV). The verb is a strong one; they literally *revoked* God's rules with their own rules. Mark adds that they *dismissed* God's words in order to keep their own traditions (Mark 7:8). And this was their *modus operandi* ('and many other such things you do').

> It is clear that this great body of Jewish tradition had failed to get to the heart of God's commands. It was supposed to fence in the law so that the people would not infringe on it. Actually, however, the tradition distorted ... the law. In fact, it had even become a means of getting around God's law (Wessell 1984, p. 678).

'Judgment is without mercy to the one who has shown no mercy' (James 2:13). They were merciless toward others who breached their rules; and however you parse Mark 7:9, Jesus' rebuke was merciless in return:

---

20. For a helpful discussion of how thorough and rigid they were on this matter, see Edersheim 1976, II:9-15.

- 'You are experts at setting aside the commandment of God in order to keep your tradition.' (NASB)

- 'You have made a fine art of departing from God's command in order to keep your tradition!' (CJB)

- 'How ingeniously you get round the commandment of God in order to preserve your own tradition!' (NJB)

The Pharisees had reduced religion to a precise and heartless science.

Once again the Pharisees were preoccupied with a purely external issue. And once again Jesus found in God's words a reliable diagnosis of their much deeper problem: they had reduced religion to a precise and heartless science.

Well did Isaiah [29:13] prophesy of you hypocrites, as it is written:
'This people honors Me with their lips,
But their heart is far from Me.
And in vain they worship Me,
Teaching as doctrines the commandments of men' (Mark 7:6-7).[21]

They were 'hypocrites' (Matt. 15:7) who professed to reverence God ('these people draw near to Me with their mouth and honor me with their lips,' Matt. 15:8) but they didn't really know or understand Him at all ('their heart is far from Me,' Matt. 15:8). So instead, they created their own sub-religion by hijacking the authority of God's words, substituting their own words as the authority, and enforcing their authority on everyone else ('in vain they worship Me, teaching as doctrines the commandments of men' Matt. 15:9).

The Jews of Jesus' day thought of themselves as preserving ancient traditions; but Jesus said that what they were actually preserving was the spirit of those whom Isaiah criticized long before (Carson 1984, p. 349).

---

21. Jesus actually says that Isaiah *prophesied* about these Pharisees (Matt. 15:7; Mark 7:6). That doesn't mean that Isaiah 29:13 didn't apply to the Jews of Isaiah's day, and that it was only a prediction about the Jews of Jesus' day. 'Rather, Jesus is saying that the prophet's words fit the people who are opposing Him so mindlessly, whatever other applications the prophet may have intended' (Morris 1992, p. 393).

When Jesus cited Isaiah, He was citing the prophet's direct quotation of God's own words; Isaiah 29:13 begins, 'Therefore the Lord said ....' When Christ made a direct practical application of Isaiah 29:13 to condemn the policies and practices of the Pharisees, He was applying God's words as the final authority and the only reliable appraiser of human religion.

Jesus and the Praising Children

After Jesus' royal entry into Jerusalem, 'when the chief priests and scribes' heard 'the children crying out in the temple, and saying "Hosanna to the son of David!" they were indignant' (Matt. 21:15). 'Son of David' was not merely a genealogical tag but a Messianic title (cf. Matt. 21:9; 22:42). The religious leaders were furious that anyone would publicly credit Jesus with Messianic status—in the temple, no less—and incredulous that Jesus would knowingly permit it: 'Do You hear what these are saying?' (Matt. 21:16). Yes, He said, He did hear. But Jesus countered their outrage with a single statement from God: 'Have you never read, "Out of the mouth of babes and nursing infants You have perfected praise"?' (Matt. 21:16, quoting Ps. 8:2a).

In Psalm 8 (addressed to 'O LORD, our Lord'), David described the praise of children to Yahweh Himself. In Matthew 21, the Son of David applied the passage to the praise of children for Himself. It was a clear and direct assertion of His identity as Yahweh. But it was also a clear, if less direct, assertion of *their* identity as Yahweh's enemies. Because once again, Jesus cut short His quotation and left them to finish the verse on their own: 'Out of the mouth of babes and nursing infants You have perfected praise ... **because of Your enemies**' (Ps 8:2b, LXX). No attentive priest or scribe could have failed to recall the rest of the line or miss Jesus' intent. It was a powerful use of God's words.

Jesus cited God's words to establish His own deity[22]

Skeptics sometimes assert that Jesus never claimed to be God. He actually did so on numerous occasions. Matthew 22:41-45 is one of them. And

---

22. Space forbids including Jesus' use of God's words in Exodus 3:6 to prove the doctrine of resurrection (Matt. 22:23-28; Mark 12:18-27; Luke 20:27-40). For a thorough discussion see my article, 'Jesus, the Sadducees, and the Resurrection: A Case Study of Systematic Theology in the Bible—The Good, the Bad, and the Ugly' in *Journal of Biblical Theology & Worldview* 1/1 (Fall 2020) at https://seminary.bju.edu/journal/.

it's a particularly gratifying one because while His enemies were trying to trip Him up with loaded questions, He turned the tables and asked them a question that so unmasked their shallow inattentiveness to God's words that 'no one was able to answer Him a word, nor from that day on did anyone dare question Him anymore' (Matt. 22:46).

On the human identity and lineage of the coming Messiah, Jesus and the Pharisees agreed; the Christ must be the descendant of David (Matt. 22:42). How then, Jesus asked, could David, the great royal patriarch, refer to the Messiah, his (presumably) lesser descendant, as 'my Lord'—a title that meant 'My Master, My Sovereign, My Better'? This turned on its head the whole cultural and biblical practice of reverencing the elders and patriarchs, unless this anointed one to come was not *merely* David's human descendant but something more, someone greater.

Jesus condemned those who refused to believe in Him not on His own authority, but on the authority of God's words

Jesus gave His enemies an amazing pledge: 'Do not think that I shall accuse you to the Father' (John 5:45a). Jesus promised not to point the finger of allegation at those Jews who rejected Him. He will not need to. Another witness will rise against them in God's court whose testimony will be more than adequate to convict them: 'there is one who accuses you—Moses, in whom you trust. For if you believed Moses, you would believe Me; for he wrote about Me. But if you do not believe his writings, how will you believe My words?' (John 5:45b-47).

On first hearing, Jesus' argument sounds illogical. 'Moses, in whom you *trust*'? And yet, Jesus implies, they did not *believe* Moses? How can that be? Jesus' language raises a question. I argued in Chapter 2 that you cannot truly trust someone if you do not believe his words. Yet here, Jesus seemed to say that these Jews were trusting in Moses, and yet not believing his words. That seems to undermine the link between trusting a person and believing his words. But Jesus' whole point was that their professed confidence in Moses was fraudulent precisely *because* they would not believe his words when those words did not conform to their own opinions and prejudices. In other words, they were trusting in a Moses of their own devising.

Jesus' warning to those Jews is a warning to those who claim to trust in God, but will not side with God's words and be governed by His words when those words conflict with their own thinking or tradition. In those cases, they either twist them and find some other way to explain them, or simply ignore them. Jesus was confident that Moses' writings alone would be sufficient to exonerate all His claims, and condemn those who knew what Moses said but wouldn't believe it when they saw it. Knowledge can be a very dangerous thing, depending on what we do with it.[23]

In Prediction

Jesus believed God's prophetic words would be fulfilled

Jesus forewarned of a day when people will 'see the "abomination of desolation", spoken of by Daniel the prophet, standing in the holy place' (Matt. 24:15). He not only implied that the event was certain but that it would be clearly identifiable; otherwise the ensuing instructions about how they were to react to that event would be meaningless (24:16-18). Jesus had every confidence that God's prophetic words were not cryptic, mysterious, and inconclusive but definite and discernible, and the events guaranteed and recognizable.

Christ also relied on God's words to predict, explain, and prepare His followers for future events in His own life. 'Behold, we are going up to Jerusalem,' He told the disciples, 'and all things that are written by the prophets concerning the Son of Man will be accomplished' (Luke 18:31). Sometimes He was more specific about which things 'written by the prophets' He had in mind. 'For I say to you,' He spoke a few days later, 'that this which is written must still be accomplished in Me: "**And he was numbered with the transgressors.**" For the things concerning Me have an end' (Luke 22:37). This is Jesus' most candid claim that Isaiah 53 is, in fact, all about Him and cannot be understood or explained apart from reference to Him.[24]

---

23. Read Romans 1 carefully and you discover that Paul argues not that all people *can* know God, but that all people *already do* know God. What do we do with that knowledge? We cannot get rid of it. Instead, we suppress it (Rom. 1:18-21) and replace it with our own foolish ideas (1:22-25). That's why it takes an operation of divine grace to overcome our fallen human disposition against God.

24. Jewish interpretation traditionally understood passages like Isaiah 53 to be Messianic until about the tenth-century A.D., when Rabbi Shlomo Yitzkhaki

Jesus made a point of using prophecy to prepare His disciples ahead of time for what was about to happen. Citing Psalm 41:9 as a prophetic reference to His imminent betrayal by Judas (something that seems to have completely blindsided the others), He said, 'I am telling you this now, before it takes place, that when it does take place you may believe that I am he' (John 13:19 ESV).[25]

He helped His followers learn to view some of the most baffling facets of His ministry—like the inexplicable hatred leveled at Him (John 15:23-24)—in the light of God's prophetic words: 'But this happened that the word might be fulfilled which is written in their law, "*They hated Me without a cause*"' (John 15:25).

Throughout His ministry, Jesus expressed utter confidence that every word of God in Scripture not only *would* be fulfilled, but *must* be fulfilled (Matt. 5:18; Mark 14:49; Luke 21:22; 24:44). Amid all the apparent chaos as His life seemed to be crumbling around Him, Jesus viewed and explained everything that was happening to Him in terms of God's words (Matt. 26:53-54, 55-56).

Christ even employed prophecy to warn the disciples of their own impending and colossal failure: 'All of you will be made to stumble because of Me this night, for it is written [Zech. 13:7], "*I will strike the Shepherd and the sheep of the flock will be scattered*"' (Matt. 26:31). And they all were (26:56).

Standing before those who were looking for any excuse to execute Him, Jesus claimed Daniel 7:13 (and hence all of Daniel 7) as a reference to Himself. On the basis of that passage, He assured His enemies with confident composure: 'Hereafter you will see the Son of Man sitting on the right hand of the Power, and coming in the clouds of heaven' (Matt. 26:64). It was an unambiguous claim to both messiahship and deity, and they knew it (26:65-66). And He paid for it (26:67-68,

---

(aka Rashi) introduced a systematic reinterpretation of such passages in an effort to counter Christian arguments from Old Testament prophecy (Rydelnik 2010, pp. 112-28).

25. Actually, there is no 'he' in the Greek text. I believe that this statement belongs in a series of seven absolute 'I am' statements in John—subtle insinuations by Jesus that He is the Yahweh (the I AM) of the OT (cf. 8:24, 28, 58; 13:19; 18:5-8; 6:20; 4:26).

27:1-2). Some things are certain enough to be worth paying for. That was Jesus' repeated testimony about God's words.

> *God's words are certain enough to be worth paying for.*

In Suffering

Jesus personalized God's words as reliable expressions of His profoundest personal experiences

Even in His direst moments, Christ found God's words a reliable reflection of His soul. 'My God, my God, why have You forsaken Me?' (Matt. 27:46) is an echo of Psalm 22:1. Indeed, much if not all of Psalm 22 finds its richest fulfillment in the experience of Christ.

With His final breath, Jesus trusted Psalm 31:5 as His own: 'Father, into your hands I commit My spirit' (Luke 23:46). The context out of which Jesus plucked His dying words is not one of anguished desperation but triumphant confidence:

> In You, O LORD, I put my trust; let me never be ashamed;
> deliver me in Your righteousness.
> Bow down Your ear to me, deliver me speedily; be my rock of
> refuge, a fortress of defense to save me.
> For You are my rock and my fortress; therefore, for Your name's
> sake, lead me and guide me.
> Pull me out of the net which they have secretly laid for me, for
> You are my strength.
> Into Your hand I commit my spirit; You have redeemed me, O
> LORD God of truth (Ps. 31:1-5).

No one knew that context better than Christ; after all, it was 'the Spirit of Christ who was in' David when he penned it (1 Pet. 1:10-11). And Jesus' quotation in part is His way of owning the whole. To Jesus, God's words were trustworthy enough to die with them on His lips.

And yet a moment's reflection on the context throws a whole new light on Jesus' quotation. It sounds to us like a resignation to death, because we are accustomed to hearing those words in the context of Jesus' crucifixion. In reality, it is nothing of the kind! It is a positive assertion of life! Read David's words again in Psalm 31. He certainly is not saying, 'Okay, Lord, if I must die, then take care of my spirit.' He is not surrendering to death; he is exulting in *deliverance* from death. That's exactly what Jesus means! 'I am the resurrection and the life,' he said; 'he who believes in Me ... shall never die. Do you believe this?' (John 11:25-26). For the believer, this shaft of light from Jesus cleaves the clouds that darken the valley of the shadow of death.

It is no accident that Christ drew on the Psalms in His darkest hours. No book is richer in its expression of spiritual experience and emotional range. Every sigh and song of the pilgrim's heart is echoed in the Psalms. It is God's hymnal for the happy soul, and the richest script for the spirit's most anguished prayer. 'The Psalms wrap nouns and verbs around our pain'—and our joy—'better than any other book' (Tada and Estes 2000, p. 157).

When things were most desperate for Him, Jesus did not fall back on His own strength or wisdom or identity as God; He anchored His soul to the sure and trustworthy words of God. So should we.

The Conclusion of the Matter

When you combine what Jesus taught about God's words, what Jesus thought about God's words, and how Jesus used God's words throughout His ministry, the full picture becomes compelling. 'What is common to all of these is a confidence that appeal to the text of the Old Testament is decisive: it settles the matter' (Thompson 2006, p. 83). Anyone inclined to abandon any of God's Old Testament words will find himself at loggerheads with Christ—an unenviable position, since He said whoever 'does not receive my words has a judge; the word that I have spoken will judge him' (John 12:48 ESV). Jesus regarded and treated God's words as entirely trustworthy for all purposes public and private. He showed us that we can fully trust God's words, and He showed us how to do it.

Review & Reflect

1. The chapter described using the Court of the Gentiles as a marketplace and turning worship into a racket. What Scriptures might we apply to contemporary worship that promises people

material prosperity while appealing for donations to millionaire preachers? How might we scripturally evaluate church music that emphasizes volume, raises the performers to rock star status, and transforms worship into an entertainment industry?

2. Jesus rebuked the Pharisees for rationalizing their way around God's words. That's not a Jewish thing; that's a human thing. We can do this as well, on both a practical level as well as a theological level. For example, you could conclude from the biblical fact of God's omniscience that it is pointless to pray, since God already knows exactly how whatever you pray for is going to turn out; what's wrong with that conclusion? Can you think of examples, practical or theological, where others have substituted or even contradicted God's words with their own words or ideas? Can you think of examples where you have done this?

PART TWO:
Practical Applications

7
Trusting God's Words about the Past

The testimony of the LORD is sure,
making wise the simple.
Psalm 19:7

The Hebrew word 'testimony' (*ēdût*) in Psalm 19:7 is one of several synonyms for God's Word. Each synonym highlights a distinctive component of God's self-revelation: instructions ('law'), stipulations ('precepts'), boundaries ('statutes'), requirements ('commandments'), and decisions ('judgments'). Especially in the context of Psalms 19 and 119 where all these synonyms appear together, it is common to flatten out the distinctions between these terms and simply make them different but equal ways of referring to the Mosaic Law *in toto*. The multiplicity of synonyms is not just for poetic variety, however; all of them 'contribute … to our total understanding of what Scripture is' and how it functions (Kidner 1973, p. 417).

So, which parts of Scripture qualify as God's 'testimonies'? A testimony is a personal attestation of what an eyewitness affirms to be so. What God says happened in the past is exactly what happened because His testimony is always 'sure' (Ps. 19:7). We've talked about that word before (*'āman*); it means faithful, dependable, reliable, trustworthy.

Human theories and assertions of what could or could not have happened often compete with God's testimony of past events. The problem is, we weren't there. We are, in that sense, *inexperienced*—which is exactly what the word 'simple' means in Psalm 19:7: 'The

115

testimony of the Lord is trustworthy, making the inexperienced wise' (HCSB).

So whom do we believe when the testimonies of man and God conflict with each other? When the two are at odds, just remember: 'there is no wisdom, or counsel, or understanding against the LORD' (Prov. 21:30). Here's a test for how you're doing with the theme of this book: are you willing to stake your reputation on the trustworthiness of a testimony from God, even when it pits you against the opinions of the wise of this world?

This is not an argument for simplistic fideism. We do not shut our eyes to evidence. But evidence inevitably involves interpretation, and interpretation assumes presuppositions. Pure, objective, presuppositionless investigation or interpretation of evidence does not exist. Presuppositions are 'invisible until disturbed' (Burroughs 1998, p. 26). We should probe and peer under every presupposition, and look askance on any interpretation of the evidence that contradicts or casts doubt on God's testimony to the facts of the case.

Fideism—the view that objects of religious belief should be accepted simply by faith regardless of reason or evidence.

I want to apply the declaration of Psalm 19 specifically in a direction suggested by the psalm's own context. Leading up to his assertion in 19:7 of the reliability of all God's testimonies, the psalmist describes the world around us as a testimony to God's creative power and activity (19:1-6). Let's explore, then, the reliability of God's testimony about creation.

The Creation: God's First Testimony to the Trustworthiness of His Words

Another name for the Ten Commandments is the Decalogue. It means Ten Words, or Sayings, or Statements. We call them the Ten *Commandments* because they all take the form of imperatives (Exod. 20; Deut. 5). But did you know the Bible contains another decalogue? In fact, the Bible *begins* with a decalogue. Ten times Genesis 1 reads, 'And God said.' These are the *first* 'ten words' from God.

God introduces Himself to us with a record—His *testimony*—of creation. All Christians believe that God is the Creator. But *how* did He create? He could have described Himself flinging the planets into orbit with the force of His almighty arm, and stamping a titanic foot on the rim of the earth, shooting a shower of life-sparks to fill the globe with living creatures. Or, He could have silently thought things into existence and willed them into being. But He chose a different way; and He chose to *tell* us—to *testify* to us—how He did it. He simply *spoke*, and it happened. 'God said' and it was. The Bible's first chapter introduces us to a God who speaks, and whose words dictate and define reality. There is heady theology in that.

What happened when God spoke, for the first time, in time? Each statement of this Creation Decalogue ('And God said') is followed by a virtual command.[1] In the first instance (1:3) God's word simply became reality. God said, 'Let light exist.' And light existed. Three times the words 'let there be' are followed by 'so God created' (1:7, 21, 27); in other words, He did exactly what He spoke. Six times God's creative statement is followed by an elegant assertion of effortlessness: 'and it was so' (1:7, 9, 11, 15, 24, 30). 'God said ... and it was so.' The Complete Jewish Bible renders it even more matter-of-factly: 'God said ... and that is how it was.'

On one level, this language conveys the creative *power* of God's words. That's an immediate, obvious, surface implication. But the corollary truth beneath the surface of those words is that what God

> *God made the Bible's first chapter an argument for trusting His words.*

says *happens*. The fact that God is *able* to do anything He says is one thing; the fact that God is *certain* to do everything He says is quite another. So, God's testimony of creation, His own description of how He created, underscores not merely His attribute of omnipotence but His attribute of trustworthiness—the reliability of His words. What He says is exactly what He does, and what He speaks is exactly how it

---

1. Eight times God's statement takes the form of a Qal imperfect jussive or cohortative implying a command (1:3, 6, 9, 11, 14, 20, 24, 26), once it is a direct imperative (1:28), and once it is a simple verb of determinative action (1:29).

happens. In other words, *God Himself made the Bible's first chapter an argument for trusting the reliability of His words.*

Psalm 33 confirms this emphasis on God's words in Genesis 1. This psalm is a magnificent hymn of worship for God's sovereign providence over every sphere of human experience. Verses 6-9 praise God for the events recorded in Genesis 1. The stanza begins by magnifying the animating energy of God's speech (33:6) and concludes by emphasizing that what God said is exactly what happened (33:9).

> By **the word of the LORD** the heavens were made,
> And all the host of them by **the breath of His mouth**.
> …
> For **He spoke** and it was **done**;
> **He commanded** and it **stood fast**.

The words 'He spoke and it was done' (literally, 'He spoke and it was' or 'He spoke and it happened') echo the refrain in Genesis 1, 'God said … and it was so.'

Genesis begins not just with a theology of creation but with *a theology of God's words.* The Bible's first chapter is not just a statement about cosmology, though it is that. It is God's testimony to the trustworthiness of His words. That must have profound ramifications for how we handle the events recorded there.

The Fall: The First Challenge to the Trustworthiness of God's Words

Genesis 1 establishes that what God says is exactly what happens. But that fact is a two-edged sword. What is true for God's creative blessings is also true for His solemn warnings. Genesis 1 cuts with the positive edge because everything God spoke into existence was 'good.' But in Genesis 2-3 the blade swivels to slice with the negative edge.

In Genesis 2:16-17, God communicates to the man and woman He created a generous permission ('of every tree of the garden you may freely eat'), a single prohibition ('but of the tree of the knowledge of good and evil you shall not eat'), and a gracious warning ('for in the day that you eat of it you shall surely die'). In Genesis 3, the reliability of those words is put to the test.

The first challenge in human history to the trustworthiness of God's words took place in the immaculate environment of Eden, when the first humans made a single but monumental decision. The theological ramifications of the Fall were many and complex. But strip that event down to the bone, and at its marrow the Fall was a decision not to trust God's words.

> *At its marrow, the Fall was a decision not to trust God's words.*

Temptation Tactics

Satan's strategy unfolded in three stages. First, he created doubt by *questioning the content of God's words*: 'Did God really say, "You can't eat from any tree in the garden"?' (Gen. 3:1, HCSB). God's speech is the only objective means we have for knowing the character and will of God. Questioning the content of those words— especially by implying their unreasonableness— sets a subtle process in motion. Maybe you've seen the bumper sticker that yells, 'Question

> *'Question Authority' is as old as dirt.*

Authority!' That may sound like the trendy motto for a brave, new world of autonomy and enlightenment; but actually, the idea is as old as dirt.[2] Literally. Doubts can sprout easily when someone fixates our attention on the alleged unreasonableness of Scripture—particularly statements deemed to be beneath our intellectual dignity, or that seem to threaten our freedom.

Second, the devil incited distrust by *contradicting the content of God's words*: 'You will not surely die!' (Gen. 3:4). In human history's

---

2. The phrase 'brave, new world' is, of course, an allusion to Shakespeare's *The Tempest*. But the context of that allusion is also pertinent to my statement here. Miranda has grown up on a deserted island with only her father and an ugly, mis-shapen, half-human creature called Caliban. When for the first time in her life she sees a whole passel of people marooned on the island by shipwreck, she exclaims, 'O Wonder! How many goodly creatures are there here. How beauteous mankind is! O brave, new world that has such creatures in't!' To which her father, Prospero, replies, ''Tis new to thee.' If you think questioning authority is a radical, new life-motto, it's new to you; but in reality it's as old as Eden.

earliest recorded conversation about God, 'the first doctrine to be denied is judgment' (Kidner 1967, p. 68). But beneath the denial of judgment lurks a more radical and sweeping agenda. The first doctrine to be denied in human history was not creation, or even the existence of God. The first doctrine to be denied in human history was the trustworthiness of God's words. Eliminate that, and all other doctrines drop like dominoes.

> *The first doctrine to be denied in human history was the trustworthiness of God's words.*

Third, Satan *engendered mistrust by maligning the motives of God*: 'For God knows that in the day you eat of it ... you will be like God, knowing good and evil' (Gen. 3:5).[3] After dismantling the message of God in Eve's mind ('you will not die'), Satan then seeks to assassinate the character of God Himself. 'The tempter pits his bare assertion against the word ... of God,' and paints 'a suicidal plunge as a leap' into enlightenment (Kidner 1967, pp. 68-69). Carl Trueman's similar reading of this event is worth citing at length.

> This is at once a more subtle and, as events reveal, a more devastating approach to the words of God. Here the serpent does not deny that the command is the word of God; rather he questions the motivation that lies behind the command .... Eve's fall from grace is facilitated by the crisis in her belief in God's trustworthiness caused by the assault of the serpent upon the relation between who God is and the words he speaks. Both of the serpent's approaches, then, call into doubt the trustworthiness of God, first by the doubting of his word and second by the doubting of the God who speaks the word. In both cases, it is the words spoken that form the focus of the attack; yet it is ultimately the integrity of the one who speaks, God himself, which is undermined .... Eve is persuaded that God is not his words, not who his words indicate that he is. The result: sin (Trueman 2002, pp. 181-82).

---

3. It is exactly the same plural word in both parts of the statement: *Elohim*. It clearly means 'God' in the first part ('God knows') and almost certainly means 'God' in the second part ('you shall be as God'). The appeal is that they would be as great as their Creator.

Satan's insinuation introduced into human history what Trueman calls a 'hermeneutic of suspicion' that has filtered our approach to God's words ever since. We learned in Eden to distrust God, and we carry it like a congenital disease. 'Human nature possesses an incurable suspicion of God' because 'that was how sin was introduced to the world' (Chambers 1941, p. 13).

God concedes that Satan's 'promise' ('you shall be as God, knowing good and evil') was technically true (Gen. 3:22). And yet it is still justly called a deception (Gen. 3:13). The deception lay in Satan's implication that this would be a good thing, and a good means of attaining it. Satan omits the details of the bargain and what it will cost; he tells them what they will gain, but not what they will lose in the process. That's how temptation usually approaches us.

So did They Die, or Not?

Since this is all about the trustworthiness of God's words, this question needs to be answered. After all, Adam and Eve didn't 'die' on 'the day' that they ate the fruit, did they? In fact, Adam lived for over nine centuries (Gen. 5:5)! If you assume a flat, simplistic definition of 'die' as physical death, it certainly looks like Satan was right. That, of course, can only mean that God (a) was wrong, or (b) changed His mind. Some, for example, argue that in the end God's pity compelled Him to renege on His words.

> God had threatened to terminate the relationship if the humans failed to trust God. But when God faces the sin, he cannot bring himself to fulfill this threat (Sanders 2007, p. 47).

Sanders does something that God never does: he sacrifices one divine attribute (God's truthfulness) on the altar of another (God's love). 'Love wins' in the end, but at too high a price: the cost of His integrity. If God is not fundamentally a person of integrity (as Chapters 2 and 4 argued), then why would we trust Him when He says He is a God of love? According to Sanders, God *really did intend* for death to be the consequence for disobedience; but when it came down to actually doing what He said, God could not bear to keep His word and inflict the punishment He had sworn. The next logical step is to apply that reasoning to the eradication of hell altogether; even if Sanders hasn't taken it, others who follow his line of thinking have.

So what is the solution? Scripture elsewhere explains that death because of sin is not merely physical and eventual (and for Adam it was physical and eventual), but also spiritual and immediate. Adam and Eve did die that day. Physical death is nothing compared to spiritual death. Separation from God and loss of divine favor is death at its worst. That's the basis for the New Testament's teaching that prior to our conversion we are all born spiritually 'dead in trespasses and sins' (Eph. 2:1, 5; Col. 2:13).[4] And that's why reconciliation—being brought back into right relationship with God—is part of the New Testament's description of what it means to be saved.

Objection: 'How could Adam and Eve possibly have understood all that? They had no basis for processing "spiritual death". Isn't it more reasonable to assume that the only kind of "death" they would have understood in Genesis 2:16 was physical death?' But on what basis could they possibly understand physical death? 'Death' of any kind was a revolutionary new concept for them, one totally outside their experience on any level. Their immediate spiritual death is the Bible's explanation for humanity's fallen, sinful condition.

To say and not do is human, not divine (Num. 23:19). For God to say and not do would be for God to lie; and that's something He is incapable of doing (Titus 1:2).

The Fall's Bottom Line

Most explanations of the Fall describe the first human sin in terms of human rebellion. That is true. But have you ever noticed that Satan 'never directly asked for disobedience' (Payne 1962, p. 217)? He never dangles the fruit in front of Eve. He never even urges her to taste it. He concentrates his attack entirely on God's words. He simply questions,

---

4. Just as physical and spiritual death are linked (Rom. 5:12), physical and spiritual life are linked as well (1 Cor. 15:22); our life in Christ is not a future gift after physical death but a present possession to replace our spiritual death, and it will be accompanied by a reversal of physical death via the resurrection.

contradicts, and insinuates—all devilish devices, to be sure. But it suggests that even now (especially now), Satan does not need to goad us to commit sinful acts. Sin usually begins as an emotional process (with our desires) but culminates in a cognitive and decisional process. God's testimony regarding the progression of the Fall reveals that *the reason they sinned is because they were persuaded that God's words were not reliable.*

Even the nature of the prohibition itself (Gen. 2:16-17) suggests that at the root of the test was not merely submission to authority but relational trust. The prohibition was utterly non-moral and, in that sense, arbitrary. Eating fruit is not inherently sinful, nor is there any indication that there was something supernatural about the fruit of *that* particular tree. 'The fruit, not in its own right, but as appointed to a function and carrying a word from God, confronts man with God's will, particular and explicit' (Kidner 1967, p. 62). Adam's and Eve's obedience, then, was purely a matter of trusting God's words; once that trust was eroded and then abandoned, the result was sin.[5]

Genesis 3 demonstrates that questioning the reasonableness of God's words leads to modifying the content of God's words, which leads to maligning the character of the God who speaks those words. As we saw earlier in Chapter 4, the person and words of God are indivisible. You cannot undermine God's words without impeaching His character.

Genesis 3 also teaches that a decision to sin is a decision to distrust God's words about that sin and its consequences. And a decision to distrust God's words is always a decision to listen to someone else, to trust their words instead. Eve

> *A decision to distrust God's words is a decision to trust someone else's words instead.*

was persuaded to trust Satan's words (3:1-6, 13) and Adam 'listened to the voice of [his] wife' (3:17 ESV); neither of them went back to God's words and relied solely on them.

---

5. I am indebted to my friend Dr David Saxon, a professor of Bible and philosophy at Maranatha Baptist University, for the gist of this paragraph.

Genesis on Trial: The Modern Challenge to the Trustworthiness of God's Words

Theologians (even liberal ones) are quick to affirm that God reveals Himself through history, including the historical events mentioned in the Bible. That does not necessarily mean, however, that they believe those events transpired just the way the Bible says. Many theologians have long conceded that God reveals Himself through history, while debunking the Bible's description of those events. There's a reason for this.

> Those who prefer God's acts to his words do so not because of anything in Scripture, but because they demand the right to consider biblical history autonomously. Divine words get in the way when human beings try to place their own interpretation on God's actions (Frame 2010, p. 29).

Divine words also get in the way when they testify to occurrences that human beings deem unlikely or unfeasible (like miracles), or contrary to the prevailing interpretation of the limited evidence we presently possess (in fields such as archaeology or geology, for example).[6] So it's not enough to say that God reveals Himself through history. He alone gets to describe the details of those historical events and to editorialize on the meaning of those acts. It is not just the acts themselves that are revelatory; God's version of those acts and the meaning of those acts is the only authoritative version. 'LORD, Your testimonies are completely reliable' (Ps. 93:5, HCSB).

This is a critical area today because Genesis is being scrutinized and re-evaluated not merely by unbelievers outside the Church (that's old news) but by otherwise evangelical theologians on the inside. It appears to be prompted by the growing embarrassment of some over God's words and their implications for three major events relating to human origins and early history: Creation and the Fall (Gen. 1–5), the Flood (Gen. 6–9), and the Tower of Babel (Gen. 10–11).

---

6. Frame (2010, p. 194) acknowledges the value and sometimes the challenge of archaeology to make us evaluate carefully both the archaeological and biblical data. 'But archaeology is not infallible, and to believers it does not speak the final word.'

I argued earlier in this chapter that Genesis begins not just with a theology of creation but with a theology of God's words, that the Bible's first chapter furnishes not only a cosmological worldview but a testimony to the reliability of His words. That's why recent interpretations of Genesis espoused by many evangelicals, arguing that the testimony of the Lord in Genesis takes the form of myth, impacts much more than one's view of the earth's origins. Such a hermeneutical overhaul of Genesis cannot avoid undercutting the emphasis on the trustworthiness of God's words, since it's woven into the very verbal fabric of God's testimony to those events.

Doubts about the believability of these events are, of course, nothing new. What is new is that even evangelicals with a history of defending the accuracy and integrity of the Scriptures are now raising those doubts themselves, but in a roundabout and seemingly scholarly way—by reclassifying the genre of Genesis 1-11 from historical narrative to myth.[7] These scholars profess to affirm the truthfulness of God. But to resurrect Calvin's observation, it is meaningless to affirm God's trustworthiness 'unless you hold that whatever proceeds from him is sacred and inviolable truth' (Calvin 1960, p. 549 [3.2.6]).

It's a bit like a woman who wanted an exact match to a particular color, and took a palette of that color to a paint store. After several failed attempts to reproduce the precise hue, the attendant hit upon an enterprising solution. He took the palette into the back, found a reasonably close shade with which he painted both his own sample and her original palette, quick-dried them, and brought them out to her. By simply altering the original, they now matched perfectly.

Some interpreters have repainted Genesis so that it can be made to match current evolutionary theory. In a kind of hermeneutical gerrymandering, they have redrawn the interpretational boundaries of Genesis in a way that allows them the flexibility to contradict the text without having to say that God was either incompetent or simply mistaken.

---

7. Representatives of this view include Peter Enns, John Walton, C. John Collins, Tremper Longman III, and Bruce Waltke.

While I was in the process of writing this chapter, a national evangelical news magazine ran an article on the BioLogos Foundation, an organization devoted to harmonizing evolution and the Bible. Their website explains 'evolutionary creation' (formerly theistic evolution) as 'the view that all life on earth came about by the God-ordained process of evolution with common descent.' BioLogos advertises itself as being 'committed to the authority of the Bible as the inspired word of God' and believes that evolutionary creation will help Christians worship God, raise their children, and evangelize more biblically and successfully.

Through a multi-million dollar grants program, BioLogos funds projects aimed specifically at countering traditional arguments against evolution from within the Christian community, and encouraging the Church to accept and embrace what BioLogos advocates see as the inevitable and infallible conclusions of evolutionary science. This work is not being done in a corner by obscure academicians. Grantees include faculty from Calvin College, Wheaton College, Fuller Theological Seminary, Oral Roberts University, and the Vineyard Church.[8]

Augustine argued long ago that

> we are bound to receive as true whatever the canon shows to have been said by even one prophet, or apostle, or evangelist. Otherwise, not a single page will be left for the guidance of human fallibility, if contempt for the wholesome authority of the canonical books either puts an end to that authority altogether, or involves it in hopeless confusion (Schaff 2007, p. 180).

In the end, it's not really Genesis that's on trial, but evangelicalism generally and evangelicals individually. The modern move to normalize an evolutionary reading of Genesis has theological reverberations far beyond an academic, esoteric debate over hermeneutics. It pulls the rug out from under God's testimony not only to the event of creation but to the reliability of His words—a subject about which, as we've already seen in multiple passages, He is profoundly passionate.

---

8. All this information can be obtained from their website at www.biologos.org

Conclusion

The biblical record is God's testimony to past events. The parting of the Red Sea was not a fortuitous low-tide marsh crossing. The sudden and widespread death of Sennacherib's army besieging Jerusalem has enough extrabiblical attestation that skeptics can no longer ignore it. As the previous chapter demonstrated, the miracles of the wilderness wanderings, Elijah's raising of the widow's son in Zarephath, and even Jonah and the great fish cannot be dismissed without impugning the credibility of Jesus Himself.

The first thing the Bible teaches us about God's words is that they are reliable—what God says is what happens (Gen. 1). The second thing the Bible teaches us about God's words is our tendency to doubt that. At the root of humanity's first sin was a failure to trust God's words (Gen. 3). Salvation begins a process aimed at (among other things) reversing that tendency. When we fail to trust God's words we not only dishonor Him, we dethrone Him because we are choosing to regard someone else as more reliable, and some other version of events as more likely than His testimony of them.

> If we receive the testimony of men, the testimony of God is greater; ... the one who does not believe God has made Him a liar, because he has not believed in the testimony that God has given ... (1 John 5:9-10 NASB).

Yes, John is talking specifically about God's testimony to Christ. But anyone who believes that God's testimony about Jesus is reliable while His testimony about anything else is open for discussion, cross-examination, and revision is in for the divine lawsuit of his life.

Review & Reflect

1. What does the word 'testimony' mean and what do passages like Psalm 19:7 and 93:5 imply about God's words?

2. What is the key introductory phrase for the Genesis Decalogue?

3. How is the Genesis Decalogue an argument for the trustworthiness of God's words?

4. How is the Satanic plan of attack in the garden of Eden (Gen 3) duplicated in temptation today?

5. Explain how the Fall was ultimately a failure to trust God's words.

6. Some interpreters (e.g., John Walton) deny that a literal interpretation of the early chapters of Genesis was ever intended, and deny that they have redrawn the interpretational boundaries in order to come to that conclusion. They believe God intended the revelation of Genesis to be understood non-literally and mythologically within the Ancient Near Eastern (ANE) context and way of thinking. One problem with that argument is that the six days in Genesis 1 are clearly interpreted literally in other parts of the Bible that fall outside the ANE cultural milieu. Trace the Bible's own interpretational trajectory of the six days of creation through the Scripture, beginning with Exodus 20:9-11, 23:12, 31:15-17. A millennium later the Levites and Nehemiah implicitly accepted the literal sense articulated in Exodus (see Nehemiah 9:13-14; 10:31). Fourteen centuries after Moses, Luke 13:14 indicates that first-century A.D. Judaism took the six days of Genesis and Exodus literally. Indeed, Jesus' sabbath observance rests on an acceptance of Exodus's literal interpretation of Genesis 1 as well. The Bible's internal interpretive trajectory throughout different 'cognitive environments' affirms and reaffirms a literal understanding of the six days of Genesis.[9]

---

9. I am indebted to my friend Phil Brown, professor at God's Bible School & College, for this observation.

8
Trusting God's Words about His Character

A trustworthy God who does no wrong
Deuteronomy 32:4 (CJB)

The glory of God is His character. When Moses implored God, 'Show me Your glory,' God replied, 'I will make all My goodness pass before you' (Exod. 33:18-19). The next morning (34:2-4) God 'descended' on Mount Sinai

> and stood with him there ... and proclaimed, 'The LORD, the LORD God, merciful and gracious, longsuffering and abounding in goodness and truth ... keeping mercy ... forgiving iniquity and transgression and sin ...' (34:5-7).

This is God's self-description on the Mountain of Law. Yes, there is also His justice and judgment: 'by no means clearing the guilty, visiting the iniquity of the fathers upon the children' (34:7). But listen to what God Himself puts first and emphasizes most when He is displaying His *glory*: mercy, grace, patience, abundant goodness, reliability, loyalty, forgiveness!

The Song of Moses in Deuteronomy 32 celebrates, among other things, that He is 'a God of truth' (Deut. 32:4)—'a faithful God' (NIV), 'a reliable God' (NET), 'a trustworthy God' (NJB). Paul affirms that even 'if we are unfaithful, He remains faithful' (2 Tim. 2:13)—the word means reliable, trustworthy. The point is not that He is faithful to unfaithful people because of them. He is faithful to the unfaithful, of course, or we'd all be in trouble; but He is not faithful to the unfaithful because we deserve it or because it's just part of His job description. The ultimate object of God's faithfulness is not unfaithful people; He is faithful to Himself, to His nature, and to His words—to His covenant obligations and promises (negative and positive)—irrespective of our unfaithfulness. That's why Paul concludes his statement with this explanation: 'He cannot deny Himself' (2 Tim. 2:13).

The point of this chapter is that because all God's words are trustworthy, we can always rely on God to be exactly what He says He is, even when it doesn't look to us like He is. I could spend the chapter citing biblical declarations of the character of God. But it will be better to learn from others who have wrestled with some of our same doubts about whether God really is the way He says He is. That's why God includes their stories and struggles in the Scriptures (Rom. 15:4; 1 Cor. 10:11).

Jacob: Forgetting God's Providence

Most people dislike risk and uncertainty. Some people take extreme measures to avoid it. Jacob had a history of manipulating circumstances. People preoccupied with trying to control life don't react well when they find they can't. They also tend to have a hard time trusting others, including God. That's the scenario being played out in Genesis 42 and 43.

With his son Joseph dead (he thought), his son Simeon held in protective custody by a powerful, shrewd, unpredictable, and eerily well-informed man in Egypt, and his youngest son Benjamin about to be taken away from him to who-knows-what-end, Jacob protested, 'All these things are against me!' (Gen. 42:36). The narrator has kept us in the know, however. We understand that all these things are totally *for* Jacob, that every apparent loss is a gain, and that every seeming step backward moves him closer not just to survival and abundant provision, but blessing and reunion with his long-lost son. God had to starve Jacob into a corner before he acknowledged—or remembered—that God and His providence was in control not Jacob, and that we do much better to rest in His running of things rather than ours.

Jacob had reason to hope in the providence of God. God had affirmed His providence to him before. It was God who multiplied Jacob's flock, he was told, not his silly pseudo-scientific genetic engineering tricks (Gen. 31:11-13). It was God who informed the whole family, twice, of His intentions for Joseph (Gen. 37:5-10).[1] And Jacob knew it (37:9-11).[2] But it's easy to lose sight of God's providence when all that you love seems suddenly at risk. That's when you most need to stake down your confidence in God's words of assurance that He is in control and that His purposes are always good.[3]

> *It's easy to lose sight of God's providence when all that you love seems suddenly at risk.*

Naomi: Overlooking God's Kindness

We don't have nearly the backstory on Naomi that we have on Jacob. Separated by about three centuries and obviously different in many ways, they are nevertheless kindred spirits in at least one respect. Both of them seriously misread the providences of God in their lives.

Surveying the dashed dreams and painful losses of her life, she was convinced (correctly) that all her sorrows came from the hand of a

---

1. 'The account of the dreams, coming at the outset, makes God, not Joseph, the "hero" of the story: it is not a tale of human success [or, I would add, of human ambition], but of divine sovereignty' (Kidner 1967, p. 180). Joseph's dreams were not reflections of his personal delusions or ambitions. They were communications from God, and a common revelatory method in that era (Gen. 20:3; 31:10, 24; 40:5ff.; 41:1ff.). But wasn't Joseph's sharing of the dreams foolish (at best) or cocky (at worst)? That's a common assumption on the part of many readers, but the narrative fails to support that view. It was essential for everyone to know about the dreams so that, in the outworking of providence, it would be clear to all that this was nothing but the hand of God bringing to pass exactly what He said would happen. The narrative goes out of its way to emphasize that (a) it was the brothers' hostile reaction to Joseph that was the problem (Gen. 37:4, 5, 8, 11), and (b) the dreams were a conscious sore point with the brothers (Gen. 37:8, 19-20) and yet they fulfilled them literally and repeatedly (Gen. 42:6, 9; 43:26, 28; 44:14; 50:18). For a fuller discussion, see Talbert 2001, 65ff.

2. 'The two attitudes in [verse 11] are those that always divide people in their reaction to news from God' (Kidner 1967, pp. 180-81).

3. For a thorough exploration of the biblical doctrine of God's providence, including dozens of verses that teach God's sovereign supervision over all our circumstances, see *Not by Chance: Learning to Trust a Sovereign God* (BJU Press, 2001).

sovereign God (Ruth 1:13, 20-21). We may surmise our own explanations for her sufferings; spectators of the sufferings of others often do. But the text is silent on that point; and if Naomi suspected a reason for these hard providences, she never said so.[4] Naomi's reading of her circumstances displays

> her sense of abandonment by God and perhaps also her lack of faith. These laments show that Naomi cannot understand the purposes of God in her life, but also that she feels that God's presence is hidden (Lau and Goswell 2016, p. 103).

Many think of Naomi as a bitter old woman (Block 1999, p. 637). After all, that's what she told people to call her: *Mara*, Bitter (1:20). But listen to her whole statement. The reason she put in for a name-change was not because *she* was bitter, but because her *life* was.

> Call me Mara, **for the Almighty has dealt very bitterly** [harshly] **with me**. I went out full but the LORD has brought me home again empty.... **the LORD has testified against me** and **the Almighty has afflicted me** (Ruth 1:20-21).

To the ear of a sympathetic listener, Naomi's words signal a woman who is grieved, weary, depressed, confused, frustrated, even despairing; but she's not angry or resentful. People who are bitter against God don't pray for God's blessings on others, like Naomi did (1:8-9); and they certainly don't attract others to the Lord, like Naomi did (1:16-17). Ruth's conversion and passionate confession of Naomi's God can only imply that amid all her loss and hardship, Naomi had a winsome enough testimony to persuade the pagan Ruth to cling to Yahweh for life.

Still, Naomi had a hard time seeing the kindness of God that shined behind the clouds of His 'frowning providences' in her life.[5] Trust is

---

4. It's a hard lesson for Bible readers to learn, but we come closest to the Bible's intent when we stick closest to what the text says instead of surmising where the text is silent. Was Naomi out of God's will because she was in Moab? There was a famine, after all; and others had left the promised land under similar constraints without censure (Abraham, Isaac, Jacob, David). In any case, you might be able to blame Elimelech but not Naomi. The bottom line is that the question is peripheral to the story; the narrative itself simply does not make it an issue.

5. For a brief but solid study on God's hard providences, see John J. Murray, *Behind a Frowning Providence* (Banner of Truth, rpr. 1990).

like an aircraft's radar—it's the only way to see through the clouds that can completely blind you to your surroundings—and hers wasn't working properly. Yes, God took her husband and both her sons, but God gave her Ruth. Yes, God brought her home 'empty,' but God brought her home. Yes, they were cast upon the mercy of others for their very sustenance, but God in mercy narrowed the 'others' to their kinsman Boaz. Yes, they were reduced to living off the land (literally!), but God saw to it that they got what they needed, and more.

> *Hardships are God's hounds to drive us to Himself.*

Eventually, the clouds began to break enough for Naomi to recognize that God was behind all this as well (Ruth 2:20). And by the end, in the providence of God, Naomi held in her lap a grandchild who would become the grandfather of King David. Who would have thought? All the time she thought of God only as 'dealing bitterly' with her, 'testifying against' her, and 'afflicting' her, He was actually nudging her toward His place of blessing and provision.

Hardships are God's hounds to drive us toward His purposes and, more importantly, Himself. He is always 'compassionate and gracious' and rich in 'loyal love and faithfulness' (Exod. 34:6 NET). If you are God's child, He always aims to do you good, even when the process is painful and His purpose is dark to you. You have His word on that.

Job: Disputing God's Fairness

Job's experience was so complex, multi-layered, and severe that it's easy to trivialize it by over-simplification.[6] His rock-solid response to suffering was gradually eroded by the wear and tear of unrelieved, unexplained suffering, and by wave after wave of wearisome insinuation from well-intentioned friends. In the face of dogged accusations of sin as the only feasible explanation, Job felt compelled to assert his innocence just as doggedly. So vigorous was his self-defense that

---

6. For a thorough treatment of the book's themes, see Layton Talbert, *Beyond Suffering: Discovering the Message of Job* (BJU Press, 2007).

God's righteousness dwindled by comparison, until Job was confident (Job 31:35-37) that God would be obliged to concede that Job was right and that He had got it wrong. 'That Job had stepped over the line at some point(s) is beyond dispute; God himself rebukes Job for doing so (40:2, 8).'[7] That's why I titled this section 'disputing God's fairness.' If you look at the verbs God uses in Job 40:8, that's exactly how He describes Job's words: 'Are you impugning my justice? Putting me in the wrong to prove yourself right?' (CJB).

Job was no smart aleck skeptic spoiling for a fight with God. He loved, served, and obeyed God more fully and faithfully than anyone else even God could think of (Job 1:8; 2:3). It's a sober reminder that the best of God's servants may come to question His character under acute pain. That doesn't excuse it, but it does help explain it.

We are most prone to question God's fairness when we are confronted with inexplicable suffering, whether ours or someone else's. But if Job learns anything from God in the end, it is that we are incompetent to pass judgment on God's ways. For one thing, we possess far too few of the facts; that's part of the point of God's answer in Job 38-39. For another, we may think that we understand what a righteously run world should look like, but we are miserably ill-equipped to make that judgment; that, too, was part of God's answer in Job 40-41.[8] And finally, God is infinitely above reproach, 'for all his ways are just. He is a reliable God who is never unjust, he is fair and upright' (Deut. 32:4 NET). That's God's trustworthy testimony to His character, a buoy marker to help us keep our thinking about God in the channel of truth amid storm and choppy water.

David: Discounting God's Promises

David, too, had dark moments of doubt and desperation. He survived multiple close encounters with death, and at least a dozen hairbreadth escapes from Saul. But one day, dogged by the maniacal monarch and under the duress of relentless running for his life, his grip on reality

---

7. Talbert 2007, p. 158.
8. Talbert 2007, pp. 211-16.

momentarily slipped: 'David said to himself, "One of these days I'll be swept away by Saul"' (1 Sam. 27:1 HCSB). *No, David, you won't. In fact, you can't. God swore you'd be king. It will take several years, but it's going to happen because God said so.* David had God's word that he would succeed Saul to the throne of Israel (1 Sam. 13:13-3; 16:12-13). If David dies, God lies. That can't happen. David didn't always remember that, especially under pressure. Some days the only way you can see your way clear is through the spectacles of God's words.

But doubt can be a dangerous thing. We can get ourselves into serious predicaments when distrust begins to drive our decisions. In 1 Samuel 27, David's irrational conclusion (any conclusion that contradicts God's words is irrational) led him to flee the country and landed him in a bizarre and awkward situation (1 Sam. 27:2-12). He became part of

> *Any conclusion that contradicts God's words is irrational.*

the personal bodyguard of Achish, King of Philistia (28:2)—Israel's inveterate enemy! Only a timely twist of providence prevented him from actually going to war against his own people (29:1-11).

Life quickly becomes confusing and convoluted when we make assumptions and decisions without reference to the reliability of God's words. There were moments in David's life on the run when it seemed only a matter of time before Saul would catch up with him. And yet, only a year and a half after his irrational decision in 1 Samuel 27:1, Saul was dead and David was sitting on the throne of Israel—just like God said.[9]

Habakkuk: Wrestling with God's Justice, Surrounded by Unrighteousness

Does the daily news ever vex you? Does it bother you when evil men triumph, dishonesty succeeds, pretentious and arrogant politicians prosper, justice is turned on its head, and sin is not only sanctioned

---

9. The timeframe is calculated by connecting 1 Samuel 27:1 with 27:7; the sixteen-month period mentioned there ended with the Philistine battle against Israel in which Saul died (cf. 1 Sam. 28:1, 4; 29:1, 11; 31:1ff.).

but celebrated? David complained, 'The wicked strut about on every side when vileness is exalted among the sons of mankind' (Ps. 12:8 NASB). Solomon observed that 'when a sentence is not executed at once against a crime, the human heart is encouraged to do evil' (Eccles. 8:11 NET). The frustrating thing is, that's not just a comment on human institutions of criminal justice; it's just as true when God refrains from judging even the most flagrant sins in society. That's what so deeply disturbed the prophet Habakkuk.

We may have trouble pronouncing his name, but we can identify with his cry of frustration over the apparent indifference and inactivity of a righteous God in a wicked world.[10]

> How long, LORD, must I cry for help? But you do not listen!
> I call out to you, 'Violence!' But you do not deliver! (Hab. 1:2 NET).

Any believer who reads a newspaper knows that feeling. We may be powerless in the face of evil, but we know God is not. And yet He seems to do so little for so long.

> Why do You force me to look at injustice? Why do You tolerate wrongdoing? Oppression and violence are right in front of me.
> Strife is ongoing, and conflict escalates (Hab. 1:3 HCSB).

Because of divine inaction, sin becomes so powerful, so prevalent, so virulent, that it doesn't just saturate society at large; it infects the very institutions that are supposed to safeguard society.

> The law has become paralyzed, and there is no justice in the courts. The wicked far outnumber the righteous, so that justice has become perverted (Hab. 1:4 NLT).

The NCV captures that final phrase even more colloquially: 'Evil people gain while good people lose; the judges no longer make fair

---

10. Habakkuk's complaint focused on his own nation of Judah, to whom God had a special covenant relationship and responsibilities. The fact that he is king of all the nations (Jer. 10:7), however, justifies broadening the application of Habakkuk's message beyond the borders of ancient Judah.

decisions.' Habakkuk was bewildered by the apparent disconnect between God's character and God's action (or inaction) in the world. How could a just God sit idly by and do nothing about the radical evil ripping society apart?

But the Lord assured Habakkuk that He had everything under control. He was neither indifferent nor inactive, and He had a plan. He would judge Habakkuk's wicked nation by delivering them into the hands of the Babylonians (Hab. 1:5-11). Habakkuk was horrified (1:12-17). Babylon was even worse! How could God punish evil by empowering those who were even more evil? God's method of dealing with sin only compounded Habakkuk's confusion, as it often does ours.

But God has His reasons, and Babylon will have its own price to pay in time. We tend to be impatient and stingy with time because we have so little of it. God has all the time in the world; He can afford to be patient and to let retribution—or repentance—fully ripen.

God's final answer to Habakkuk puts everything into perspective (Hab. 2:2-20). It can be summed up in four exhortations: *wait on Me* (2:2-3); *have faith in Me* (2:4); *leave it to Me* (2:6-20); and *rest in Me* (2:20). All of these are expressions of *trust* grounded in nothing but the words of God.

Habakkuk adopts God's counsel and applies it in the form of a final prayer (3:1): a *petition* that God would make His work clear to all and yet temper His wrath with mercy (3:2); *praise* for God's glorious acts of sovereign intervention in the past (3:3-15); and *personal resolve* to 'rest in the day of trouble' and 'rejoice in the LORD' alone whatever the future holds, because the Lord alone holds the future (3:16-19).

Habakkuk begins the book in frustration and confusion over God's ways and ends with a steady, joyful trust in God's character. 'The theme of the book is doubting and then trusting God's justice' (Bell 2010, p. 439). It is when we do not understand God's ways that we most need to rely and rest on His character and what His words reveal Him to be.

Righteous people long to see the triumph of righteousness. By 'righteous people' I don't mean 'superior' or even 'good' people. 'The righteous' in the Bible are not inherently moral people. Righteous people are merely rebel sinners who were at odds with God but have been reconciled and transformed by the grace of God in Christ, and whose affections and choices are now informed and defined by God's words (Ps. 32; Rom. 4).

Righteous people know those moments when our souls cry out with Isaiah:

> Oh, that You would rend the heavens! That You would come
> down ... to make Your name known to Your adversaries, that
> the nations may tremble at Your presence! (Isa. 64:1-2)

That cry will be answered when Christ acts finally and decisively in time and on earth for all to see. In the meantime, we will be frustrated by the domination of sin and wonder why God would 'remain silent when the wicked swallows up the man more righteous than he' (Hab. 1:13 ESV). That's when we need to reaffirm our trust that God is every bit as just as He says He is. His sense of timing is just a little different than ours.

Lamentations: Doubting God's Mercy amid Severe Chastisement

In hindsight, the catastrophic blizzard that swept the American Midwest in January 1888 was predictable, certainly explicable. In early January, a sea of undisturbed and unusually frigid air massed and stagnated over the Canadian plains, like 'a blob of invisible subzero mercury sealed and quivering over a quarter of a continent' (Laskin 2004, p. 76). Finally, a complex of weather events conspired to pry the system loose and shove it hurtling toward the United States with deadly velocity and minimal warning. As the meteorological monster soared southward, 'all the elements of the storm suddenly began to feed off each other, bloating up hugely with every bite.' Instead of snow, it produced 'slick-surfaced crystals ... hard as rock and fine as dust,' driven horizontally by high winds (ibid., pp. 119-20). What made it even more deadly was that it followed on the heels of a temperature spike that sent many children to school that morning in shirtsleeves. As the storm rolled across the prairies, temperatures plunged 18 degrees in three minutes, and kept plummeting from there.

To those standing outside, it looked like the northwest corner
of the sky was suddenly filling and bulging and ripping open.
In account after account there runs the same thread, often the
same words: There had never been anything like it.... 'Suddenly
we looked up and saw something coming rolling toward us with
great fury from the northwest, and making a loud noise.... we
saw what appeared to be a huge cloud rolling over and over
along the ground, blotting out the view of the nearby hills and
covering everything in that direction as with a blanket. There
was scarcely time to exclaim at the unusual appearance when
the cloud struck us with awful violence and in an instant the
warm and quiet day was changed into a howling pandemonium
of ice and snow (ibid., pp. 128-30).[11]

Shift scenes now from nineteenth-century America to Israel in the
sixth-century B.C. The gathering storm of God's wrath against Judah
hovered ominously to their north for decades, growing in provocation as
each successive generation ignored His prophetic warnings and basked
in the artificial warmth of delayed retribution due to periodic revival,
prophetic prayer, and divine patience. Once it was unleashed, however,
Babylon came hurtling from the north like 'a howling pandemonium'
with death and mayhem in its wake. Lamentations gives voice to the
emotional aftermath, as Jeremiah ghost-writes Judah's response to
God's calamitous chastisement on the nation. In some passages he
describes Judah's sin and suffering in the third person (Lam. 1:1-11); in
others, he speaks for the nation in the first person, venting her misery
and acknowledging the rebellion that brought God's wrath upon her
(1:12-16, 18-22).

When the curtain rises in Lamentations, Jerusalem is a smoldering
ruin. The temple has been gutted and plundered. The streets are deserted
except for a few scattered refugees rummaging through the rubble for
scraps of food. The book's verbal snapshots of the city's wretchedness

---

11. I have quoted Laskin's *The Children's Blizzard* at length because I know of no
more vivid illustration of the divine judgment on Judah through Babylon. Laskin's
book is a riveting read in its own right, mapping out the meteorological ingredients
of this historical storm and tracing the true-life stories of its victims and survivors.

are vivid. The effects of God's pent-up wrath[12] are so devastating that the lament tentatively broaches the question: what now? Is there any point in repentance or any way back to God? Hasn't He cast us off forever? 'Your ruin is spread wide as the sea; who can heal you?' (2:13). Just as the writer resigns with a sigh, 'My strength and my hope have perished from the LORD' (3:18), he recalls the character of God.

> Through the LORD'S **mercies** we are not consumed, because His **compassions** fail not. They are new every morning; great is Your **faithfulness**. 'The LORD is my portion,' says my soul, 'Therefore I hope in Him!' The LORD is **good** to those who wait for Him, to the soul who seeks Him…. Let him put his mouth in the dust—there may yet be hope. Let him give his cheek to the one who strikes him, and be full of reproach. For the LORD will not cast off forever. Though He causes grief, yet He will show **compassion** according to the multitude of His **mercies** (Lam. 3:22-32).

For the chastised child of God, the path back to God mapped out by the prophet is not an easy one, but it is simple: genuine repentance toward God and confident hope in His character. Chastisement does not signify hatred or rejection; it is the sign of relational love and intended restoration (Heb. 12:5-11). The very fact that Jerusalem's destruction was *from the Lord* is, itself, the basis for hope. God is the cause of chastisement and, therefore, the only source of relief; for chastisement is, by definition, restorative in aim. There is hope for restoration not because we deserve another chance but because God delights in it. Everything turns on your willingness to trust that God really is the way He says He is. When your sin and obstinacy reduce your life to wreck and ruin, His testimony to His own character is still trustworthy.

Chastisement does not signify hatred; it is the sign of relational love.

---

12. God's wrath is a dominating topic in the book, expressed by at least seven different Hebrew words used eighteen times. God is also the subject of thirty-three distinct and graphic acts of judgment in Lamentations 2:1-9, and of twenty-six such acts in Lamentations 3:1-18.

Martha and Mary: Questioning the Timing and Love of God amid Delay

When Lazarus fell ill, his sisters sent an urgent appeal to Jesus: 'Lord, behold, he whom You love is sick' (John 11:3). This was no seasonal virus. Clearly, they were concerned. Jesus, on the other hand, seemed not to be. His response was so casual that we might suppose He felt no particular attachment or obligation to this family. But John counters that misimpression: 'Now Jesus loved Martha and her sister and Lazarus' (11:5). And yet, knowing that Lazarus is ill and loving them as He does, He stays put (11:6). For two more days! John offers no defense; he doesn't suggest that Jesus would have gone immediately but other pressing business prevented Him. Jesus just decides to delay.

Jesus loved ... *and yet* ... He stayed? Those two statements seem to clash. That's why I connected them with the phrase 'and yet.' But that's not how John connects those two verses. Look at the conjunction he uses in 11:6. (And if you think conjunctions are insignificant, think again! Even a conjunction can carry significant theological freight.) John's choice of conjunction seems awkward, unnatural, counter-intuitive—which is additional evidence that it was deliberate, not accidental. John's connector between 11:5 and 6 is not a contrastive term like 'yet' or 'despite' or 'nevertheless'—as though Jesus' action was somehow paradoxical to His love. He uses a matter-of-fact term of explanation: 'So [*therefore, consequently, for this reason*], when He heard that he was sick, He stayed two more days in the place where He was' (11:6).[13] Until He knew that Lazarus was dead (11:14). Jesus' delay was prompted by His love. He didn't delay *despite* His love; he delayed *because* of His love. 'Now Jesus loved [them] ... therefore ... He stayed two more days in the place where He was.'

---

13. Translators and commentators who ignore the force of this Spirit-directed word choice do a disservice to the sacred text and short-circuit its theology. Concerned to rescue Jesus from a charge of calculated cruelty (knowingly causing grief through delay), some suggestions end up judging God by our priorities rather than judging us by His. The passage calls us to a higher theology. There are higher concerns (like the glory of God, John 11:4, 40) and greater goals (like the good of others, 11:15, 42, 45). That's not cruelty; that's Christlikeness.

That juxtaposition of thoughts is jarring. True love always acts immediately and races to the rescue, doesn't it? Not necessarily. Not omnipotent love. Not love that is also in complete control. My sense of grief or loss is not the measure of the rightness or wrongness of God's actions, or God could *never* send illness or take life. There are higher concerns than my immediate pain, and greater needs than my immediate relief.

Jesus' love prompted His delay—in this case because He intended to do something far greater for this family than merely raise Lazarus from a sickbed. Others needed the impact of this incident as well: 'I am glad **for your sakes** that I was not there,' He told the disciples, 'that you may believe' (John 11:15). But our focus here is on the sisters.

It is no stretch to draw a parallel between this passage—Martha and Mary appealing to the absent Jesus via a messenger—and prayer. Especially the kind of prayer that can't seem to break this world's gravitational pull, and finally lies on the ground lifeless and silenced by lack of reply. What answerless questions hounded their thoughts during those interminable days before Jesus finally arrived, four days too late? Don't you think they talked about that around their lamp-lit kitchen table every night after the messenger returned, and Jesus didn't come? You can hear the echo of those late-night talks when both of them, independently, greeted Jesus with the same words: 'Lord, if You had been here, my brother would not have died' (John 11:21, 32).

The unasked question that hangs in the air when those words are uttered—'if You had been here'—is a question about timing. They had no doubts about His power ('my brother would not have died'). But they could not fathom His timing. They'd sent for Him. Why had He not come sooner? And what else did that delay at least seem to imply?

There is some dispute over exactly where Jesus was when He received the message from Bethany. Some say He was only a day's journey away, just across the Jordan in Perea, and therefore that Lazarus must have died even before Jesus received word of his illness (Morris 1971, pp. 538, 548). Others believe He was in the northeast trans-Jordan region of Batanea, as much as four days away so that even if Jesus had left immediately he would still have arrived after Lazarus's death (Carson, 1991, pp. 407-08).

Both explanations seem eager to exonerate Jesus for His delay. The fact is, we are given Jesus' whereabouts in such broad terms (John 10:40) that even scholars cannot dogmatize or agree on exactly where He was. I'm all for background data and exegetical precision, but sometimes we can be so clever and complicated that we miss a text's simple point.

The structure of John's account seems specifically calculated to call attention to the issue of *timing*, without relying on abstruse and uncertain computations of exactly how far away Jesus was. John's report of the illness (11:1), the message sent to Jesus (11:3), the careful mention of Jesus' love (11:5) sandwiched between His diagnosis (11:4) and intentional delay (11:6), and the words of both Martha and Mary highlighting what could have been averted had He not delayed—all the details coalesce to emphasize that God may be 'late' but never too late, His purposes beyond our comprehension, His ultimate answer beyond our expectation, His reasons righteous, and His motivation love.

It's true that they did not question His compassion or His concern like the disciples did on another occasion ('Teacher, do You not care that we are perishing?')—at least not overtly. But John, guided by God's Spirit in how he penned this narrative, anticipated that we might. That's why the narrative takes pains to point our attention to Jesus' love for this family, not once or even twice but three times (11:3, 5, 36). And if we need that reassurance, probably Lazarus's sisters did too.

Delay on the front end looks like failure, but it's not at all the same thing.

We don't recognize delay as merely delay until after the fact. Delay on the front end looks exactly like failure, silence, absence, non-answer; but as Martha and Mary discovered, they're not at all the same thing.

Jesus countered Martha's words by grounding her hope not just in an event ('Your brother will rise again') but in Himself: 'I am the resurrection and the life!' (John 11:25). And He followed it with a pointed and personal question that you have to answer for yourself: 'Do you believe this?' (11:26).

To say that there is no such thing as unanswered prayer is not a mere truism; it is a truth. Every prayer is always answered, and you know all the possible answers: *yes, no,* and *not yet.* Richly colored threads of theology and doctrine are woven into the pattern of this passage. But lying right on the surface of the text, within easy reach of the simplest reader, is an assurance about God's timing in answer to our needs and pleas: God's delays, however painful and disconcerting, are always timely, purposeful, and never at odds with His love.

What To Do with All This

Every disciple faces times when he needs to rest his head upon the breast of God's character (cf. John 21:20). When storms threaten to push you out onto a sea of uncertainty and insecurity, God's attributes are the unseen rocks and ridges on the ocean floor to which you can anchor your soul. Learn to lash your ship to a word from God about the character of God and refuse to let go of it.

This is not about wishful thinking, believing what you want to be true. It is about living life by unseen realities rather than by appearances. In legal language, that's called circumstantial evidence. Circumstantial evidence is not conclusive because it allows for more than one explanation.

We've just surveyed several examples of people who lapsed into living life by circumstantial evidence. Jacob was convinced everything was against him when it wasn't; he was misreading practically everything that was happening to him. Naomi thought God was testifying against her when He was actually advocating for her. Job concluded that God had turned against him when God's view was, 'there is none like him on the earth' (Job 1:8). David sometimes couldn't hear God's promises for the sound of Saul's threats in his ears. To Habakkuk, God seemed indifferent to the surrounding society's sin and chaos when, in reality, He was anything but. Judah despaired that God had finally forsaken them, yet the character of God was their only hope. Two sisters confused by Christ's delay found Him to be all that He said He was, and more. We are all inclined to misread the character of God through circumstantial evidence. What we know is too easily unseated by what we see.

God has filled His word with testimonies to His character. 'The name of the LORD is a strong tower; the righteous run to it and are safe' (Prov. 18:10). The 'name of the Lord,' you may remember from Chapter 4, is a metonymy for the person and character of God. It is God Himself, and God's character, that is the refuge of the righteous. What quality of God do you most need to lean your weight on?

> *The character of God is the refuge of the righteous.*

His sovereignty over all your circumstances?

- 'Who is he who speaks and it comes to pass, when the Lord has not commanded it?' (Lam. 3:37)

- Christ is 'the blessed and only Potentate, the King of kings and Lord of lords.' (1 Tim. 6:15)

His presence when you feel forsaken and alone?

- 'For thus says the One who is high and lifted up, who inhabits eternity, whose name is Holy: "I dwell in the high and holy place, and also with him who is of a contrite and lowly spirit, to revive the spirit of the lowly, and to revive the heart of the contrite."' (Isa. 57:15 ESV)

- 'He Himself has said, "I will never leave you nor forsake you."' (Heb. 13:5c)

His sufficiency to satisfy your soul's needs and desires?

- 'The LORD is my portion, says my soul, therefore I hope in Him.' (Lam. 3:24)

- 'Be content with what you have, for he has said, "I will never leave you nor forsake you."' (Heb. 13:5b-c ESV)

His protection and deliverance?

- 'Call upon Me in the day of trouble; I will deliver you, and you shall glorify Me.' (Ps. 50:15)

- 'He Himself has said, "I will never leave you nor forsake you." So we may boldly say: The LORD is my helper; I will not fear. What can man do to me?' (Heb. 13:5c-6)[14]

---

14. I have purposely used this passage three times in a row not for convenience or lack of other Scripture, but because the passage itself grounds our confidence in

His provision?

- 'Those who seek the Lord shall not lack any good thing.' (Ps. 34:10)

- 'Look at the birds of the air, for they neither sow nor reap nor gather into barns; yet your heavenly Father feeds them. Are you not of more value than they?' (Matt. 6:26)

His wisdom?

- 'With Him are wisdom and might; to Him belong counsel and understanding' (Job 12:13 NASB).

- 'the foolishness of God is wiser than men' (1 Cor. 1:25).

His compassion?

- 'The LORD is gracious and full of compassion, slow to anger and great in mercy.' (Ps. 145:8)

- 'The Lord is very compassionate and merciful.' (James 5:11)

His love?

- 'I have loved you with an everlasting love.' (Jer. 31:3)

- Nothing 'shall be able to separate us from the love of God which is in Christ Jesus our Lord.' (Rom. 8:39)

His forgiveness?

- 'To the Lord our God belong mercy and forgiveness, though we have rebelled against Him.' (Dan. 9:9)

- 'Of him all the prophets bear witness that through His name everyone who believes in Him receives forgiveness of sins.' (Acts 10:43 NASB)

His goodness?

- 'The LORD is good, a stronghold in the day of trouble, and He knows those who trust in Him.' (Nahum 1:7)

God's presence, our material contentment, and our personal security in this one word from God.

- 'How much more will your heavenly Father give good gifts to those who ask Him.' (Matt 7:11 NLT)

His righteousness and justice?

- 'I, the LORD, speak righteousness; I declare things that are right.... I the LORD love justice; I hate robbery and wrong.' (Isa. 45:19; 61:8 ESV)

- 'Righteous and true are Your ways, King of the nations.' (Rev. 15:3 NASB)

His changelessness?

- 'I am the LORD; I do not change.' (Mal. 3:6)

- With God 'there is no variation, or the slightest hint of change.' (James 1:17 NET)

I've included one verse from both the Old Testament and New Testament, but it was difficult to limit myself to just one. I also tried to select out-of-the-ordinary passages and, when I could find them, statements made directly by the Lord. Each is only the tip of an iceberg of revelation in which God both demonstrates and declares the characters He bears.

To shift metaphors, the character of God is like a massive, sprawling, southern oak.[15] Each mighty limb is an attribute of God, and each of these words from the Lord is a single leaf in the expansive canopy of God's character that covers those who take their refuge in him. Search Him out! Climb all over this colossal tree, explore every bough and branch. His character is your hope, and His trustworthy words are the only fuel that will keep your confidence in Him burning brightly.

Review & Reflect

1. Mount Sinai is where God displayed His holiness (Exod. 19) and revealed His law (Exod. 20). When Moses later asked to see God's

---

15. I don't know what you think of when you hear this analogy. I grew up in the South Carolina low country, a land of mammoth oak trees with limbs so large and long they rest on the ground. If you want a mental image, search the internet for 'Angel Oak,' a tree about six miles from where I grew up.

glory, what attribute did God most highlight, what terms did He use to do so, and why is that self-revelation so significant in that context?

2. Are there any characters in this chapter with which you can particularly identify in your personal experience? What do you think God intends you to learn from their example?

3. Are there any other attributes of God that you have been tempted to question? Find specific Bible statements to which to anchor your confidence in God's character in that regard.

9

Trusting God's Unbelievable Words

Is any word too hard for the LORD?
Genesis 18:14 (literal)

Many people erroneously assume that God's omnipotence means that He can do anything. That assumption is not only unbiblical, but also illogical. Scripture specifies several things that God cannot do. He cannot do evil (Jer. 9:24; James 1:13). He cannot tempt man to do evil (James 1:13). He cannot deny Himself (2 Tim. 2:13). He cannot lie (Num. 23:19; 1 Sam. 15:29; Titus 1:2; Heb. 6:18). And He cannot fail to do what He says (Isa. 55:11). The things God cannot do have nothing to do with God's ability and everything to do with God's character. God can do anything consistent with His character. God's character prohibits Him from doing certain things and, likewise, compels Him to other actions.[1]

When we really need God to supply the necessary funds to pay a debt, to open a door of employment for us, to heal an illness, or to intervene in a predicament, few of us wrestle with the question, 'Can He do this?' We know He *could* do it. He's *God*. Our question is not so much 'Can He?' but 'Will He? Will He do this *for me*? And how can I know He will do this for me?'

In other words, is God *merely omnipotent*, so that He *can* do *anything*? Or is He something more than that? Is He *reliable*, so that I can know that He *will* do *whatever He says*?

---

1. For an original and thoughtful investigation of classes of actions God is unable to perform, see Frame 2013, pp. 339-41.

The Bible answers those questions with a rhetorical question: *Is anything too hard for the Lord?* The expression occurs four times in three different passages—Genesis 18, Jeremiah 32, and Luke 1.[2] But we have short-changed ourselves in how we understand and apply these words. It's an expression that is not so much misunderstood, as not understood fully enough. Systematic theologies routinely cite this statement as a proof text for God's omnipotence. Commentators, with rare exceptions, explain it the same way. The driving conviction of this chapter, however, is that omnipotence, though not absent from the statement, is in the background. Genesis 18, Jeremiah 32, and Luke 1 are primarily not about the omnipotence of God but about the trustworthiness of God's words.

Genesis 18—An Impossible Birth

Here is the first occurrence of this thematic statement: 'Is anything too hard for the LORD?' (Gen. 18:14). On its grammatical surface this is a question; but it's a rhetorical question, and rhetorical questions are actually declarations. In much the same way, what sounds on the surface of most translations like an appeal to God's omnipotence is in fact something much more specific and practical.

The original question was not posed as a matter for theological conjecture, tossed out as a theoretical brainteaser to seminary profs seated comfortably around a table of polished walnut. The question was first posed amid the smell of roasted meat and fresh-baked bread, while a warm wind rippled the tent of an aged and childless couple who had just been promised—*for the twelfth time in twenty-five years*—that they would have a child.[3] And the answer is not speculative, but profoundly personal and practical.

---

2. If you will take a few moments to read each of those chapters for yourself, you will get a great deal more out of the discussion that follows.

3. Genesis 12:1-3; 12:7; 13:15-16; 15:4-5, 13, 18; 17:7-8, 16, 19, 21; 18:10, 14. These passages represent a total of twelve explicit promises on at least six separate occasions. The earlier passages do not specify a son but they assume it, since the promise to establish Abraham's family line would require the birth of a son. Likewise, the earlier passages do not specify the involvement of Sarah but they assume it, and that detail begins to be specified in Genesis 17:16 (after the Hagar episode).

Abraham was ninety-nine, Sarah eighty-nine. Think about that. Picture your grandparents coming to visit and excitedly announcing, 'Guess what! Gramps and I are going to have a baby!' Sounds like a headline at the grocery store checkout, right? ('Nonagenarian Couple Announces Conception of Miracle Baby! Doctors Suspect Alien Intervention!')[4]

But this couple isn't like your grandparents. Sarah is reproductively dead twice over—physiologically barren all through her youth and, now, biologically too old. Her womb is 'dead' and Abraham is 'as good as dead' (Rom. 4:19 ESV), reproductively speaking. God purposely waited for the obstacles to mount up until it was impossible, 'to bring the promise to the brink of failure.' Why? 'To demonstrate that the promise, when fulfilled, came from God alone' (Sailhamer 1990, 2:147-48).

Of course, it displays His power; but more important to the story line—both the micro (Abrahamic) story line as well as the macro (biblical) story line—it proves His reliability. Remember, this is the twelfth time God has laid His credibility on the line by promising this aging couple a child. Such a promise is nothing less than a word from God.

Nothing God Says …

In the question, the word *anything* translates the Hebrew term *dābār*—a term so common and so flexible that it 'is translated in eighty-five different ways in the KJV!' (Kalland 1980, 1:178). A common translation is the generic word *thing* or *matter*.[5] That is the sense almost universally reflected in translations of Genesis 18:14.[6] But that's usually a secondary option when the primary meaning of the word does not seem (to the translators) to make sense in the context.

---

4. An internet search for the oldest mother on record produces mixed results. According to Guinness, the oldest confirmed mother is said to have been sixty-six; other sources report an Indian woman giving birth at sixty-nine or seventy—still twenty years younger than Sarah.

5. See, for example, Genesis 22:1; Exodus 1:18; 2:14; 9:4.

6. Leupold's remark (1942, 1:542) is representative of most commentators; *dābār* 'here is the equivalent of the indefinite pronoun: "thing"—"anything".'

The primary meaning of *dābār* is 'word,'[7] as in the phrase 'the word of the LORD.' So, its normal sense is a *spoken thing*, a *statement* or *saying*—if the context supports that sense. In many places where *dābār* is routinely translated 'thing,' if you simply poke around in the passage a little, you discover that the 'thing' in view is something that was said. (For examples, see Appendix 3.) That is exactly the situation in Genesis 18.[8]

God[9] had just *given His word* that Sarah herself, despite the physiological and biological impossibilities, would bear a son of her own. This rhetorical question in 18:14 is tied directly to the explicit statement God had just made in 18:10. Given that context, Genesis 18:14 could be translated literally and quite accurately, 'Is any **word** too hard for the LORD?'[10]—meaning (remember, rhetorical questions are actually emphatic declarations), God has said so and He cannot possibly fail to do something that He has said!

God had gone on record multiple times promising to give them an heir. The issue is not merely whether He is *powerful* enough to enable a ninety-year-old barren woman to have a child, but whether *this* ninety-year-old barren woman will have a child *because God promised it*.

> One great reason of the long delay of the fulfillment of the promise of the birth of the child ... was because God wanted to lay a supernatural basis for the history of Israel; and that both Israel and the nations of the future might learn that the things which are naturally impossible are not

---

7. The verb form is translated with about thirty different words, but nearly all are synonyms for some form of speaking.

8. Despite his more traditional rendering of the verse, Andrew Steinmann recognizes that the text reveals God's identity as 'the Yahweh who can do *what he has stated*' (Steinmann 2019, p. 194 emphasis added).

9. That the speaker in 18:10 and 13-14 is Yahweh is clear from a careful reading of the text: (1) the differentiation between speakers in chapter 18 referred to as 'they' and 'He'; (2) the reference to Yahweh in 18:17–33 (note 17, 20, 22, 33); (3) the clear indication that Yahweh is one of the three who came to visit Abraham (cf. 18:22 and 19:1); (4) the differentiation again in chapter 19 between speakers referred to as 'they' (19:2–4, 9–13, 15–17) and 'He' (19:21–22); and (5) the identification of the one calling down the judgment on Sodom and Gomorrah as Yahweh (19:24).

10. John Frame 2010, p. 51 also calls attention to this literal rendering.

supernaturally impossible, and that *nothing which Jehovah has ever spoken is 'too hard' for him to accomplish* (Baron 1988, p. 236 emphasis added).

The New Testament confirms that this is the point in Genesis 18. Citing Abraham as an example of faith, Paul does not say that Abraham was convinced he could have a child because God was omnipotent, but that Abraham was 'fully convinced that **what He had promised** He was also able to perform' (Rom. 4:21). The gospel context of Romans 3 and 4 supplies a compelling parallel. Believing the gospel is not about believing that salvation is possible because God is omnipotent; it is about believing that God *will do* for *me* all that He has graciously promised in Christ.

… Is Too Good to Be True

Now look at the next phrase: 'too hard for the LORD' (KJV, ESV, NIV). The NASB similarly reads 'too difficult,' but a marginal note suggests, 'Or, wonderful.' That's a strange word here: *is any word too wonderful?* Where does that marginal suggestion come from?

The Hebrew verb *pālā'* usually describes something as 'marvelous, amazing.'[11] The noun form is one of the Old Testament words for a miracle (a 'wonder'). When you read in the Old Testament (especially in Psalms) about God's 'wonders' or His 'marvelous works', it's usually

---

11. Victor Hamilton (1995, pp. 13-14) notes, 'On many occasions the verb means not "to be difficult" but "to be wonderful". Thus, one might render Genesis 18:14a "is a matter too wonderful for me?" But almost all instances of *pālā'* meaning "to be wonderful" are confined to Niphal participles and uses of the verb in the Hiphil stem.' So, Hamilton thinks 'difficult' is the more likely rendering here. Hamilton's observation is technically correct; however, those 'instances of *pālā'* meaning "to be wonderful"' that he singles out account for 85 per cent of its total occurrences, when you include the occurrences of the Niphal perfect where it also always means 'to be wonderful' (2 Sam. 1:26; Ps. 118:23; Prov. 30:18). The only reason for doubting the meaning 'wonderful' in Genesis 18:14 and (as we will see) in Jeremiah 32:17, 27 is that these passages use a Niphal imperfect which pretty clearly means 'to be difficult' in Deuteronomy 17:8 and 2 Samuel 13:2. However, the only other occurrence of the Niphal imperfect is Zechariah 8:6, where there is considerable consensus for translating it 'to be marvelous, wonderful.' In short, there is sound basis for rendering it 'too wonderful' in our passages rather than 'too hard, too difficult.'

this word.[12] So again, the verse could quite literally and accurately be translated, 'Is any word too wonderful for the Lord (to perform)?'

We've all used or heard the expression, 'That's just too good to be true!' That's the idea here. Is there anything God has given His word on that is simply too high to hope for, too much to actually count on? Is there anything that is just too good to be true if God has said it?

The answer to that question in Genesis 18 comes three chapters (and nine months!) later: 'And the LORD visited Sarah **as He had said**, and the LORD did for Sarah **as He had spoken**. For Sarah conceived and bore Abraham a son in his old age at the set time **of which God had spoken to him**' (Gen. 21:1-2). Do you hear the emphasis? It's not God's omnipotence that is exalted and celebrated in the birth of this miracle baby. Three times over the conclusion to the story underscores the absolute trustworthiness of God's words.

Everything in the text and context demonstrates that Genesis 18:14 really isn't primarily about God's omnipotence—that He *can* do *anything*. It is more wonderfully specific than that. It is the assurance that God *will* do *anything He says*. Divine ability is obviously included, but it is a secondary emphasis; the primary emphasis is divine reliability.

Again, the New Testament confirms this understanding of Genesis 18:14 when it explains the object of Sarah's faith. Hebrews 11 does not say that Sarah received strength to conceive because God is omnipotent and can do anything, but rather '**because she judged Him faithful who had promised**' (Heb. 11:11). Her faith was not merely in God's omnipotence (that He *could* do this); her faith was in God's faithfulness to His words (that He *would* do this because He *promised* to). God's words are guaranteed. You can lean all your weight on a word from God, no matter how unlikely or impossible it may sound.

Jeremiah 32—An Improbable Prediction

Jeremiah declares, 'Ah, Lord GOD! behold, You have made the heavens and the earth by Your great power and outstretched arm. **There is nothing too hard for You**' (Jer. 32:17). God replies by affirming, 'Behold,

---

12. See, for example, Exod. 15:11; Pss. 77:11, 14; 78:12; 88:10, 12; 89:5.

I am the LORD, the God of all flesh. **Is there anything too hard for Me?'** (32:27). Both statements use the same language as Genesis 18:14 (*dābār* and *pālā'*). What's going on in this passage?

We've hurdled about fourteen centuries from the time of Abraham and Sarah. The year is 587 B.C. (Jer. 32:1). Judah is about to be gobbled up by Nebuchadnezzar who will, within a year, demolish Jerusalem, dismantle the Solomonic temple, over-run the land of Judah, and forcibly march multitudes of Jews back to Babylon as captives (32:2-5). God tells Jeremiah what's about to happen, and Jeremiah tells the people.

Then God does something very strange. He instructs Jeremiah to purchase some land in Judah, and file the deed publicly so that everyone can see (32:6-8). It's one of those vivid prophetic actions that God sometimes uses to arouse curiosity and underscore a point. With Nebuchadnezzar's legions poised on the doorstep, real estate is one of the worst investments imaginable. Nevertheless, Jeremiah does what God says (32:9-12).

Why? Because God wants to accentuate His promise that, in spite of the impending Babylonian takeover, He *will* bring His people back again and Jews (not foreigners) *will* own the houses and fields and vineyards of Judah (32:13-15). Elsewhere God caps the Babylonian captivity at seventy years and no more (25:11-12, 29:10). How likely is this, really? Genesis 18 was a biological impossibility; this is, at best, a historical improbability. Yet God goes on record verbally once again and makes the point as publicly as possible.

Jeremiah's response to this acted prophecy is a magnificent prayer (32:16-25). Practically the first thing out of his mouth is this confession: 'There is nothing too hard for You!' (32:17). Guess how that reads literally. 'There is no **word** too wonderful for you [to perform]!'[13] In the first part of that verse Jeremiah talks about how God made heaven and earth by His great power and outstretched arm. That sounds like Jeremiah has God's *power* in mind more than His reliability. But look at the broader context:

---

13. The Latin Vulgate consciously reflects this sense by translating *dābār* as *verbum* ('word') in Jeremiah 32:17 and 27.

- 32:1—'the word (*dābār*) that came to Jeremiah from the LORD'
- 32:6—'the word (*dābār*) of the LORD'
- 32:8—'the word (*dābār*) of the LORD' (twice)
- 32:17—'there is no word (*dābār*) too hard for You'
- 32:24—'what You have spoken (*dābār*) has happened'

All this is followed by a restatement of the New Covenant (first introduced back in Jeremiah 31:31):

> Behold, I will gather them out of all countries where I have driven them in My anger, in My fury, and in great wrath; I will bring them back to this place, and I will cause them to dwell safely. They shall be My people, and I will be their God; then I will give them one heart and one way, that they may fear Me forever, for the good of them and their children after them. And I will make an everlasting covenant with them, that I will not turn away from doing them good; but I will put My fear in their hearts so that they will not depart from Me. Yes, I will rejoice over them to do them good, and I will assuredly plant them in this land, with all My heart and with all My soul. For thus says the LORD: Just as I have brought all this great calamity on this people, so I will bring on them all the good **that I have promised them** (Jer. 32:37-42).

That word *promised* in 32:42 is the verb form of *dābār*—'all the good that I have **spoken** to them.' All the surrounding emphasis on the *dābār* of God in Jeremiah 32 conditions how we read not only Jeremiah's exclamation (32:17) but also God's reaffirmation (32:26-27):

> Then the word (*dābār*) of the LORD came to Jeremiah, saying, Behold, I am the LORD, the God of all flesh. Is there anything (any word, *dābār*) too hard for Me?

The passage continues, 'Therefore thus says the LORD …' (32:28)— more words from God, as He elaborates even further His already improbable-sounding prophecy.

Now listen to Ezra—'In the first year of Cyrus, king of Persia, **so that the word of the LORD spoken by the mouth of Jeremiah**

156

the prophet might be fulfilled' (1:1). Improbable as it sounded back in 587 B.C., God began in 539 B.C. to do exactly what He said—not just because He was *powerful* and *could* do it, but because He *said* that He *would* do it.

It's not that God's rhetorical question (Gen. 18:14), Jeremiah's exclamation (Jer. 32:17), and God's reaffirmation (Jer. 32:27) have *nothing* to do with divine omnipotence (see Chapter 5); but they're not primarily statements of omnipotence. His reliability is backed up by His infinite ability. There is no disputing His power. Our question is not 'Can He?' but 'Will He?' Will He really do the amazing, improbable, impossible things He says? Yes! He can and He will because He must, and He must because His integrity is on the line. He has put it there, quite unnecessarily but also quite purposefully.

Luke 1—A *More* Impossible Birth

You know the story well. So well, perhaps, that every Christmas the familiar language slips past you like a lazy river with mesmerizing monotony. The angel Gabriel appears to a young woman named Mary, informing this betrothed virgin that she would become a pregnant virgin and, as a virgin, give birth to God's Messiah. Ever known anyone like that?

Genesis 18 was a *statistical* biological impossibility, but at least Abraham and Sarah had relations. Luke 1 is an *absolute* biological impossibility. Mary was the first one to understand that impossibility and ask about it: 'How can this be, since I do not know a man?' (Luke 1:34). But biological impossibilities don't stand a chance against a word from the God who created biology.

In answering her question, Gabriel explains that it would be an act of miraculous, divine intervention (1:35). 'And look,' he adds by way of confirmation, 'your relative Elizabeth has also become pregnant with a son in her old age—although she was called barren, she is now in her sixth month!' (1:36, NET). Gabriel offers Elizabeth as proof to Mary that God will do exactly what He said—impossible as it may sound—because He promised and then performed something almost as impossible for Elizabeth just six months earlier.

Finally, to seal the certainty of his message, Gabriel adds, 'For with God nothing shall be impossible' (Luke 1:37 KJV). Guess how that reads literally: *For with God no saying will be impossible.*[14] Like Genesis 18:14 and Jeremiah 32:17 and 27, this verse is usually cited as a declaration of divine omnipotence. But it's more than that: 'this remark means that God can and will *perform his word. His promise can be trusted*' (Bock 1996, p. 58, emphasis added). Elizabeth later confirmed that very assurance to Mary: 'for there will be a fulfillment of those things which were told her from the Lord' (Luke 1:45). Mary experienced the impossible not because God is omnipotent (after all, no other virgins have ever conceived), but because God promised her that she would.

Joel Green (who translates Luke 1:37, 'For no word from God will be impossible') captures the theological significance of this interchange between Gabriel and Mary. What we should hear in Gabriel's words is not an affirmation of divine omnipotence ('God can do anything') but, rather,

> Gabriel's denial of the impotency of any *word of God*; this point is taken up immediately by Mary ('let it be to me *according to your word*,' v. 38), then underscored by Elizabeth ('and blessed is she who believed ... *what was spoken to her by the Lord*,' v. 45).[15]

---

14. John Frame cites this literal rendering of Luke 1:37 (2010, p. 51). The term translated 'nothing' is the Greek word *rhēma*, and its parallels to *dābār* in the Old Testament are remarkable. (1) Its primary meaning is 'word' or 'saying'; the word occurs seventy times in the New Testament, and sixty-six times it is translated by one of those terms. (2) Like *dābār* its secondary translation is 'thing' but, also like *dābār*, even when it is translated that way it often clearly refers to something *spoken* in the context. (For examples, see Appendix 3.) (3) It is an important New Testament term for a 'word' from God (e.g., Rom. 10:17). And (4) it is the very Greek word used to translate *dābār* in Genesis 18:14 in the Greek version of the Old Testament (known as the Septuagint, or LXX).

15. Green 1997, p. 92 emphasis added. In addition to the statements of Joel Green and Darrell Bock already cited, I. Howard Marshall (1978, p. 72) concedes that Luke 1:37 could be translated 'no word from God will be powerless,' citing Grundmann, Tasker, and the NEB for corroboration. I find it fascinating that this considerable body of opinion on Luke 1:37 has virtually no parallel in commentary opinions on Genesis 18 or Jeremiah 32, even though all these passages are clearly saying exactly the same thing in identical language: not that God can do anything because He is omnipotent, but that God can be counted upon to do anything He says because He is reliable. I do not know why some New Testament interpreters see it but Old Testament interpreters do not.

No one doubts that Luke 1:37 *means* the same thing as Genesis 18:14 and Jeremiah 32:17, and 27. These four statements are all cut from the same grammatical cloth. The parallels between the language and the contexts support seeing these passages not as generic assertions of God's *ability* to do the unbelievable but specific affirmations of God's *reliability* to do everything He says.

Drawing Conclusions

Where Do We Go with This?

This chapter has been devoted to one of the Bible's most astonishing assertions. You could hardly ask for a more authoritative collection of speakers.

- Yahweh: *Is any word too wonderful for the Lord to perform?* (Gen. 18:14).

- Jeremiah: *Ah, Lord God, behold, there is no statement too amazing for You to fulfill* (Jer. 32:17).

- Yahweh: *Is anything I say too amazing for Me to fulfill?* (Jer. 32:27).

- Gabriel: *No saying from God will be impossible* (Luke 1:37).

What is the relevance, for you and me, of this emphasis on the utter *reliability* of God's words? First, this truth is applicable *historically*. Did God *really* create everything out of nothing by His word? Well, did He *say* He did? Then it's trustworthy. What about the Flood? The Exodus with all those miraculous plagues? The splitting of the Red Sea? If God is, indeed, not only omnipotent but reliable, why should we balk at affirming that everything recorded in the Bible happened just the way God *says* it did?

Don't limit God's words by your puny imagination.

Second, this truth is applicable *prophetically*. Are there some prophecies that seem just too fantastical to expect to come to pass as stated? Again, did God *say* He would do it? No words He utters are too good to be true nor too amazing for Him to perform. Don't limit God's words by your puny imagination.

Third, this truth is applicable *presently* and *personally*, in terms of promises God makes to you in the book of His words that we call the Bible. The general categorical assertion that God *can* do *any*thing is a comfort; but it is a very limited comfort when you need some specific intervention from God. We know that He can; but can we know that He will? If He hasn't promised it, He could and He might. But if He has promised it, He will and He must—no matter how impossible it may seem to us.

Applying the Trustworthiness of God's Words

Let me start with an admittedly facetious application, but one I hope makes the point effectively. How do you apply Luke 1:37 (or Gen. 18:14) directly to yourself? Suppose you say, 'I'm a virgin (or a ninety-year-old). Can I trust God that I will have a miraculous conception and bear a child?' Did God say you would? 'Me? Well, no. At least not yet.' Then, no, you don't have any basis for believing that God will do that for you. History demonstrates it's not impossible. God has done it before, but only for those to whom He gave His word on it.

But suppose you're in real financial need. You know God *can* meet anyone's need because He's omnipotent. But *will* He do it for *you*? Did He say He would? Paul could promise the believers in Philippi (who had been giving sacrificially to meet his needs), 'My God will supply all your need according to His riches in glory by Christ Jesus' (Phil. 4:19). So yes, absolutely; you have His word on it.[16]

Someone reading this may be desperate for God's healing—for yourself, or a child, or a spouse. You know He *can* so you know He *could*. But *will* He? I don't know; did He say He would? Does He ever promise that He will always physically heal you? Actually, no; if He

---

16. The guarantee is for needs, not whims or luxuries, nor even necessarily for foolish financial imbroglios. Also, context is important for promises too. The context of Philippians 4:19 suggests that this is not a blanket promise to just anyone. Because the Philippians have given sacrificially time and again to his needs, Paul has the liberty to assure them that God will meet their needs just as faithfully as they have met Paul's. I'm not sure that believers who are covetous, stingy, and ungenerous with their money toward God's work and God's ministers have any basis for confidence in this promise. This is not about earning God's favor, but it is about God making certain promises to certain kinds of people.

did then no Christian would ever die of disease or even old age. But He does promise that He is always in absolute control of everything that happens to you—not Satan, not doctors, not nature, and not chance (Talbert 2001, pp. 18-26). If you're a believer, that's a promise from your Father that you can climb into and rest securely and serenely, no matter what happens.

Maybe your life is in chaos, falling apart, spinning out of control. You don't know what to do or where to turn. Of course, you know God *could* step in and restore order and bring peace ... if He chose to. But *would* He? *Will* He? Did He say He would?

- 'Come to Me ... and I will give you rest,' Jesus said. (Matt. 11:28)

- 'Be anxious for nothing, but in everything by prayer and supplication, with thanksgiving let your requests be made known to God; and the peace of God, which surpasses all understanding, will guard your hearts and minds through Christ Jesus.' (Phil. 4:6-7)

- 'Trust in Him at all times, you people; pour out your heart before Him; God is a refuge for us.' (Ps. 62:8)

You can count on these words from God. His credibility and character are on the line. He *can*—but more importantly, He *will*.

A defeated Christian says, 'But I've been so unfaithful for so long, I'm embarrassed to even go to the Lord in prayer. I know God *can* forgive. I'm sure He's forgiven others, but how can I be confident that He really will receive *me*?' Did He say He would? Yes! 'If we confess our sins, He is faithful and just to forgive us our sins, and to cleanse us from all unrighteousness' (1 John 1:9). Then He *has* to—not because we deserve it, but because He has promised it. And nothing He has promised is too good to be true.

Of course, this reliability of God's words cuts both ways. Will God really chasten me if I ignore His warnings about certain sins? I know He *could*, but nothing has happened (yet). Well, what does God say about that? 'For whom the Lord loves He chastens, and scourges every son' (Heb. 12:6). Don't mistake the longsuffering of God for ignorance or negligence or forgetfulness to keep His word. He is a faithful Father who loves His children too much to leave them alone when they persist in sin.

Will God really keep me and preserve me as His child? He's omnipotent, so He *could* do it, but I struggle so much with sin and with doubt. How can I know He won't tire of my failures and decide I'm not worth the trouble anymore? Because when you put your faith in Christ, 'having believed, you were sealed with the Holy Spirit of promise, who is the guarantee of our inheritance' (Eph. 1:13-14). If you are a believer you are *in Christ*. That means, among other things, that your position before God is as secured as Christ's. That's why God can say, 'I will never leave you nor forsake you' (Heb. 13:5).

Responding to the Trustworthiness of God's Words

Whatever word God addresses to your need is utterly reliable. You have three options. First, you can reject it outright and invest your trust in someone else's words. That's a real option, but an unhappy one because the Lord is the only one who can meet your needs and satisfy your deepest desires. And trusting submission to His words is the only way of obtaining it.

Second, you might balk in doubt—skepticism aimed either at God (that He really will do what He says) or skepticism aimed at yourself (that He really will do it for *you*). That was Zechariah's reaction in Luke 1 to God's promise that his barren wife would become a mother in her old age. 'How shall I know this?' (Luke 1:18) is a question of skepticism, a question that expects further confirmation that God's words to him (through an angelic messenger, no less!) would *really* happen before he was prepared to embrace that hope. Gabriel's response indicates that Zechariah's question is inappropriate and mistrustful (Luke 1:19-20). God granted him confirmation alright, but not the kind he had in mind (1:21-22). What God said still happened, because God's words were not just for him but for his wife. But Zechariah would 'nevertheless bear the sign of his doubt' for the next nine months (Liefeld 1984: 8:828).

The third option is to embrace His words with the arms of faith. Collapse the whole weight of your trust on His words, like Mary did in the face of an utterly impossible-sounding promise: 'Behold, the maidservant of the Lord! May it be to me **according to your word**' (Luke 1:38).[17] The result of this response is blessing. Elizabeth put it this way: 'Blessed is she who believed, for **there will be a fulfillment** of those things **which were told her from the Lord**' (Luke 1:45). That's not an abstract, theoretical assurance; that's the experiential affirmation of an old and impossibly pregnant woman whose husband had been literally speechless for the past six months (with three more months of muteness to go) because he couldn't bring himself to trust God's words. How you respond to God's words is up to you.

A Final Appeal

The case I have tried to make in this chapter—that these passages are *primarily* declarations of God's trustworthiness, and only secondarily references to God's omnipotence—is not widely reflected in the commentary literature on Genesis or Jeremiah. It's not that the emphasis I'm arguing for is considered and dismissed; it's never even considered. Not until one surveys the commentaries on Luke does this appreciation for God's trustworthiness as the central thrust begin to show up.

But even in the books and commentaries that assume this is a statement of omnipotence, the applications you will find are still valid. Why? Because inevitably the applications (forgiveness, salvation, provision, etc.) are not just random actions we think God should be *able* to do because He is omnipotent. They are actions God has *said* He will do for any who comes to Him. 'There is no promise too great to be fulfilled. Christ's words never pass away, and what he has promised he is able to perform' (Ryle 1986, 1:29). In other words, even the applications within the scriptural contexts of Genesis 18, Jeremiah 32, and Luke 1 demonstrate that the real point of this statement is not the omnipotence of God but the trustworthiness of His words.

---

17. Zechariah's question ('How shall I know this?') expressed doubt, requesting additional evidence. Mary's question ('How shall this be?') expressed confusion, requesting additional explanation. Gabriel's response in each case confirms the difference between their questions.

Besides all the grammatical arguments rehearsed in this chapter, there's one more weighty theological argument against viewing these as first and foremost statements of omnipotence. As I showed at the beginning of the chapter, the fact is that some things *are* impossible for God. But *nothing He says* ever falls into that category. With God, no saying will prove to be impossible for Him, and none of His words are too good to be true.

A Final Illustration

In Bunyan's classic, *The Pilgrim's Progress*, Christian and Hopeful lose their way and wander into the realm of a giant named Despair, who captures them and throws them into the dungeon of Doubting Castle. Despair drubs them severely and even urges them to commit suicide as the only escape from their wretchedness, because he has no intention of ever releasing them. This is serious stuff Bunyan is writing!

Caged by their doubts and pummeled by depression, they lie in that dismal dungeon from Wednesday to Saturday (Bunyan is quite specific about the timing). Then, on Sunday morning, Christian

> broke out in a passionate speech: 'What a fool am I thus to lie in a stinking dungeon when I may as well walk at liberty! I have a key in my bosom called PROMISE that will, I am persuaded, open any lock in Doubting Castle.' Then Christian pulled it out of his bosom and began to try at the dungeon door, whose bolt [as he turned the key] gave back, and the door flew open with ease, and Christian and Hopeful both came out (Bunyan 1990, pp. 128-34).

What is the *key* called *promise* but a *word from God* that you are meant to believe and trust? It is the only means of escape from doubt and despair. Find out what God promises you in your need. Then claim that, cling to that, pray those words back to God, and believe not only that He *can* do it, but that He *will* do it for you because He *said* He would. No word from God is too good to be true. To be sure, He is omnipotent; but better than that, He is unfailingly, reliably true to His words.

164

Review & Reflect

1. Are there any passages of Scripture that you struggle to accept because they seem too good to be true? Or too fantastical? Or too incredible? What are they?

2. Is there something in particular that you need the Lord to do in your life right now? Can you find passages that, interpreted contextually, address those needs?

3. How are Zechariah's (Luke 1:5-20) and Mary's (Luke 1:26-38) situations, angelic messages, and responses both similar and different?

10
Trusting God's Words in Action

Now the just shall live by faith
Hebrews 10:38

Some of the largest and longest-living things on earth are found along the northern coast of California. The coastal redwoods (*Sequoia sempervirens*) are the tallest. Many are over 350 feet, with the current record-holder at 379 feet high and a girth of about 48 feet. At 305 feet, the Statue of Liberty would be lost to view in a forest of these giants. Some are estimated to be 2000 years old. The Sierra redwoods or giant sequoias (*Sequoiadendron giganteum*) are located in the heart of California. Though shorter (the tallest is a mere 275 feet, the equivalent of a 25-story building), the girth of the largest specimens is at least twice that of their taller northern cousins.

Hebrews 11 takes the reader on a tour through an avenue of human redwoods. These believers stand out against the skyline of history not because they were powerful or popular, but because they believed that God would do what He said even when it seemed unlikely, if not impossible. When Hebrews was written, some of their testimonies were as long-lived as today's redwoods; since then they yet have another two thousand years under their belts. That's some serious girth.

Such giants can be intimidating and discouraging. How could we ever be like them? We don't think of ourselves as redwoods. (Maybe dogwoods.) But neither did they. Every redwood started out as a little sapling. They were as full as we are of weakness and fear and

167

trembling, as aware as we are of deficiencies and failings. They tower over the generations not because they were extraordinary individuals; every one of them had sins, flaws, failures, and times of unbelief and unfaithfulness. They tower over the generations *in God's estimation*— that's the writer's point, after all—because of ordinary trust in the words of an extraordinary God.

Why is Hebrews 11 in the Bible? Why this content? And why here rather than earlier in the letter? What exactly is the argument of this chapter and how does it factor into the larger message of the book of Hebrews? Hebrews 11 is a casebook designed to demonstrate the kind of faith that evokes God's pleasure and approval. But how the writer gets to this point is crucial to understand if we are to get the full impact.[1]

The Bigger Picture of the Book of Hebrews

The letter to the Hebrews appears to have targeted first-century Jews who had professed faith in Jesus as the Messiah, many of whom were experiencing severe persecution from their unbelieving Jewish brethren (10:32-39). Two decades earlier, James taught his Hebrew brothers that such trials are 'a testing of your faith' designed to produce endurance (James 1:1-3).[2] The test of authenticity is endurance under stress over time.

You can draw a direct line from the letter's opening statement in 1:1-2 ('God ... has spoken to us by His Son') to 12:25 ('See that you do not refuse Him who speaks'). Those two statements embody the letter's most foundational theological thesis: the same God who spoke His words in the Old Testament through His prophets has now spoken with finality through His Son.

Bolstering that fundamental assertion is a sustained emphasis on the reliability of God's words and the necessity of clinging to those words in total trust. In fact, Hebrews highlights a particular form of

---

1. For a helpfully condensed version of the entire epistle, see Bruce 1964, pp. xix-xxii.

2. Interestingly, the same word for 'endurance' bookends Hebrews 11 (between Heb. 10:32, 36; and 12:1, 2, 3, 7).

divine speech that specifically invites trust. The word 'promise' (both the noun and the verb) occurs more frequently in Hebrews than in any other New Testament book—and always with reference to God's promises.[3] I'll develop the importance of that word later in this chapter. But for now, it's not amiss to say that Hebrews grounds its call to believe and obey God specifically in the trustworthiness of His words.

The argument of the letter can be summed up in three movements: (1) God, who has spoken in the past through prophets, has now given His final revelation through a Son; (2) the Son has filled full all the Old Covenant shadows and inaugurated the New Covenant, so that everything necessary for deliverance from sin and acceptance with God has been completed in and by the Son; so, (3) hold fast to that confidence and confession in spite of hardship, persecution, doubt, or any other temptation to turn back because, now that Christ has come, there is nothing to turn back to.

The writer's application of that message (point 3 above) is the engine that drives the letter. That's why he can sum up the whole communique as a 'word of exhortation' in Hebrews 13:22 (Lane 1991, c). That exhortation is a persistent and impassioned appeal to continue to cling to Christ because there is no way back, and no other way to God. Here is just a sampling from Hebrews to demonstrate the pattern:

- 'Therefore **we must give the more earnest heed to the things that we have heard, lest we drift away**' (2:1).

- We are Christ's '**if we hold fast the confidence and the rejoicing of the hope firmly to the end**' (3:6).

- 'We have become partakers of Christ **if we hold the beginning of our confidence steadfast to the end**' (3:14).

- 'Seeing then that we have a great High Priest who has passed through the heavens, Jesus the Son of God, **let us hold fast our confession**' (4:14).

---

3. The noun and verb combined occur eighteen times in the book. I could give you the references but it will mean more if you find them and mark them on your own. Cf. Kaiser 2008, p. 397.

- 'And we desire each of you to **show the same earnestness to have the full assurance of hope until the end**' (6:11, ESV).

- '**Let us hold fast the confession of our hope without wavering**, for He who promised is faithful' (10:23).

- 'Therefore **do not cast away your confidence**, which has great reward' (10:35).

The exhortation crescendos in chapter 10 (10:32-39), buttressed by a bevy of illustrations in chapter 11, before climaxing in chapter 12. Hebrews 11 reinforces this running exhortation by cataloging cases of those who 'by faith' acted solely on a word from God. With this collection of real-life men and women who have proved the trustworthiness of God's words, the writer grasps his Jewish readers firmly by the shoulders, looks them in the eye, and says, 'Look at your own ancestors! This is your heritage—dogged trust in a clear word from God, in spite of cost or consequence! You have a family history of living by trust in God's words. Follow their example! Cling to what God has said, come what may!'[4]

That this is all about *faith* is clear when you follow the trail of that keyword. 'Faith' appears only sparsely in the earlier chapters of Hebrews (4:2; 6:1, 12). The subject is reintroduced in chapter 10 (10:22, 38, 39) and becomes *the* topic of conversation in chapter 11, where the word occurs twenty-four times (more than any entire New Testament book except for Romans).

That this is all about faith *in a word from God* is clear when you pay attention to the details. Like the gold that was hammered flat, cut into fine strips, and threaded into the fabric of the priestly garments (Exod. 39:3), the thread of faith based on God's words is what gives Hebrews 11 its glitter.

- 11:7—Noah was '**warned** by God.'

- 11:8—Abraham was '**called** by God.'

---

4. This is the essence of his appeal as chapter 12 opens: 'Therefore, since we are surrounded by so great a cloud of witnesses [*all those just mentioned in chapter 11*], let us also [*like them*] lay aside every weight, and sin … and let us run with endurance the race that is set before us [*like they ran theirs*]' (Heb. 12:1 ESV).

- 11:9, KJV—Abraham 'sojourned in the land of **promise**.'

- 11:9—Isaac and Jacob were 'heirs with him of the same **promise**.'

- 11:11—Sarah judged God 'faithful who had **promised**.'

- 11:13—The patriarchs died with faith in God's **promises**.

- 11:17-18—Abraham 'had received the **promises**' centered in Isaac.

- 11:33—Many Old Testament believers 'obtained **promises**.'

- 11:39—Still others obtained God's approval for a life of faith in a '**promise**' they did not receive in their lifetime.

All these expressions explicitly make God's words the focal point of their faith. In other statements, the linkage between their actions and their trust in a word from God is not directly stated but nevertheless implicit.

- 11:22—Joseph's 'by faith' expectation of Israel's departure from Egypt can only be traced back to God's promise (Gen. 15:13).

- 11:28—Moses' 'by faith' observance of the Passover was motivated by God's warning and instruction (Exod. 12).

- 11:29—Israel's 'by faith' passage through the Red Sea was based on God's command (Exod. 14:15-18).

- 11:30—Israel's 'by faith' tumbling of Jericho's walls was grounded on God's directions (Josh. 6:1-5).

- 11:31—Rahab's 'by faith' deliverance from destruction was rooted in her faith in God's promise to Israel (Josh. 2:9).[5]

There's much more to the book of Hebrews, of course, but what we've seen is adequate to contextualize chapter 11 in terms of its role in the

---

5. 'I know that the LORD has given you the land,' she told the spies (cf. Deut. 1:8). We do not know how she knew this, only that she believed it and acted on it—saving not only herself but also her family. Rahab is a particularly remarkable example because her faith was in *a divine promise of her own annihilation* made *to someone else* (Israel); rather than fighting it or complaining about it, she trusted it, embraced it, and submitted to it.

message of Hebrews and its contribution to our exploration of what it looks like to trust in the reliability of God's words.

Faith Is Defined by God's Words (11:1-3)

What is faith, and how does it work? The writer addresses this question in general (11:1-3) before putting faith on display in specific, real-life situations from the past.

First, *faith is the only way to relate to things future and invisible*: 'Faith is the substance of things hoped for, the evidence of things not seen' (11:1). This is not a technical definition of faith but a description, a statement of how faith works. What's the difference? If I say, *a tree is a woody perennial plant having a single usually elongated main stem and upper limbs or branches bearing leaves*, I'm defining what a tree is. But if I say, *a tree is a provider of shade*, or *a source of lumber*, or *a supplier of food*, I'm describing what a tree *does*. That's what Hebrews 11:1 is doing with faith.

Descriptively, faith is the *basis* of hoped-for things, the *certainty* of unseen things. That doesn't mean faith creates its own reality; things do not happen simply because we believe in them hard enough. It simply means that the reason believers *expect* certain things to happen in the future is *because God has said they will*; and the reason we are *confident* about the reality of things that we admit we cannot see is *because God has said they are so*. Faith is the sole connecting link between our limited physical sense, or our present experience, and what God says is so, including things that we cannot yet see (because they are invisible) or experience (because they are future). One translation captures it well: 'Faith means being sure of the things we hope for, and knowing that something is real even if we do not see it' (11:1 NCV). The certainty of realities that we cannot yet see or experience is grounded in the words of God. That's why we can sing with confidence,

> Things that are not now, nor could be,
> Soon shall be our own.

The rest of Hebrews 11 reinforces this understanding of faith as the basis on which God's people hope for future things and can be certain of unseen things. For example, Noah acted on faith in God's warning 'of things **not yet seen**' (11:7). Abraham (11:8) acted on faith in God's promise of a possession that was both future ('a place he would **later** receive as an inheritance' NET) and unseen ('he went out, **not knowing where he was going**'). By faith, Isaac (11:20) blessed Jacob and Esau 'concerning **things to come**' (future).

Second, *faith is necessary to obtain the pleasure and approving testimony of God*. It was by faith that 'the elders obtained a good testimony' (11:2). A good testimony with whom? Their neighbours and contemporaries? The answer comes in 11:4, where Abel 'obtained the **testimony** that he was righteous, **God testifying** about his gifts' (NASB). God is ultimately the only one whose testimony about you matters. Whatever other failures plagued the men and women in this chapter, they all 'obtained a good **testimony**' from God because of their faith in His words (11:39).[6] In fact, 'without faith, it is impossible to please Him' (11:6).

C. S. Lewis expressed his surprise at how many historical Christian writers explained the scriptural concept of 'glory,'

> taking heavenly glory in the sense of fame or good report. But not fame conferred by our fellow creatures—fame with God, approval or (I might say) 'appreciation' by God. And then, when I thought it over, I saw that this view was scriptural; nothing can eliminate from the parable the divine *accolade*, 'Well done, thou good and faithful servant.' ... I suddenly remembered that no one can enter heaven except as a child; and nothing is so obvious in a child ... as its great and undisguised pleasure in being praised. ... And that is enough to raise our thoughts to what may happen when the redeemed soul, beyond all hope and nearly beyond belief, learns at last that she has pleased Him whom she was created to please (Lewis 1976, pp. 36-37).

The Holy Spirit reveals that this divine pleasure, this testimony of divine *approval*, comes through trusting God's words over anyone and everyone else's.

---

6. Despite the variety of translation to be found in different Bible versions, the same Greek word (*martureō,* to witness or testify) underlies all three of the italicized terms in this paragraph from 11:4 and 39.

Third, *faith is also the way we relate to things past that we have not seen or experienced.* 'By faith we understand that the worlds[7] were framed by the word of God, so that the things which are seen were not made of things which are visible' (Heb. 11:3). The writer takes us back to the beginning of everything, linking creation not merely to the power of God but to 'a word from God' (11:3 NJB), and linking our ability to understand how everything began to faith in God's record of it (see Chapter 7).[8]

Biblical faith is not natural optimism, positive thinking, self-persuasion, imagination, or hopeful uncertainty. Biblical faith is believing what God says. Biblical faith is *always* rooted ultimately in a word from God. By biblical definition and demonstration, 'faith always presupposes a divine revelation to which it is a response' (Griffith-Thomas 1976, p. 55).

Trusting God's Words Works Itself Out in Our Actions

Hebrews 11 is a real-life exhibit of a living faith that manifests itself in trusting a word from God, come what may. Biblical faith inevitably manifests itself in how we live life. Just scan down through the chapter and listen to the verbs that grow out of the faith of these ordinary people. 'By faith,' that is, because of faith in a word from God,

- Abel offered a better sacrifice (11:4)

- Enoch pleased God (11:5-6)[9]

- Noah prepared an ark (11:7)

---

7. Literally 'the ages,' referring to 'the universe of space and time' (Bruce 1964, p. 280). The same term appears in the same sense in Hebrews 1:2.

8. 'The detail that the world was ordered ... "by means of the word of God" alludes to the creative commands of God in Gen. 1' (Lane 1991, p. 331).

9. Hebrews 11:5 reads, 'By faith Enoch was translated'—referring, of course, to an action God performed, not Enoch. The passage clarifies, however, that the reason he was translated was because 'he pleased God,' and immediately adds that 'without faith it is impossible to please Him.' That succession of ideas makes the point that if Enoch pleased God, it could only be by his faith. The gist, then, is that by faith Enoch pleased God.

- Abraham obeyed and sojourned (11:8-9)

- Sarah received strength (11:11)

- Abraham offered Isaac (11:17)

- Isaac blessed (11:20)

- Jacob blessed (11:21)

- Joseph made mention and gave commandment (11:22)

- Moses' parents hid him (11:23)

- Moses refused (11:24), forsook (11:27), and kept (11:28)

- Israel passed through the Red Sea (11:29) and felled the walls of Jericho (11:30)

- Rahab perished not (11:31)

And the list continues with more verbs piled on top of each other (11:32-37) of things that people accomplished and endured, conquered and suffered *by faith*—that is, all because of their trust in a word from God. Faith in God's words (or the lack of it), drives our decisions (Moses), animates our actions (Abraham), and feeds our hope (Isaac, Jacob, and Joseph). It determines how we worship God (Abel), whether we satisfy God (Enoch), and even whether we escape divine judgment (Noah, Rahab). What (or rather whom, whose words) you believe has everything to do with how you will live and how you will die.

Hebrews 11 showcases far too many examples of faith to include in this chapter. We'll survey only a few of those who model what it looks like to live by trust in God's words.

Noah: Trusting God's Words Means Preparing for Future Judgment (Heb. 11:7)

'By faith Noah, being warned by God [*the **basis** of faith—a word from God*] about things not yet seen [*the **realm** where faith operates—things future and things unseen*], in reverence prepared an ark for the salvation of his household [*the **action** of faith—obedience to God's direction*], by which he condemned the world [*the **consequence** of faith—distinction*

175

from the world], and became an heir of the righteousness which is according to faith [*the result of faith—righteousness in God's view*] (Heb. 11:7 NASB).

Strip out all the modifying phrases and what's left is this kernel statement: 'By faith Noah ... prepared an ark.' By faith Noah built a boat? Building the ark was a work of faith not because it was a grand, extraordinary risk venture, nor because it entailed a lifetime of activity that appeared absurd to everyone else or was blatantly out-of-step with his culture. It was an expression of faith because the only reason he did it was a warning from God about something future and as yet unseen (Gen. 6:13-21). Contrary to all his senses, all his experience, and all the opinions of everyone around him, Noah regarded God's words as trustworthy and acted on them (Gen 6:22). That trust in God's words ended up directing his entire life. And saving his family.

Noah's trust in God's words was instrumental in his family's security and deliverance from certain, coming judgment ('to the saving of his house'). What would have become of his family if he had not regarded God's words about future and unseen things to be trustworthy? A parent's unwillingness to trust God's words is not a purely personal matter; it can jeopardize the spiritual life and welfare of the children as well.

God has warned us of coming judgment, too (Heb. 9:27; 2 Cor. 5:10). If we trust God's words about that judgment to come, we will live life in a certain way that will impact our families, our priorities, our choices, our relationships with people—all on the basis of God's statements about a future and unseen reality, even though it is a long time in coming, and there is no visible precedent or proof.

By virtue of his trust in God's words, Noah also 'condemned the world ....' In what way did he do that? God's words surely sounded foolish to Noah's generation. His trust in God's words distinguished Noah from all those around him. Noah's faith condemned the world simply because his believing response to God's words stood in contrast to their unbelief, even though they all had access to the divine warning (2 Pet. 2:5). The trustworthiness of God's words vindicated Noah's trust and condemned the world's unbelief.

'By which [faith] ... he became heir of the righteousness which is according to faith.' James 2:18 can help us here. 'Show me your faith without your works' (James 2:18a). What if Noah had said he believed God, but didn't build the ark? 'I will show you my faith by my works' (James 2:18b). It was the building of the ark that demonstrated Noah's trust in God's words, because 'faith without works is dead' (James 2:20).

The Patriarchs: Trusting God's Words Means Living as Sojourners (Heb. 11:8-10, 13-16)

The primary feature of the faith of Abraham, Isaac, and Jacob highlighted here is its pilgrim character. Faith-based sojourning is emphasized through a variety of expressions.

- 'he went out, not knowing where he was going' (11:8)

- 'he sojourned in the land of promise' (11:9 KJV)

- 'as in a foreign country' (11:9)

- 'dwelling in tents' (11:9)—implying transience, temporariness

- 'for he waited for the city' (11:10)—expresses anticipation, a quest

- 'confessed that they were strangers and pilgrims' not just in the land of Canaan but 'on the earth' (11:13)

- 'those who say such things declare plainly that they seek a homeland' (11:14)

When God called Abraham out of Ur with the promise of a land inheritance, he had no idea where he was going and no GPS to get there. No notion of what it would look like when he arrived—no travel brochures or reports from Mesopotamian vacationers just back from holiday in Canaan. No itinerary of what would happen when he arrived. No idea that, once there, God would lead him into a famine (Gen. 12:10), make him wait twenty-five *more* years before the arrival of a son and heir (Gen. 21:5), and then ask him to give up that son (Gen. 22). And no inkling that it would take nearly seven hundred years before his descendants even began to inherit the land God had promised.[10]

Trusting God's words always entails an element of uncertainty; that's the nature of faith. Uncertainty about specifics and circumstances and maybe even immediate consequences; but not uncertainty about God or the ultimate outcome. Abraham's call was not merely a call to a specific place; it was a call to radical trust and loyalty to a new God. Isn't that the essence of Christianity—of following Christ? It is the very lack of sight that constituted his obedience as an act of trust. Trust is that principle by which a believer, on the basis of God's words, lives for what he does not yet possess and in light of realities he cannot see.

Abraham traveled a thousand miles on the basis of a promise that God would give him descendants and, one day, give Canaan to him and to his descendants—a promise God reconfirmed to his son Isaac and later to his grandson Jacob.[11] That's why they lived in tents, moved into no city, and never built any permanent settlement structures. A pilgrim lives for another time and another place. How do we do that? How do we reach out mentally (Heb. 11:15) and emotionally (11:16) and embrace what is future (another time) and unseen (another place)? By trusting God's words about the transitory nature of this present life and the certainty, reality, and glory of what is to come. How does that work?

First, *trusting God's words about future and unseen realities equips us to live a life that is both engaged in and yet unattached to this present world* ('by faith he sojourned in the land of promise, as in a strange [foreign] country,' Heb. 11:9 KJV). That word 'sojourn' is a crucial word; it embodies a mindset, a worldview. We are called to live as pilgrims and sojourners (1 Pet. 1:17; 2:11),[12] pitching our tents

---

10. Abraham's departure from Haran is dated at 2092 or 2091 B.C. (Merrill 2008, p. 47; Kaiser 1998, p. 55). Israel's conquest of the land of Canaan after the exodus from Egypt occurred about 1400 B.C. (Merrill 2008, p. 125; Kaiser 1998, p. 154).

11. Abraham lived seventy-five more years after Isaac was born (Gen. 21:5; 25:7); he saw Isaac become a husband (Gen. 25:20) and a father (Gen. 25:26), and died when Jacob was fifteen.

12. First Peter's fundamental description of believers is that we are 'pilgrims and sojourners'—temporary dwellers in a foreign country—the same words used

temporarily in a sin-filled world that is hostile to God, while living for another world and a higher reality. We are pilgrims and sojourners here and now precisely because one of those unseen realities is that we are citizens elsewhere. The New Testament elsewhere confirms this outlook that we, though living here, hold our ultimate citizenship 'in heaven' (Phil. 1:27, 3:20-21).[13]

Here's the irony. Abraham sojourned as a stranger in the very land God promised to give to him (and his descendants). Likewise, we sojourn as strangers on an earth that God created for His people and still intends to give to them (Ps. 37:11; Matt. 5:5). At a minimum, that certainly includes the 'reforged' new earth; but some (including me) believe it also includes this present earth as well. In any case, this life is just the front porch of our eternity (2 Cor. 4:16; 5:1). But it still takes faith to trust and follow God on the front porch, because it involves present realities that we can't see and future realities we don't yet have.

Second, *trusting God's words about future and unseen realities prompts us to pass along to our families the legacy of a pilgrim mindset* ('with Isaac and Jacob, the heirs with him of the same promise'). Your attitudes, values, and priorities—communicated by the way you live and the choices you make and don't make—are communicated to your children and grandchildren. We can teach what we know, and we should; but we will reproduce what we are.

> *We teach what we know; we reproduce what we are.*

---

in Heb. 11:9, 13. Peter gives us specific guidance on how to live out that identity in an alien and hostile world.

13. In Philippians, Paul reminds us that we actually belong to another world. He uses a verb (*politeuomai*, 1:27) that carries the idea of conducting oneself according to one's citizenship. Then in 3:20 Paul informs us that 'our citizenship (*politeuma*) is in heaven.' This language was particularly relevant for residents of the city of Philippi which was designated as a Roman colony (cf. Acts 16:12). Beyond merely being part of the Roman Empire, a colony was considered an extension of the city of Rome itself (though it was 800 miles away), a satellite city of Rome. This privileged status 'provided the inhabitants with numerous advantages, including autonomous government, immunity from tribute, and treatment as if they actually lived in Italy' (Kent 1978, p. 95; Johnson 2013, pp. 5, 85-86). Philippi becomes a striking illustration of what it means for us to live as citizens of heaven while temporarily inhabiting this present earth.

Finally, *trusting God's words about future and unseen realities enables us to anticipate and live for realities that are certain and enduring* ('for he waited for the city that has foundations, whose builder and maker is God'). 'Waiting' does not suggest killing time while we hang around to see what happens; it depicts positive expectation. It's the difference between waiting on a random street hoping a bus might come by and pick you up, and waiting at the bus stop; even if you're early and have to wait a long time, you know the bus is coming. The writer of Hebrews himself applies this Abrahamic expectation to all of us (Heb. 13:13-14). And John gives that city a name: New Jerusalem (Rev. 21).

Sarah: Trusting God's Words Means Participating in the Performance of God's Promises (Heb. 11:11-12)

The example of Sarah's faith is sandwiched right in the middle of the discussion of the patriarchs, perhaps because she was the vital link between Abraham and his heirs. Dissect the details of Sarah's story, and it's as if God had decided: 'I will give this couple a child and build from them a great nation. But that's too easy. First, I'll also make her physiologically barren. Then I'll wait until they're both reproductively dead. *Then* I'll give them a child.' He promises Abraham a descendent—a promise He makes twelve times over the next quarter-century. All the while, from all appearances, nothing is happening.

Hebrews 11:11-12 is a highly compressed summary of what is, in Genesis, a protracted story with multiple twists and turns over the space of twenty-five years and ten chapters. But it will help to explore briefly that fuller backstory.

Genesis opens three windows into Sarah's relationship to Abraham and the divine promise. The first is her *barrenness* (Gen. 11:29-30); that's not particularly problematic until we encounter God's promise to Abraham (Gen. 12:1-3). The second is her *beauty*—even at sixty-five—and Abraham's not-so-trusting example in Egypt (Gen. 12:10-20). Abraham's rationalization ('when the Egyptians see you ... they will kill me,' Gen. 12:12) shows just how faltering his faith could be. The fact is, they can't kill Abraham without undermining the integrity of God. The third is her *pragmatism*—her ploy to facilitate God's plan, prompted by a misinterpretation of God's providences (Gen. 16:1-3). You can read her rationalization right there in the text: God promised a child, but 'the LORD has restrained me from bearing.' So she proposes a solution, one of the earliest displays of the God-helps-those-who-help-themselves philosophy.

We're usually pretty hard on Sarah for her suggestion of her servant, Hagar, as a surrogate mother. In her defense, Sarah's pragmatism is actually a sign of faith in God's promise! Why would she even suggest this if she didn't believe God's promise to Abraham in the first place? But time is not standing still. She is seventy-five and barren. Abraham is eighty-five. And it's worth pointing out that as far as the biblical record is concerned, though God said Abraham would have descendants (Gen. 12:7; 13:15-16; 15:4-5), He never specified that Abraham *and Sarah* would have a child until *after* the Hagar incident (Gen.17:16, 19, 21). So Sarah devises a pragmatic solution—the only one under the circumstances that seemed reasonable and workable (and, for what it's worth, culturally normal and legal).

But there are several problems with pragmatism. (1) It replaces patience with activity, which is always much easier and (to us) more sensible than waiting on the Lord. (2) It replaces God's perfect timing with a chronology that makes more sense to us (usually now). (3) It replaces God as the object of trust with self as the object of trust—my plan, my strategy, my ingenuity, my ability to figure out a way to make this work. (4) It is often willing to rationalize a questionable method in order to accomplish a worthy goal. And, (5) it often creates unintended and undesirable consequences. You can see all of these factors play out in Genesis 16 and its aftermath.[14]

---

14. Sarah's own daughter-in-law was later faced with a similar dilemma at the time of Isaac's blessing of Jacob and Esau; and she, too, chose a wrong solution. By contrast, David conscientiously passed up several providential and humanly defensible opportunities (to kill Saul) in order to achieve God's *known* will (David's accession to the throne). Instead, he trusted in God's way and God's time to bring about God's words.

Obviously, God often employs our use of the means He has put at our disposal to accomplish His will. It is possible, however, to bring into the chemistry of a situation something that violates the will of God at some other point, or that simply isn't God's intended means and method (often because it does not sufficiently magnify Him exclusively). Sarah's scheme may have been prompted by faith, arguably selfless, culturally acceptable, and even providentially incorporated in the divine purpose; but in retrospect, it was clearly not the way God intended to fulfill His promise (Gen. 17:18-21).

But sometimes these things take time to shake out. It's amazing how long we can operate on a total misunderstanding of God's purposes and providences. Long after the fallout of the Hagar debacle, both Sarah and Abraham seem to have assumed that Ishmael was the fulfillment of God's promise. Thirteen years later when God, apparently for the first time, clarified to Abraham that Sarah would be the one to bear the promised child (Gen. 17:16), his reaction was the same as Sarah's: laughter (Gen. 17:17; 18:12). Eventually, however, the laughter of disbelief turned to the wide-eyed wonder of trust in God's unbelievable promise (Heb. 11:11), then back into the laughter of incredulous celebration when the divinely-promised impossibility became reality (Gen. 21:6-7).

This New Testament summary in Hebrews 11:11-12 fast-forwards to the end of that story to focus attention on Sarah's submissive trust in the way God said it would happen, and the role of Sarah's faith in the realization of God's promise to Abraham.[15] What was that role?

The first word of verse 12 ('therefore') provides a hint. 'Therefore' is a causal word and when you turn it around, so to speak, it spells 'because.' So the connection of 11:11-12 can be restated like this: *Because of Sarah's faith, an innumerable offspring came from one man (and him as good as dead).* It's remarkable that Abraham is not only

---

15. A few translations and commentators have understood 11:11-12 to refer not to Sarah's faith but to Abraham's. There are several reasons for this, some of them very technical and grammatical. This book is not the place to delve into such abstruse debates. I will simply say that I agree with most translations that the focus is on Sarah's faith (11:11) as a necessary link to Abraham's reception of God's promise of an innumerable progeny—namely, the nation of Israel (11:12).

unnamed in this passage, but passive. It's not too much to say that these verses essentially credit the birth of the nation Israel to the faith of Sarah!

In the silence of the days following God's final clear announcement in Genesis 18, Sarah came to the conclusion that the one who had promised was utterly reliable to do what He said. As a result, *she received strength in connection with her husband, and **therefore** God then fulfilled His promise to her husband* (Heb. 11:12). Sarah had to reach a verdict about God in her heart: Was He trustworthy? The question was not, 'Can I trust my husband in this?' The question was not, 'Can I figure out a way through this?' The question was, 'Can I trust God to do what He said?' Charles Wesley famously wrote,

> Faith, mighty faith, the promise sees
> And looks to that alone,
> Laughs at impossibilities
> And cries, 'It shall be done!'[16]

What makes faith 'mighty'? Is it up to us to somehow find a way to muster in ourselves a forceful faith that persuades God to fulfill His promise? Jesus said that even a mustard-seed-sized faith is sufficient to move mountains. The mightiness of faith does not reside in us; faith is mighty when it clings doggedly to the promise of God. You don't need a big faith in God; you just need trust in a big God. And the more you exercise it, the stronger it grows and the more habitual it becomes.

Abraham: Trusting God's Words Means Always Giving His Words the Benefit of the Doubt (Heb. 11:17-19)

Probably when most of us think of Abraham's offering of Isaac, we think of it especially as an example of his obedience. That's where Genesis 22 seems to focus our attention. But Hebrews 11 specifically

---

16. Some versions read, 'And looks to God alone': but Wesley originally wrote it as I have quoted it. It is appropriate, given the indivisibility of God and His words. To look to God is to look to His promise; to look to God's promise is to look to the one who performs it.

spotlights Abraham's *faith* in sacrificing Isaac.[17] This passage lets us eavesdrop on how faith reasons and talks, especially when it involves enormous personal loss or seems to contradict everything we thought God was doing and saying up to that point.

The fulcrum of this passage is Abraham's trust in God's promise. It's right in the text. Abraham is identified as 'he who had received the **promise**' (11:17); and Isaac *is* the promise, the one 'of whom **it was said**, "In Isaac your seed shall be called"' (11:18). The passage plasters God's promise on a placard and holds it up for us to see that, in the end, *this* is what Genesis 22 was about. Abraham's dilemma was the apparent contradiction between God's *promise* and God's *command*.

The same God who said,

> Sarah your wife shall bear you a son, and you shall call his name Isaac; I will establish My covenant with him for an everlasting covenant, and with his descendants after him (Gen. 17:19),

now said,

> Take now your son, your only son Isaac, whom you love, and go to the land of Moriah, and offer him there as a burnt offering on one of the mountains of which I shall tell you (Gen. 22:2).[18]

---

17. Lane comes within an inch of putting his finger on the pulse of this passage: 'It is the faithfulness of God to his promises, more than the ~~faith and~~ obedience of Abraham, that is the primary thrust of the writer in vv. 17-19' (Lane 1991, p. 363). My strike-through represents a necessary corrective, in my opinion. Abraham's obedience was certainly the necessary expression of his faith in God's promises, and Genesis 22 places that obedience center stage. But here in this passage the writer weds the trustworthiness of God's words with Abraham's faith in those words; it is impossible to divorce Abraham's trust from God's promise and feel the full force of these verses.

18. How could God command human sacrifice when He elsewhere expresses total abhorrence of the practice? (1) God always intended to halt the sacrifice. (2) Abraham's expectation of Isaac's immediate resurrection (expressed implicitly in Gen. 22:5 and explicitly in Heb. 11:19) means that, in any case, this would not have been a 'normal' human sacrifice. (3) God intended to display through the episode a number of theological truths (faith, obedience, substitution, resurrection, and so on.). And, (4) God designed it to portray typological and prophetic truth regarding Messiah, even down to the very location (the mount on which the Temple would be built and where the *unaborted* sacrifice of His Son would take place).

Abraham's conundrum wasn't, 'How can I obey these two conflicting commands?' but, 'If I obey this command, how can God possibly keep that promise?' Obedience to God's clear command would, it seemed, undermine God's equally clear pledge. The temptation, in short, was to worry about God's part.

But to read the Genesis account, there was no conflict or quandary for Abraham at all. He never questions, never vacillates. It takes the sudden call of the angel of the Lord to stop him (Gen. 22:10-11). How could Abraham be so unhesitatingly resolute?

By now Abraham's trust in God's words was so reflexive, so instinctive and unwavering, that he had already reached an astonishing and unprecedented conclusion: 'God was able to raise [Isaac] up even from the dead' if that's what it would take for God to keep His promise (Heb. 11:19). We might be tempted to ask, 'How could the writer of Hebrews infer Abraham's thinking from the Genesis narrative?' Even apart from the text's inspiration (which guarantees its accuracy), it can actually be deduced from an attentive reading of the Genesis narrative. Abraham told his servant, 'the lad and I will go yonder and worship, **and we will come back to you**' (Gen. 22:5). If Isaac was to be the sacrifice, there's only one way that could happen.

What makes this act of faith so extraordinary is that Abraham had no basis for expecting this outcome or believing that God even did such a thing as raising up dead people. So far as we know, he had no revelation, or personal experience, or historical precedent that would lead him to this conclusion. But *he was so thoroughly convinced of the reliability of God's words that it was easier for him to imagine that God would do something utterly unprecedented than that He would fail to fulfill His words, to the letter.*

Abraham's willingness to reason outside-the-box is one of the most striking examples of a legitimately 'sanctified imagination.' It is instructive for what we do with God's personal promises, but also for how we interpret His prophetic promises. (The covenant promises to Abraham were both personal and prophetic.) Abraham's instinct was not to reinterpret God's prophetic promises. It apparently never occurred to him to think, 'Maybe God's promises are referring to *spiritual* descendants, and the land God promised is really a *spiritual* inheritance.' Abraham clung to the straightforward jots and tittles of God's words. God may have to do something utterly unexpected in order to do what He said, but He can never abandon His words.

> Abraham possessed the *promises* of God, as yet unrealized, when he possessed the God of the promises and his trustworthy *word* (Kaiser 2008, p. 60 original emphasis).

When we are confronted with a clear word from God, trust thinks like Abraham did in Hebrews 11:19. God will always find a way to keep all His promises, even if it means doing something unprecedented, unheard of, or otherwise impossible.

'What More Shall I Say?'

As he winds down this section, the writer of Hebrews exclaims, 'What more shall I say? For the time would fail me to tell of [others] who through faith ... obtained promises ...' (11:32-33). He then launches into a staccato bullet list of names and circumstances that divide into two classes.

There were those whose faith enabled them to achieve what they never could have accomplished apart from trust in God's words (11:32-35a). They conquered kingdoms, did righteousness, obtained promises, shut lions' mouths, doused raging fires, escaped the edge of the sword, gained strength when they were weak, became mighty in battle, and put foreign armies to flight. Some mothers even had their dead children raised back to life.

But then there were the 'others.' Those whose faith enabled them not to achieve but to *endure* (11:35b-38). Some accepted torture rather than recant their faith because they were confident in the greater reality of their resurrection.[19] 'Still others' were mocked and

---

19. Hebrews 11:35-36 links the reader to a historical era underappreciated by most Christians—the intertestamental period. The word 'tortured' literally refers to being stretched out on a rack and beaten with rods. And the story the writer has in mind comes from the apocryphal book of 2 Maccabees. While not part of the inspired canon, the books of Maccabees are one of our most valuable sources of

beaten, chained and imprisoned. Some were executed by stones, or saws, or swords. And others lived out their days roaming the earth in sheepskins and goatskins—destitute, afflicted, tormented—living in deserts, mountains, dens, and caves, bearing what they never could have endured without a sustaining trust in God's words.

Most of us find our lives a mixture of conquest and suffering. Few people spend their lives in only one class of experiences, though some seem to be called to a greater share of hardship and loss than others. We are inclined to pry into the whys of providence, and pit our lot against that of others. When Jesus foretold Peter's martyrdom, Peter glanced back at John and asked, 'Lord, what about him?' Jesus replied, 'If I want him to live until I come back, what concern is that of yours? You follow me!' (John 21:21-22 NET).

In *The Horse and his Boy* when Shasta questions Aslan's dealings with Aravis, the Lion replies, 'Child, I am telling you your story, not hers; I tell no one any story but his own' (Lewis 1970, p. 159). In his own way the writer of Hebrews makes the same point when he exhorts, 'Let us run with endurance the race that is set before *us*' (12:1; italics added). The nature and length of that race varies from person to person.

You and I are prone to be too preoccupied with the here-and-now. Too often we don't really trust God's words about eternity enough. We tend to gauge our success or failure by our present experiences and their immediate and visible outcomes. Hebrews 11 thrusts us into a larger reality and shows us what it looks like to navigate our way through this present, visible world by trusting God's words about the larger realities—future things and unseen things. God never intended this life to provide the bulk of our reward or satisfaction, only the smallest foretaste. This life is not the whole story. It's not even most of the story.

Trust in the trustworthiness of God's words is essential to doing, or to enduring, whatever course God lays before you, and to receiving the

---

intertestamental Jewish history. Conservative commentators old and recent agree that the writer is clearly referring to events from 2 Maccabees 6 and 7 that were well-known to his readers.

testimony and approval of God in both doing and enduring whatever He calls you to do or to endure.

Review & Reflect

1. What are some of the future realities that God's words teach believers to have confidence in? What are some of the present but unseen realities that God says are so? Don't just generalize; try to connect each example with a specific statement in God's words.

2. Hebrews 11:32-38 refer to quite a variety of people and situations that the writer clearly must have had in mind, though he doesn't identify them by name. Using a good cross-reference Bible, find examples of people who had some of those experiences.

3. Hezekiah is a great example of someone who trusted in God's word in the face of personal mockery and national threat. See 2 Kings 18, 19; 2 Chronicles 32; Isaiah 36, 37, where *bātach* occurs twenty times combined.

11
Prophets, Kings, and the Words of God

Know now that nothing shall fall to the earth
of the word of the LORD ...
2 Kings 10:10

In my book *Not by Chance: Learning to Trust a Sovereign God*, I spent a chapter exploring the books of Kings as a kind of historical museum of God's providence. I likened 1 and 2 Kings to the well-stocked workshop of a master craftsman, where the tools of divine providence fill the walls in staggering multiplicity and variety. God sometimes displays His dominion by direct supernatural intervention; but often, as in the books of Kings, the instruments of His sovereignty are secondary means like people and animals, weather and inanimate objects. I want to examine that same body of revelation again, but through a very different lens and in the context of this book's distinctive focus. Because one of the most important ways God demonstrates His sovereignty is through the unfailing reliability of His words.

No other book of the Bible goes so out of its way to cite God's words as the driving force and explanation behind the events of human history as the record of 1 and 2 Kings. God's words overshadow and shape war and peace between nations, the whims of the great and powerful, feast and famine, the deeds and deaths of kings and prophets alike. Let me take just one paragraph to try to quantify that theme in concrete terms as it appears in the books of Kings.

189

The phrase 'the word of the LORD' occurs fifty-one times in Kings and the phrase 'thus says the LORD' thirty-three times.[1] (By comparison, the same phrases in the record of Chronicles—which is 14 per cent longer and covers essentially the same history—occur only fifteen times and twelve times respectively.) In addition, about a dozen nearly synonymous phrases also call attention to God's words in Kings. Combined, these phrases uniquely highlight the role of God's words about a hundred times throughout this historical record. Along the way, the books of Kings document dozens of specific prophecy-fulfillments.[2] Some of these are blessings, others judgments. Some occur within just a few hours of the pronouncement of 'the word of the LORD,' while others take years, decades, or even centuries to materialize. The larger theological point of the writer of Kings is unmistakable: for good or ill, and however long in coming, *all God's words are totally trustworthy.* What follows is only a representative sampling of passages intended by God to bolster our confidence in the reliability of all His words.

The Man of God & the Word of the Lord (1 Kings 13)

One paragraph of context. By the time we reach 1 Kings 13, God has already maneuvered a number of events exactly as He previously said He would. Eli's descendant Abiathar was removed from the priesthood per a word the Lord uttered some fifty years earlier (1 Kings 2:27). Solomon's throne was established after David, just as God said (8:20, 24). After Solomon, however, God engineered the division of the kingdom 'that he might fulfill His word' of judgment for Solomon's twilight defection (12:15). Jeroboam, the beneficiary of that split, repaid the privilege by promptly steering the newly seceded northern kingdom straight into a quagmire of deviant worship from which they never emerged (12:25-33).

---

1. These phrases are certainly prominent in prophetic literature, notably Jeremiah and Ezekiel. What is distinctive about Kings, however, is the casting of human events as the fulfillment of the word of the Lord.

2. See the chart in Appendix 4, 'Fulfillment of "The Word of the Lord" in Kings.' For a similar chart see Bell 2010, pp. 150-51.

Enter an unnamed 'man of God' sent 'by **the word of the LORD**' from Judah to Bethel, one of Jeroboam's new religious capitals. Not so coincidentally, Jeroboam was at that moment offering incense at the altar of one of his infamous golden calf idols (13:1). The nameless prophet 'cried out against the altar by **the word of the LORD** and said, "O altar, altar! **Thus says the LORD**: Behold, a child, Josiah by name, shall be born to the house of David"' (13:2).

Stop right there and you already have a pretty remarkable prophecy; but there's more. The as-yet unborn child would, *according to the word of the LORD*, defile the sanctity of Jeroboam's idolatrous altar by burning upon it the bones of its pagan priests. The time was unspecified, but to guarantee the certainty of God's words the event would be signified in stone: 'This is the sign which **the LORD has spoken**: surely the altar shall split apart and the ashes on it shall be poured out' (13:3). In the time it took Jeroboam to thrust out his arm and cry 'Seize that man!' a crack of lightning, invisible and thunderless, pierced the air, the stone split, and the altar tumbled in a cloud of ash, 'according to the sign which the man of God had given by **the word of the LORD**' (13:5). What about this future child named 'Josiah'? Back to him in a moment.

Just when it seems the episode should be over, the story takes a curious twist. King Jeroboam invited the man of God to stay for a meal before returning to Judah. That's when we get a peek at the fine print in the prophet's mission statement: 'it was commanded me by **the word of the LORD**, saying, "You shall not eat bread, nor drink water, nor return by the same way you came" (13:9).' So he departed by another route (13:10).

But 'an old prophet' in Bethel got wind of everything that had happened, pursued the man of God, and countered the word of the Lord with one of his own: 'an angel spoke to me by **the word of the LORD**, saying, "Bring him back with you to your house, that he may eat bread and drink water"'—but the old prophet 'was lying to him' (13:18). Why? The text never answers that question. So, any solutions we supply are sheer speculation and, therefore, irrelevant to the point of the story, which resumes when the two men sit down to eat.

Mid-meal, *the word of the Lord* really did come to the old prophet this time (13:20), rebuking the man of God for disobeying what he knew to be *the word of the Lord* to him (13:21) and issuing a stiff sentence (13:22). Too harsh, some might think, for a guy who exhibited such courage and faithfulness by venturing into enemy territory with such an unpopular message. But disregarding the words of the Lord is a serious business, sometimes a matter of life and death, especially for a prophet. The sentence's execution when he set out for home later that day was almost Aslanesque—eerie, uncanny, and unmistakably supernatural (13:23-25).

On hearing the news of a lion-mauled traveler on the southbound road out of Bethel, the old prophet didn't need to wait for the name of the unfortunate victim to be released by the authorities. 'It is the man of God who was disobedient to **the word of the LORD**. Therefore the LORD has delivered him to the lion, which has torn and killed him, **according to the word of the LORD** which He spoke to him' (13:26). What the old prophet did next was just as unexpected and inexplicable as the lie he told earlier. He collected the corpse (torn by the lion but uneaten), mourned over him, buried him in his own tomb, and said: 'When I am dead, then bury me in the tomb where the man of God is buried; lay my bones beside his bones' (13:31). Why? Because 'the saying which he cried out by **the word of the LORD** against the altar in Bethel ... **will surely come to pass**' (13:32).

> *This story is about the cast-iron, copper-bottomed dependability of God's words.*

And it did. Jeroboam had the supernaturally split altar repaired, and idolators continued to worship there until a future king demolished it, exhumed the nearby tombs and, on the wreckage of the altar, burned the bones of those idolatrous priests. By the way, that king came to the throne as an eight-year-old named Josiah (2 Kings 22:1). It took thirty-two chapters and 300 years, but everything happened 'according to **the word of the LORD** which the man of God proclaimed' (2 Kings 23:15-16).

The story has an almost O. Henry ironic twist to it. And it raises as many questions as it answers. So what's it all about? It is the message of Kings in microcosm, the whole theme wrapped up in one vividly illustrated chapter. Every conversation and action in the story hinges on *the word of the Lord*. The primary purpose of the story is not to deliver an anti-idolatry message, important as that is. It's not about Jeroboam or Josiah. It's not even about either of the prophets (whose very namelessness helps universalize the point of the narrative). The central 'actor' throughout the narrative is *the word of the Lord*.

> The word of Yahweh is the theme of the story. If we keep that as our compass point we can't go astray no matter how many unanswered questions litter our study (Davis 2007, p. 148).[3]

This is a story about the cast-iron, copper-bottomed dependability of God's words. Never doubt them, even if someone of stature contradicts them. The story's punchline comes in the old prophet's final words: '**the word of the LORD ... will certainly come true**' (13:32 NIV).

The *word of the Lord* theme in Kings is clearly intended to elicit trust in all of God's words. Every time God's words are confirmed by an immediate and visible fulfillment, it conditions us to accept all the other words of the Lord as equally reliable, even when they seem incredible, unlikely, or delayed. 'God's short-term prophecies ... should convince us to trust his long-term prophecies' (Bell 2010, p. 157). That is exactly the conclusion we are expected to draw. The old prophet connected the dots: if the man of God died *according to the word of the Lord* because he disobeyed *the word of the Lord*, then no one should doubt his earlier prophecy *by the word of the Lord*. The fulfillments we can see guarantee the certainty of those we can't.

Elijah & the Word of the Lord (1 Kings 17-21)

The *word of the Lord* theme in Kings is like rain; the drops are scattered everywhere, but in certain places it pools into puddles. The next puddle after the man of God episode is the Elijah chronicle. On our way there, let me just spotlight a few more outworkings of the word of the Lord. Jeroboam's son (apparently the one godly exception in

---

3. For an engaging explanation, illustration, and application of this passage see Davis 2007, pp. 145-56.

the whole Jeroboam clan, 1 Kings 14:13) died and was mourned by Israel 'according to the word of the LORD which He spoke through His servant Ahijah the prophet' (14:18). Baasha eliminated the rest of Jeroboam's descendant's 'according to the word of the LORD which He had spoken through His servant Ahijah the Shilonite' (15:29). Then Zimri, in turn, performed the same service toward Baasha 'according to the word of the LORD which He spoke against Baasha by Jehu the prophet' (16:12).

Suddenly, out of the blue, the writer inserts a mere footnote, a one-verse, matter-of-fact, by-the-way reminder that God's words have no expiration date. It comes in the form of the fulfillment of a word from God that had been sitting quietly in a forgotten corner of the Bible for six centuries. Finally, someone during the reign of Ahab (we might have guessed) mustered the temerity to ignore God's ancient warning about rebuilding Jericho (Josh 6:26-27). His name was Hiel, and he paid the price: the loss of his oldest and youngest sons, 'according to the word of the LORD, which He had spoken through Joshua' (1 Kings 16:34).

All these thematic raindrops are scattered reminders that despite the noisy movers and shakers who attract all the attention and think they're calling the shots, God's words are the wheels on which history rolls along. But *the word of the Lord* theme begins to pool again when a prophet named Elijah steps onstage.

One day this prophet stood on King Ahab's royal doorstep with a nervy announcement: 'there shall not be dew nor rain these years, except at my word' (17:1). This, by the way, was not brash presumption or prophetic megalomania; when speaking on behalf of the Lord, the word of the prophet *was* the word of the Lord (2 Chron. 20:20; Isa. 44:26). *The word of the Lord* then directed him to a hideout by a brook where God promised to airlift food supplies to him (17:2-4). 'So he went and did **according to the word of the LORD**,' and that was exactly what happened (17:5-7).

When there's no rain, pretty soon there's no brook. That's when '**the word of the LORD** came to him' again (17:8-12) and sent him to be fed by a widow who was, herself, on the verge of starvation. (God's supply of irony is infinite.) When she objected that she couldn't postpone her own death just to feed him, Elijah assured her that she could, 'for **thus says the LORD God** of Israel': her food would last until God sent rain. And it did, '**according to the word of the LORD** which He spoke by Elijah' (17:13-16).

If Elijah was forty when he first set foot on Ahab's front porch (I merely surmise), he's now forty-three when '**the word of the LORD** came to Elijah' again, informing him that a storm was brewing (18:1). But first, there was a small matter of protocol to attend to. God wanted to make the point, as sharply as possible, that Baal (the alleged god of fields and fertility who hadn't managed to muster a drop of rain on his worshippers in three years) was an impotent imposter, and that Yahweh alone was still Israel's God. Even this sometimes farcical confrontation is footnoted with passing reminders of *the word of the Lord* (18:31, 36). Once Elijah had executed God's words and will, a rain cut loose (according to *the word of the Lord*, 18:1) that would have sent Noah scurrying to Home Depot (18:45).

After 1 Kings 19, Elijah's story is suspended for a chapter and a half, but resumes when '**the word of the LORD**' directed him back to Ahab once again—this time not to the royal veranda but to a robbed vineyard (21:17-18). Elijah confronted Ahab with a double-barreled 'thus says the LORD' (21:19), promising a notoriously undignified demise for a crowned head: dogs would lick up his blood in the same place they licked the blood of the murdered Naboth. God then added a word for Jezebel as well (21:23). He had an even more inelegant end in mind for the Queen—dogs would eat her.

Are you sensing the pattern in how this narrative of Kings was written? Would it surprise you to learn that Ahab's post-mortem indignity happened exactly '**according to the word of the LORD** which He had spoken' (22:38)?[4] Or that, Jezebel's grisly disgrace

---

4. Some have noted the apparent discrepancy in location between the prophecy (Jezreel, 1 Kings 21:19) and the fulfillment (Samaria, 1 Kings 23:37-38). The solution is remarkably simple. Virtually all the information needed to unravel the alleged tangle between 21:19 and 22:38 can be found in 21:1, along with a rudimentary knowledge of geography. Samaria was not only the name of a city but also the name of the region over which Ahab ruled. The Lord told Elijah to go meet Ahab, 'who is in Samaria; behold, he is in the vineyard of Naboth' (21:18).

matched God's words so precisely, even though it happened fifteen years later? Or that even the idolatrous King Jehu recognized, 'This is **the word of the LORD** which He spoke by His servant Elijah the Tishbite' (2 Kings 9:36)?

Nowhere is the authoritative reliability of God's words more apparent than when He pits them against the powerful of the earth. Shakespeare's Richard II reflects on the illusion of pomp and power attached to human rulers; all their days they are dogged by death and, in the end, even the mightiest monarch may be dispatched with exquisite effortlessness:

> for within the hollow crown
> That rounds the mortal temples of a king
> Keeps Death his court, and there the antic sits,
> Scoffing his state and grinning at his pomp,
> Allowing him a breath, a little scene,
> To monarchize, be fear'd, and kill with looks,
> Infusing him with self and vain conceit,
> As if this flesh which walls about our life
> Were brass impregnable; and humour'd thus,
> Comes at the last and with a little pin
> Bores through his castle wall, and farewell king![5]

But death is not the ultimate sovereign; over death God 'keeps his court'. Indeed, the whole soliloquy could be turned on its head to mock the vanity and impotence of death itself. As the books of Kings frequently illustrate, even death is a slave to the words of the King of kings.[6]

We know from 21:1 that Naboth's vineyard is not in the city of Samaria but in the city of Jezreel, which is in the *region* of Samaria. I.e., 21:18 is plainly saying that Ahab was in Samaria *and* in Jezreel simultaneously. And since the Samaria mentioned in the giving of the prophecy (21:18-19) is the region of Samaria (not the city of Samaria), then we should expect the Samaria mentioned in recounting the prophecy's fulfillment (22:38) to refer to the region of Samaria, which is where Jezreel was. God's words are exactly right, down to every detail.

5. *Richard II*, Act 3, Scene 2. Text from Evans 1997, p. 865.

6. At least fourteen of the *word of the Lord* fulfillments in Kings have to do directly with someone's death. See chart in Appendix 4.

Elisha & the Word of the Lord (2 Kings 1-9)

The *word of the Lord* theme wends its way through the ministry of Elisha as well, but it begins to sprout new growth in a slightly different direction. Things begin to happen by the word of the Lord not only directly but indirectly, through the word of His prophet. God evidently wants to tutor us as readers that the words of His prophets are the words of the Lord.

After Ahab's son 'Ahaziah died **according to the word of the LORD** which Elijah had spoken' (2 Kings 1:17; cf. 1:4, 6), Elisha inherited Elijah's ministry (2:1-18). That's when *the word of the Lord* theme takes a new twist. Miraculous events begin to materialize '**according to the saying of Elisha**' (2:22). Sometimes it is explicitly linked to a 'thus says the LORD' (2:21), sometimes not (2:23-24).

The words of the Lord still govern human affairs, from deliverance on the battlefield (2 Kings 3:16-18ff.) to miraculous provision for His people (4:42-44; 7:1, 16), from the anointing of kings (9:1-13) to the execution of kings (9:24-26; 10:8-11). But the narrative begins braiding together the reliability of God's

> *The words of God's prophets are the words of God.*

words and the reliability of the words of His prophets. Childless women became mothers (4:14-17), lepers were cleansed (5:14), and cynics silenced (7:2, 17-20) because the words of the prophet were the words of the Lord.

One example of this binary emphasis on the word of the Lord and the word of the prophet will be sufficient. When Samaria was under crisis siege conditions, Elisha predicted '**by the word of the LORD**' an overnight reversal: within twenty-four hours Samaria would be wallowing in food surpluses at rock-bottom prices (2 Kings 7:1). 'Even if the LORD made windows in heaven,' scoffed a king's aide, 'how could this be?' It was not a question of curiosity but cynicism; perhaps he thought Elisha was just shrewdly playing for more time (see 2 Kings 6:30-33). Elisha offered no explanation for how the prophecy might materialize; he only attached an addendum aimed at the king's aide: 'You shall see it with your eyes but you shall not eat of it' (2 Kings 7:2). The manner of fulfillment, as it turned out, was bizarre and utterly unpredictable. A divinely induced auditory experience incited mass panic in the besieging army,[7] prompting an immediate twilight evacuation without so much as packing (7:6-7). When four starving lepers wandered into the camp that evening to surrender in exchange for some food, they discovered the depopulated camp (7:3-5, 8-9), and by morning Samaria was feasting on the food left behind (7:10-20). The correlation between prediction and fulfillment was precise and literal down to every detail, 'according to the word of the LORD' (7:16) and 'just as the man of God had said' (7:17, 18). God will always do exactly what He says, however inconceivable the mechanics of a prediction may seem to us on this side of the fulfillment. This is a critically important principle to keep in mind when it comes to future prophecy as well. But that will have to be another book.

Hezekiah & the Astonishing Exception (2 Kings 20)

One of the subthemes that emerges from a study of the life of Hezekiah is that he had the ear of God in a remarkable way. When he encouraged the northern Israelites to come back to the Lord and celebrate the Passover in Judah, it emerged that they had not properly cleansed themselves (apparently out of ignorance). Hezekiah prayed that God would unilaterally provide atonement for them and, despite their technical offense, accept those who had set their hearts to seek Him—and the Lord listened to Hezekiah (2 Chron. 30:18-20).

After the Assyrians had swallowed up every neighboring kingdom, and much of Judah as well, they laid siege to Jerusalem. Hezekiah prayed

---

7. I have previously described this as an auditory hallucination (Talbert 2001, pp. 112-113); but I am not at all sure that's an accurate depiction of the event. Hallucination implies something that wasn't really there; but perhaps there was. In 2 Kings 6:17, there was an actual, invisible angelic army—literal, though not physical—that could be seen (complete with chariots!). Might there not have been an invisible angelic army—literal though not physical— that could be heard in 2 Kings 7 (complete with chariots!)? Maybe it wasn't a supernatural hallucination at all. Maybe God simply enabled them to hear what was really there (just as Elisha and his servant *saw* what was really there), though they misidentified the source. The proximity of the passages seems intentional, not just coincidental.

for the impossible—that God would deliver the city (2 Kings 19:15-19). The 'word of the LORD' (19:21) replied through Isaiah the prophet with a witheringly derisive message for high-and-mighty Sennacherib (19:21-34); and in the end, God did the impossible (19:35-36) because Hezekiah prayed (19:20).

When Hezekiah fell ill at the age of thirty-nine,[8] however, an astonishing intersection between the prayer of Hezekiah and the word of the Lord occurred. Back in 2 Kings 1, Elijah had told King Ahaziah, 'Thus says the LORD: "You shall not come down from the bed to which you have gone up, but you shall surely die"' (2 Kings 1:4), and Ahaziah died (1:17). But when Isaiah told King Hezekiah, 'Thus says the LORD: "Set your house in order, for you shall die and not live"' (2 Kings 20:1), something very different happened. Hezekiah prayed that God would spare him (20:2-3), and God answered. Immediately. Before Isaiah had even gotten out of the palace 'the word of the LORD came to him saying, Return and tell Hezekiah ... thus says the LORD ... I have heard your prayer, I have seen your tears; surely I will heal you' (20:4-5).[9]

Because of Hezekiah's prayer, 'Thus says the LORD, you shall surely die and not live' was transmuted to 'Thus says the LORD, surely I will heal you.' Doesn't that undermine the absolute reliability of God's words? No, because God responds to human prayer, and even to human change. When God gave Ahab a blistering message of judgment, Ahab's sincere expression of grief and humility—even though apparently short of full repentance—prompted God to mitigate His pronounced judgment so that the full judgment on his posterity would not come in Ahab's day (2 Kings 21:27-29).

---

8. Hezekiah became co-regent under his father Ahaz in 729 at the age of eleven, and began his sole regency at age twenty-five when Ahaz died in 715. His illness can be dated with confidence to 702-701. He reigned fifteen more years before he died in 686 at the age of fifty-four.

9. Many have said that Hezekiah's prayer was wrong and selfish. Nothing in the text indicates that God saw it that way at all. True, Hezekiah responded to his healing with a degree of presumption and foolishness, of which he repented (2 Chron. 32:25-26). The notion, however, that Manasseh, Judah's wickedest king, was born during Hezekiah's fifteen-year reprieve from the Lord is mistaken; a careful study of the chronology shows that Manasseh was already seven years old when Hezekiah fell sick.

God is immutable. That means He never changes. But built into His immutability is an exception clause: a willingness to change when people do. In short, 'God deals differently with us when we deal differently with him' (Butterfield 2015, p. 17). God spells out this exception clause Himself. Notice His own references to His speech.

> The instant I **speak** concerning a nation and concerning a kingdom, to pluck up, to pull down, and to destroy it, if that nation against whom **I have spoken** turns from its evil, I will relent of the disaster that I thought to bring upon it. And the instant I **speak** concerning a nation and concerning a kingdom, to build and to plant it, if it does evil in My sight so that it does not obey My voice, then I will relent concerning the good with which **I said** I would benefit it (Jer. 18:7-10).

Passages like 2 Kings 20 demonstrate that one of the factors that can mitigate a *word of the Lord* is the pleasure of God in answering the prayer of His people.

Conclusion

It's a little—just a little, mind you—like the relationship between Lawrence Anthony and Nana. A conservationist and owner of the 5,000 acre Thula Thula wildlife reserve near the eastern coast of South Africa, Anthony took in a small herd of rogue wild elephants that otherwise would have been terminated. Nana, the 5-ton matriarch of the herd, wasted no love on humans; she threatened, charged, and constantly expressed her antipathy toward anything on two legs. Over a period of time, however, Anthony and Nana formed a profound and unusual bond. She actually began responding visibly to Anthony's vocalizations—not the words, but the tone and emotion in his voice.

'Elephants operate on the steadfast principle that all other life forms must give way to them' (Anthony 2009, p. 198). Translation: Elephants *always* have the right of way; and they know it. The lion may be the king of the jungle, but the elephant is the boss. Yet there were times when Anthony was able to dissuade this 10-foot-tall, 10,000 pound behemoth from a certain course of action with nothing more than words.

One evening, in the middle of an outdoor candlelit dinner complete with white tablecloths and French cuisine on fine china, the herd ambled leisurely up toward the reserve's guest lodge. When it became apparent that the elephants weren't going to just stop and observe, the guests scrambled for the (relative) safety of the lodge. Nana moseyed up to where Anthony stood beside a pole supporting the patio roof, gently touching his chest with her trunk. Speaking to her affectionately but earnestly, he implored her to take the herd and move off. But she wasn't ready to leave yet.

> Moving forward she leaned her head on the support pole in front of me, and gave a heave. With that the lodge's whole roof shifted and controlling my urge to shout I quickly moved forward again and resumed stroking her trunk speaking soothingly to her. Incredibly, she leaned forward again, this time with more force and … it seemed the whole structure was on the verge of collapsing. I instinctively did the only thing I could and putting both my hands high on her trunk pushed back on her with all my strength pleading with her not to destroy our livelihood. And there we stayed, her leaning on the pole and me pushing back on her for an eternal thirty seconds before she stepped back … and walked away. … Nana could have collapsed the pole easily, and my puny effort at pushing her off was but a feather in the wind. She was just making a point (Anthony 2009, pp. 201-02).[10]

Don't think Nana was domesticated, like a circus elephant. As C. S. Lewis might put it, she was not a tame elephant. In terms of physical power and willpower, she was still the boss. She retained her wildness and independence. But she conceded to respond to the pleas of a pint-sized person, though she was fifty times his match and could do pretty much whatever she wanted.

I'm not comparing God to a wild matriarchal pachyderm. I'm trying to illustrate, however feebly, the nature of a relationship in which power yields to the pleas of powerlessness. In something like the same way,

---

10. Lawrence Anthony's fascinating book is titled *The Elephant Whisperer* not, he explains, for his skill in teaching and communicating with them, but vice versa.

omnipotence responds to impotence when God hears our prayers—and sometimes He even changes His spoken intentions as a result. I can't pretend to understand or explain that. But if there's no room to fit that into your theology, your theology is not yet as big as the Bible.

Review & Reflect

1. The books of Kings include many examples of prophecies that are first pronounced and then fulfilled to the detail (see Appendix 4). What impression should that make on us as readers when we come across other prophecies that have not yet been fulfilled?

2. Here's a personal Bible study project. Find (and mark) every reference to 'the word of the LORD' in 1 Kings 13. Do the same for all of 1, 2 Kings.

PART THREE:
Worldview Implications

12
Trusting God's Narrative of Reality: Introducing the Big Picture

What is truth? ~ *Pilate*
John 18:38

Your word is truth. ~ *Jesus*
John 17:17

It's easy to mock the scientific ignorance of the ancients. But have you ever had the sensation of moving at 70,000 miles per hour? If so, you should stop reading and seek medical help immediately. If not, you ought to be able to agree that geocentrism (the theory that the universe revolves around the earth), in a sense, makes complete sense to our senses.

Every personal observation we can muster tells us that, from all appearances, we are situated on a stationary, motionless planet around which everything else revolves. It stands to reason that if the earth were actually hurtling over 1,000 miles per second through space (like a cosmic baseball) and simultaneously spinning (like a curveball) at over 1,000 miles per hour, we'd feel something, right? After all, you feel it when you stick your head out the window of a car traveling a paltry 60 mph; and you probably know how it feels to spin on a carnival ride at considerably less than 1,000 mph (though it may feel that fast at the time).

From everything that the vast majority of the world's population can personally see and feel, the universe *must* be geocentric. And yet the vast majority of all eight billion of us believe that geocentrism is completely wrong.

In other words, in contradiction to all our everyday senses, we hold a worldview called heliocentrism—the notion that everything in our solar system revolves around the sun. It is, in large measure, a worldview based on faith in things most of us have never personally seen. It is an *interpretation* of reality that we have come to embrace on the basis of certain evidences. And yet, it completely transforms how we view our world and everything around us; it dictates our knowledge base, directs our entire educational system, and even shapes how we live our lives and talk about reality. (It wasn't called the Copernican *Revolution* for nothing.) When geocentrism was turned on its head, tossed out, and replaced with heliocentrism, it even had profound theological implications. It suggested that earth (and, by implication, man) was perhaps not at the center of everything after all.[1]

That rather pedestrian illustration of physical worldview is suggestive for one's metaphysical worldview. In that more philosophical sense, 'a worldview is 1. a set of basic beliefs, assumptions, and values, 2. which arises from a big story about the world and 3. produces individual and group action—human culture' (Ward et al. 2016, p. 15).[2]

> *Your worldview defines everything you think about everything.*

Not everyone's worldview is equally well-defined, or thought-through, or even self-consistent. Yet everyone has one. Your worldview shapes everything you think, from origins to aliens to morality, and is ultimately the rationale behind everything you do.

That's why worldviews deserve such careful scrutiny. They are so pervasively influential that they even shape our statements about worldviews. Stephen Jay Gould, famous American paleontologist, evolutionary biologist, and science historian, made the oft-quoted assertion,

---

1. Curiously, evolution has yet to find a way to filter residual geocentrism out of the human gene pool. Every child is still a born 'geocentrist' and has to grow out of the assumption that he or she is the center of everything. Some are more successful at it than others.

2. This definition comes from a superb high-school textbook on worldview titled *Biblical Worldview: Creation, Fall, Redemption* and authored in large part by two of my former doctoral students.

> Nothing is more dangerous than a dogmatic worldview—
> nothing more constraining, more blinding to innovation, more
> destructive of openness to novelty (Gould 1995, p. 96).

Let the irony and absurdity of Gould's statement sink in. Actually, one thing is more dangerous than a dogmatic worldview: someone who pretends *their* worldview is not dogmatic. But the real thrust of this chapter lies in another direction.

Where do we find our 'big story' that feeds our 'beliefs, assumption, and values' and shapes our interpretation of reality and our reactions to the world around us? Many find it in evolutionary theory. Or the musings of a favourite author. Or even the philosophy of a screenwriter, made disproportionately influential because it is cinematically rendered bigger than life and backed up by an emotionally convincing soundtrack. Others take theirs from the *Bhagavad-Vita* or the *Quran*. Most people stitch together a willy-nilly worldview from whatever seems popular, sounds sensible, and makes them feel good. Christians find theirs (or ought to) in the Bible.

Plotting the Biblical Storyline

The Bible is not a random collection of unrelated, or even loosely related, sacred writings that happen to come from one predominant people group (the Jews). One of the most revolutionary concepts to understand about the Bible is that it is, from beginning to end, a story. A long story. A single, unified narrative of reality that flows like the river out of Eden, tumbles down through time, and deltas into distant vistas beyond the book of Revelation. Sometimes rushing headlong, sometimes meandering slow and silent, but always moving, always growing as each narrative along the way, each psalm and sermon, each prophecy and poem, trickle into it like tributaries to swell the stream. It's not just a true story; it is *the* true story. (I know that may sound like a dogmatic worldview.) How you view the world drives how you live. The Bible is God's record of reality to help us see and interpret our experience through His eyes, because He is the only one who sees everything, and sees it as it really is.

Stories can be very complex, especially long ones. You may have learned in high school or college the distinction between a short story and a novel. The difference is not merely length, but the level of character development, plot complexity, and thematic intricacy. Think of some of the longest stories you may know—by Dostoevsky, Dickens, or Tolstoy. The Bible is longer than any of those.[3]

That's why there are several ways of summarizing the Bible's overarching message, identifying its seams, and tracing the progression of its story. Because the Bible possesses multiple organizing themes, its story can be viewed from a variety of different angles.

The Glory of God

Many have suggested that the grandest and most overarching theme in the Bible is God's desire to display—and share—His own glory. It's a challenging read, to be sure, but one of Jonathan Edwards's most insightful and influential essays is titled 'The End for Which God Created the World.'[4] In it he demonstrates scripturally that the ultimate goal of God through human history—the end for which He made all things—is to show and to share the glories of His attributes and character.

So, the Bible can be explored as the record of God's revelation of His own glory in human history.

Creation, Fall, Redemption

The story of the Bible is the story of God's *Creation* of a world peopled by creatures like Himself in important ways, the *Fall* of that race into mistrust and rebellion against their Creator, and the extraordinary steps God takes to *Redeem* us from the consequences of our fallen-ness.

At first glance, the storyline might sound a bit unbalanced and top-heavy. After all, creation covers Genesis 1–2 and the Fall happens

---

3. A quick internet check informs me that Tolstoy's *War and Peace* has 587,287 words; the Bible has 782,815 words (NASB).

4. The most accessible version of this, complete with organizational divisions and explanatory notes, can be found in John Piper's *God's Passion for His Glory* (Wheaton: Crossway, 1998).

in Genesis 3. Doesn't that mean that everything else (Gen. 4–Rev. 22) is about redemption? Actually, no.

The creation theme has threads that run all the way through the Bible and impact many other passages and doctrines and applications along the way. Try studying creation all the way through the Bible sometime. Here's just a handful of the creation threads you'll come across after Genesis 2.

- Psalm 33:1-9—Creation is a reason for ongoing praise of the Creator and ongoing confidence in His word because it was the means by which He created.

- Eccles. 12:1—Remembering your Creator in your youth is intended to impact how you live and the choices you make.

- Isa. 40:26-31—Remembering God as Creator should encourage you in His control over all things, His awareness of your suffering, and His ability to empower you in your weakness.

- Mark 10:6-9—Creation is the basis for the unchanging sanctity and definition of marriage.

- 2 Cor. 5—Conversion is described as making us a *new* creation in Christ.

- Rev. 21-22—A future new creation will replace this fallen creation.

Similarly, the theme of the Fall and its consequences runs all the way through the Bible. Scripture is constantly reminding us and showing us what we are. It is, in fact, the Bible's explanation for why Christ died. That's the final theme.

Redemption is where all this is going. Beginning with the Fall in Genesis 3, the Bible is full of God's acts and aims and images of redemption. God redeems Israel from bondage in Egypt—a picture of Christ's greater redemption at Calvary.[5] Such acts and images of

---

5. In Luke 9:30-31, Moses and Elijah appeared at Jesus' transfiguration 'and spoke of His decease [literally, his exodus] which he was about to accomplish at Jerusalem.'

redemption run all through the Old Testament, from the sacrificial system of the temple to the story of Ruth. God's role as Redeemer is endemic to what the New Covenant is all about (Isa. 54:8; 59:20; 60:16; 62:12). In biblical parlance, the 'New Testament' *means* the 'New Covenant' because it introduces the inauguration of that New Covenant through the redemptive work of Christ.[6]

So, the storyline of the Bible can also be summarized as God's redemption of His fallen creation.

The Covenants

The Bible can also be organized covenantally. The Bible divides itself between the Old Covenant (Old Testament) and the New Covenant (New Testament). The distinction between these two divisions is not merely chronological but covenantal. The Old and New Covenants form an organizational framework intrinsic to the theological structure of the Bible. In addition, the story of God's relationship with man can be told in terms of the series of covenantal arrangements recorded in the Bible (Noahic, Abrahamic, Mosaic [Old], Davidic, and New).

So, the division of the Bible into Old and New Covenants is yet another rubric under which one can trace the Bible's organically connected storyline.

Other Themes

Other big themes dominate the scriptural landscape and span both testaments: dominion, worship, divine presence, promise and fulfillment, the people of God, and many more. Even a human creation—like a Dickens novel—can have a highly complex, multi-layered, multi-themed, multi-storylined structure. It would be overly simplistic to say

---

6. In discussing the concept of worldview, Greg Koukl argues that *everyone's* worldview includes, in some form or other, the creation-fall-redemption (CFR) pattern. First, everyone believes *something* about where everything came from. Second, everyone recognizes that *something* is wrong with the world as it is. Third, everyone has *some* theory about what would fix whatever is wrong with the world, and that if that solution were applied, the world could be what it should be. So, atheists, unbelievers, and idolators all have their own version of CFR (though, of course, they would never use those words to describe it). It's just that the Bible's version is the most coherent. See Koukl 2017, pp. 25-27.

that *David Copperfield* is 'about' David Copperfield, or even that it is 'about' Charles Dickens in a semi-autobiographical sense. It is about money, and love, and power, and hypocrisy, and forgiveness, and a dozen other themes, each of which could function as a lens to magnify those respective themes as they surface and resurface throughout the story. Life is complex and richly textured, and so is good writing that is true to life. Where do you suppose we get the ability to do that? From the one who created us in His image and gave us the greatest, complex, multi-layered, multi-themed, multi-storylined Book.

These overarching paradigms are not in competition with each other, and none is more right than the others. All of them emerge from the Bible and function like gears in a complex machine, all of different sizes and shapes and speeds and moving in different but complementary directions. Or like spirographs[7]—overlapping, intersecting, and complementary outlines of redemptive history. Each of them contributes something distinctive to our understanding of what is going on in the Bible and how it relates to us in multiple ways and on multiple levels.

We've talked about trusting God's words in spheres big and small, personal and panoramic. In this chapter I'd like to back out about as far as we can and take in as broad a scope as possible, as wide as all of human history, and encourage you to trust God's narrative of reality. The Big Picture storyline I want to use to do that is one we haven't talked about yet.

The Kingdom

Kingdom is one of the major, overarching, framing themes that God has woven into His revelation of reality, and one of the thematic threads woven most closely to the core of the Bible's storyline. I think the next

---

7. I would worry that some readers might miss this illustration, but anyone my age grew up with it, the generation before me bought it for their kids, and this 'geometric drawing toy' was relaunched in 2013. So everyone either knows or can easily discover the image behind the allusion. Just check Wikipedia. Who would have thought a device 'that produces mathematical roulette curves of the variety technically known as hypotrochoids and epitrochoids' would make a wildly popular children's toy?

two chapters validates that claim, but let me take just a moment to justify it on the front end.

The kingdom was a persistent and predominant focus of the ministry of Christ. How many times do you suppose all four Gospels record Jesus using words like 'kingdom' or 'king,' specifically with reference to God's kingdom? The answer is about a hundred and sixty. Granted, many of those occurrences are parallels in more than one Gospel, but that does not dilute the point; it only means that God saw to it that the final form of His revelation should include massive and repeated attention to the concept of God's kingdom. In addition, the rest of the New Testament includes dozens of other references to the divine kingdom.

God Himself has chosen to describe reality in kingdom terms. It is the primary model He uses across both testaments to describe His relationship not only to His people but to the world and humanity at large. Here's just a brief sampling:

- Ps. 10:16, 'the LORD is King forever and ever'
- Ps. 45:6, 'Your throne, O God, is forever and ever'
- Jer. 10:7, 'who would not fear You, O King of the nations?'
- Dan. 4:34, 'His kingdom is from generation to generation'
- Mal. 1:14, 'For I am a great King, says the LORD of hosts, and My name is to be feared among the nations.'
- Luke 1:33, 'of His kingdom there will be no end'
- 1 Tim. 1:17, 'Now to the King eternal'
- 2 Pet. 1:11, 'the everlasting kingdom of our Lord and Saviour Jesus Christ'
- Rev. 19:16, 'King of kings and Lord of lords'

Kingdom language is God's way of expressing the nature of His relationship to creation, His claims on creation, and His purpose for creation. It is also the language God uses to explain the meaning and significance of human history. And it furnishes the setting in which we are intended to view our own lives in the context of history. We are not citizens in a heavenly democracy; we are subjects of a King within a kingdom.

All the freedoms and self-determination of modern democracies render a kingdom mentality very foreign to us. (Our confusion over the concept is illustrated by the bumper sticker I saw in a church parking lot: 'Elect Jesus King of your life.') Yet the kingdom model has been in place and predominant for most of human history, and was endemic to the biblical world. In a fallen world, power corrupts and absolute power corrupts absolutely (an expression credited to the nineteenth-century British politician and author Lord Acton). Monarchy represents absolute power, which is why sooner or later you get really evil kings who do great damage. But what if there could be a monarchy with a perfectly just, sinless, guileless Monarch?

From the Bible's beginning to its end, the history of the world is framed as the story of the kingdom of God. The view of creation as a kingdom commences in Genesis and climaxes in Revelation. By the time you reach that final chapter in the story, you become aware that there is a vast historical background to all of the events it describes—events that fill out the final landscape of human history, events that have been in preparation and in prophecy for a long, long time.

The next two chapters trace this kingdom theme woven into the very fabric of the storyline of Scripture that runs through both the Old and New Testaments.

When we trust God's narrative of reality, it has massive ramifications for all of life, and beyond.

13
Trusting God's Narrative of Reality: Tracing the Big Picture (OT)

Yours is the kingdom, O LORD, and You are exalted as
head over all ... and You reign over all.
1 Chronicles 29:11-12

These next two chapters can only skim along the surface of this biblical storyline of God's kingdom plans and purposes. We'll plot a course through every successive segment of each testament. Many other passages than we will be able to survey factor into this concept. This is strictly a flyover view, but the scenery is spectacular and worldview-altering.[1]

Old Testament
Pentateuch

Historically, canonically, and theologically it all starts here. God created all things, but fashioned humanity alone in His own image and granted him dominion over all creation (Gen. 1:26-31). Dominion is a kingdom concept—the sub-delegation of authority to mankind as God's vice-regents.[2] The first expression of God's relationship to

---

1. I am indebted to my pastor, Dr Mark Minnick, for the idea of the thematic survey that follows. He once preached through just such a survey to demonstrate the pervasive kingdom theme in the storyline of Scripture.

2. Any expression of the Creation component of the CFR storyline should incorporate the concept of dominion because the intentionality of human dominion is expressly built into God's first statement regarding the creation of humanity. God did not create man for purely redemptive purposes but for dominion purposes. Likewise, any expression of the Redemption component of the CFR storyline should incorporate the concept of restoration because one of

man—if we are going by the words that God Himself actually uses—is not couched as a covenant but a command (Gen. 2:16-17).[3] It involved no bilateral agreement, no mutuality. It is the word—in fact, the first recorded relational word—of an absolute sovereign to His created subject.

Later Scripture will confirm that God has the kingdom concept in mind in these opening chapters of Genesis. But the first humans were seduced by a sly and seditious serpent, the first creature to challenge the word and rule of the Sovereign (Gen. 3:1-5). He succeeds in swaying them to join his mutiny (3:6-7), though he's not identified definitively until the final chapter of the story (Rev. 12:9; 20:2). Their revolt against God's authority twisted their divine image, marred their ability to exercise righteous dominion over creation, and constitutionally altered their posture towards the King and their relationship to His kingdom. They became banished rebels. And what quickly becomes apparent is that this penchant for defying God became habitual and pervasive (Gen. 4:1-15, 16-24; 6:1-13).

But God, even in pronouncing their punishment, planted a seed-promise to counter their rebellion and its effects. To the serpent He said, 'I will put enmity between you and the woman, and between your seed and her Seed; He shall bruise your head, and you shall bruise His heel' (Gen, 3:15). That's what you call a pregnant promise. Like subtle foreshadowing in a well-crafted book that you don't entirely understand until later in the story, God doesn't explain here what all that means. It was a promise that would end up costing Him dearly—a veiled pledge that He, through the woman's seed (Christ), would do all that was necessary to restore to us our divine image, our divine grant of dominion over creation, and our relationship to our King and His kingdom.

The first actual occurrence of the word 'kingdom' is a reference to Nimrod's realm in the land of Shinar, called Babel (Gen. 10:10). This may not strike the first-time reader as particularly ominous or

---

the core goals of redemption is the restoration of human dominion over creation as originally intended.

3. The first reference to a designated 'covenant' does not show up until Genesis 6:18.

even significant. But the next chapter commences a history of that kingdom that will run nearly to the end of Revelation. God had said 'Fill the earth' (Gen. 1:28; 9:7). Instead, man expressly defied God's authority ... again.

> Now the whole earth had one language and one speech. And it came to pass, as they journeyed from the east, that they found a plain in the land of Shinar, and they dwelt there. Then they said to one another, ... Come, let us build ourselves a city, and a tower whose top is in the heavens; let us make a name for ourselves, lest we be scattered abroad over the face of the whole earth. But **the LORD came down** to see the city and the tower which the sons of men had built.... So **the LORD scattered** them abroad from there over the face of all the earth, and they ceased building the city. Therefore its name is called Babel, because there **the LORD confused** the language of all the earth; and from there **the LORD scattered** them abroad over the face of all the earth (Gen. 11:1-9).

The passage makes clear who is still in control. But keep Babel simmering on the back burner of your mind, because it is the same name in Hebrew that will show up later in the story as Babylon. It appears here as the first manifestation of organized kingdom rebellion against God's authority. In Revelation 17–18 it will resurface as the final manifestation of organized kingdom rebellion against God's authority.

In time, God narrowed down His kingdom purposes to the descendants of one man, Abraham (Gen. 12:1-3), whom He promised would become a father of kings (Gen. 17:6, 16), repeating the same pledge to his grandson Jacob (Gen. 35:11). God eventually further funneled His kingdom plan into one particular descendent of Abraham's seed. Jacob's prophetic bequest to the line of Judah echoes with kingdom overtones: 'The **scepter** shall not depart from Judah, nor the **ruler's staff** from between his feet, until Shiloh comes, and to him shall be **the obedience of the peoples**' (Gen. 49:10 NASB).

The first direct reference to God's reign comes on the heels of His destruction of the most powerful kingdom on earth. God's rule is not argued for; it is simply declared: 'the LORD shall **reign** forever and ever' (Exod. 15:18). The first explicit reference to God as King (Num. 23:21) is similarly matter-of-fact, almost taken for granted, cloaked in a poetic parallelism:

> the LORD his God is with him [Israel],
> and the shout of a **King** is among them [Israel].

The 'LORD his God' in line 1 is the 'King' in line 2. As their King, he legislated the rules for their future monarchy (Deut. 17:14-20). It would be another delegation of God's rule into human hands.

In summary, then, the opening chapters of this story depict God as Sovereign, the earth as (part of) His realm, and humans as His subjects who are also endowed with vice-regency status. The race went rogue, however, and established the first vestiges of a human kingdom in opposition to the will and purposes of God. But God set in motion a plan to counter and conquer human rebellion, and simultaneously restore humanity's place in His kingdom.

Historical Books

God had plans to establish a kingdom among His people (Deut. 17, above). But when Israel stubbornly insisted that Samuel appoint a king over them, here's how God interpreted that demand: 'they have rejected Me, that I should not **reign** over them' (1 Sam. 8:7). Why would God say that, if He'd already made provision for a kingdom? Because the 'when' is as much a part of God's will as the 'what.' Israel wanted what God intended, but they wanted it *now*. That's always dangerous, and always more trouble than it's worth. Still, even though they rejected His reign God retained His rule. It was God who appointed Saul as their king (1 Sam. 9:15-17)—the best available at the time but, as it turned out, far from ideal. And when he failed, it was God who deposed him and anointed David to replace him (1 Sam. 13:14; 16:1).

When David wanted to build a 'house' (temple) for God, God replied that He would build a 'house' (dynasty) for David:

> When your days are fulfilled and you rest with your fathers,
> I will set up your seed after you, who will come from your
> body, and I will establish his **kingdom**. He shall build a house

> for My name, and I will establish the **throne** of his **kingdom**
> forever (2 Sam. 7:12-13).

On the other end of the historical spectrum, King Cyrus of Persia recognized on some level that the ultimate King was the Lord God of Israel, who had 'given' to him 'all the kingdoms of the earth' (Ezra 1:2). As we discover in the prophets, it was God who raised up Cyrus in the first place (Isa. 45:1) and, like Cyrus, convinced Nebuchadnezzar before him that 'the Most High **rules** in the kingdoms of men, and gives it to whomever He wills' (Dan. 4:25, 32), whose '**dominion** is an everlasting **dominion**' and whose '**kingdom** is from generation to generation' (Dan. 4:34). Indeed, any and every such display of God's authority over the kings of the earth is a display of His ultimate kingship; the very concept of God's supreme *reign* is at the heart of God's sove*reig*nty.

The Historical Books are, of course, all about the kingdom as it is played out in the nation of Israel; so there are lots of passages in this section that highlight this theme. I will touch on just one more. A kingdom requires three components: a ruler, a realm, and a reign. You can see all three in this passage: 'Yours is the **kingdom**, O LORD, and You are exalted as **head** [ruler] **over all** [realm]. Both riches and honor come from You, and You **reign** [rule] **over all**' (1 Chron. 29:11-12).

Poetical Books

Psalms is, among other things, the Royal Hymnbook. I cited some passages from Psalms above that underscore the Kingdom theme. A few passages, however, soar above the others in their significance for this theme. Psalm 2 can hardly be overemphasized in this regard, with its 'buoyant, fierce delight in God's dominion and his promise to his King' (Kidner 1973, p. 50). Not only is it classed as a 'royal psalm'[4] (making its connection to the kingdom trajectory obvious), but it encompasses the Bible's entire kingdom-history storyline in microcosm.

The psalm first summarizes the history of human rebellion against God's rule (Ps. 2:1-3):

---

4. Royal psalms traditionally include 2, 18, 20, 21, 45, 72, 89, 101, 110, 132, and 144 (Jacobson 2014, p. 65). I am inclined to include Ps. 8.

Why do the nations rage, and the people plot a vain thing? The **kings of the earth** set themselves, and the **rulers** take counsel together, against the LORD and against His Anointed, saying, 'Let us break Their bonds in pieces and cast away Their cords from us.'

God's counter-determination is to establish His own King in Jerusalem who will inherit and subdue the international rebellion against Him (2:4-9):

He who sits in the heavens [the Father] shall laugh; the LORD shall hold them in derision. Then He shall speak to them in His wrath, and distress them in His deep displeasure: 'Yet I have set **My King** on My holy hill of Zion.'

[The Son responds] 'I will declare the decree: The LORD has said to Me, "You are my Son, today I have begotten You. Ask of Me, and **I will give You the nations for Your inheritance**, and **the ends of the earth for Your possession**. You shall break them with a rod of iron; You shall dash them to pieces like a potter's vessel."'

Finally, God issues His gracious ultimatum to submit to His King before that judgment begins (2:10-12):

Now therefore, be wise, O **kings**; be instructed, you **judges of the earth**. Serve the LORD with fear, and rejoice with trembling. Kiss the Son, lest He be angry, and you perish in the way, when His wrath is kindled but a little. Blessed are all those who put their trust in Him.

> *Psalm 2 encompasses the Bible's kingdom storyline in microcosm.*

'As an example of redemptive-historical drama,' Psalm 2 'gives a theological perspective for interpreting world events' (VanGemeren 1991, p. 65); and it does so within an explicitly kingdom-oriented framework.

Psalm 8 revisits the theme of God-ordained human *dominion* over creation (vv. 6-8). Its significance, however, becomes especially apparent in retrospect once you reach the epistles, so we will explore it more fully when we get there. Psalm 89 reconfirms the pre-eminence of the Davidic dynasty over all other kings of the earth (89:27-29) and reaffirms the eternality of David's descendants and dynasty (89:3-4, 36). Psalm 110 (the most quoted Old Testament passage in the New Testament), depicts David's descendant, heir, and 'Lord' (Jesus the Messiah, Matt. 22:41-46) as *ruling* in the midst of His enemies until 'the day of His power' when 'He shall execute the **heads** of many countries' and 'execute **kings** in the day of His wrath' (just as Ps. 2:11 warns).

Many of the Psalms also draw attention to the reality of God's present reign over nations and creation as 'the great **King** above all gods' (95:3) who 'has established His **throne** in heaven, and His **kingdom rules** over all' (103:19). Psalm 22 looks ahead to the final triumph of God's kingdom, when 'all the ends of the world shall remember and turn to the LORD, and all the families of the nations shall worship before You. For the **kingdom** is the LORD'S, and He **rules** over the nations' (22:27-28). Indeed, 'Your **kingdom** is an everlasting **kingdom**, and Your **dominion** endures throughout all generations' (145:13). God's kingdom is a dominant theme throughout the Psalms.

Prophetical Books

Isaiah leads us almost immediately into the court of the King. The irony of the historical context is not accidental.

> In the year that **King Uzziah** died I saw the Lord **sitting upon a throne**, high and lifted up; and the train of His **robe** filled the temple.... And I said: 'Woe is me! ... for mine eyes have seen the **King**, the LORD of hosts!' (6:1, 5).

The Bible features two stunning throne-room scenes; one of those is Isaiah 6 (the other is Revelation 4–5). Even when God's good earthly kings (like Uzziah) die, God is still on His throne governing the affairs of men and nations. But God is not content to merely rule *in absentia*, from a distance. Isaiah 9 reiterates His promise of the unending success of Messiah's government via the establishment of David's throne and kingdom. God remembers His promises to Eve (Gen. 3), to Abraham (Gen. 12), to David (2 Sam. 7), and to His own Son (Ps. 2). In the end, He has vowed, 'to Me **every knee shall bow**' (Isa. 45:23)—a gesture of acknowledgement and submission that Paul will attribute to Christ as God's anointed King (Phil. 2:9-11), just like Psalm 2 says.

In Daniel 2, Nebuchadnezzar's symbolic dream of a towering statue, representing the progression of earthly kingdoms, ends abruptly when a great boulder, supernaturally sculpted ('without hands') out of a mountain, strikes the 'feet and toes' and collapses the entire image. This is a living stone, because after it demolishes the succession of secular earthly kingdoms it grows into a massive mountain, a divine empire that fills the earth (Dan. 2:44-45)—signifying the end of independent human kingdoms and the establishment of God's kingdom on earth over all the nations.

Until then, God still rules over and over-rules the current kings of the nations: 'He removes **kings** and raises up **kings**' (Dan. 2:21) and 'the Most High **rules** in the **kingdoms** of men and gives it to whomever He chooses' (Dan. 4:25, 32; 5:21). That doesn't mean He always chooses the best of men; sometimes He appoints the basest (4:17). While the kingdoms of the earth remain in rebellion against Him so that He is ruling in the midst of His enemies (Ps. 110:2), He rules by containment and management rather than reclamation.

Daniel 7 is another Himalayan height in the Kingdom mountain range that runs from Genesis to Revelation. Daniel 7 is to the Prophets what Psalm 2 is to the Psalms.

> I was watching in the night visions, and behold, One like the Son of Man, coming with the clouds of heaven! He came to the Ancient of Days, and they brought Him near before Him. Then to Him was given **dominion** and **glory** and a **kingdom**, that all peoples, nations, and languages should **serve Him**. His **dominion** is an everlasting **dominion**, which shall not pass away, and His **kingdom** the one which shall not be destroyed.... Then the **kingdom** and **dominion**, and the greatness of the **kingdoms** under the whole heaven, shall be given to the people, the saints of the Most High. His **kingdom** is an everlasting **kingdom**, and all **dominions** shall **serve and obey Him** (Dan. 7:13-14, 27).

Whereas Psalm 2 summarizes history as a conflict between kingdoms (human and divine), Daniel 7 describes the eschatological nature and progression of that conflict. It returns to the dominion theme of Genesis 1, granting universal dominion to 'one like a son of man' (7:9-14)—the title Jesus will claim for Himself (Matt. 24:30, 26:64). A confederacy of rebellious human kingdoms will challenge the Son of Man's universal dominion (7:15-25). That ultimate expression of human rebellion against divine authority (described in Psalm 2) will culminate in a single personage (7:20-21), identified in the New Testament as the anti-messiah, who will blaspheme God and terrorize His people (7:25). But 7:26-27 describe the triumph and transfer of kingdom dominion to 'the people, the saints of the Most High' under the Son of Man. Throughout it all, the determination of the Ancient of Days stands—this universal dominion and kingdom that is granted to this Son of Man is shared with the saints of the Most High (7:18, 22, 26-27). That's why believers will be called 'joint-heirs with Christ' (Rom. 8:17).

> **Eschatological**—pertaining to the end times.

> Dominion over all the earth and its creatures was humanity's first commission (Gen. 1:28), but man lost it through disobedience.... The perfect Man regains everything that the first man lost. Daniel saw dominion belonging to beasts, an arrangement contrary to creation's mandate. He sees dominion returned to man, an arrangement that fulfills God's purpose (Barrett 2003, p. 85).

Other prophets contribute to this kingdom theme. 'I will overthrow the **throne** of **kingdoms**; I will destroy the strength of the Gentile **kingdoms**' (Hag. 2:22). 'And the LORD shall be **King** over all the earth' (Zech. 14:9). 'For I am a great **King**, says the LORD of hosts, and My name is to be feared among the nations' (Mal. 1:14). Folded into the New Covenant is the ultimate fulfillment of the kingdom promises in the Davidic Covenant (Jer.33:14-26; Ezek. 37:24-25). These and many other passages in the prophets generate the anticipation to see this storyline come to fruition. When will God set these kingdom promises in motion? The kingdom promises are wrapped up in the person of

God's anointed, Jesus the Messiah, and inaugurated with His coming recorded in the New Testament.

Review & Reflect

1. Summarize how Psalm 2 'encompasses the Bible's entire kingdom-history storyline in microcosm.'

2. Since God originally granted righteous dominion over this earth to mankind (which we subsequently forfeited because of sin), what significance might that have for the messianic title 'Son of Man' in Daniel 7. What does Daniel 7 contribute to the resolution of that part of the kingdom storyline?

3. Read Isaiah 45:18-23. The speaker is identified (vv. 18-19) as the LORD (Yahweh, Jehovah). Now read Philippians 2:5-11, where Paul cites Isa. 45:22-23 directly with reference to Jesus Christ. What might that suggest about the specific identity of the speaker in Isaiah 45?

14

Trusting God's Narrative of Reality: Tracing the Big Picture (NT)

For he has rescued us from the dominion of darkness and
brought us into the kingdom of the Son he loves
Colossians 1:13 NIV

The New Testament is the sequel to a story begun centuries before. Much of it makes only incomplete sense if it is severed from the earlier part of the story. In some ways, however, it is also a prequel. It includes windows into earlier parts of the story, explaining the causes behind previous events and the fuller truth underlying ancient statements. Here the kingdom story that began in Genesis 1 comes to its fulfilling fruition.

New Testament

The Gospels

The Gospels announce the arrival of God's Messiah and King, but not quite as people expected. For the sake of space, we'll survey the kingdom theme only in Matthew,[1] which purposefully introduces itself as 'the book of the genealogy of Jesus Christ, the son of David' (1:1). At His birth, Gentile magi came asking 'where is He that is born **king** of the Jews?' (2:1-2). John the Baptist, Messiah's forerunner (Isa. 40; Mal. 3), declared that 'the **kingdom** of heaven is at hand' (3:2)—an announcement Jesus Himself took up (4:17), proclaiming it as good news (4:23; 9:35). In fact, He offered his Spirit-empowered ministry

---

1. Unless otherwise noted, all references in this section are to Matthew.

as proof that the kingdom had arrived (12:28). Jesus instructed His followers to pray for the kingdom to come (6:10) and exhorted them to 'seek first the **kingdom** of God' (6:33). He claimed sole discretion over who enters the kingdom (7:21), clarified that access was not on the basis of personal righteousness (5:20; 18:3; cf. John 3:3), and gave his disciples 'the keys of the **kingdom**' (16:19; 18:18-19). Gentiles will swell the numbers of the kingdom while many Jews will be excluded from it (8:11-12). The kingdom parables emphasize a spiritual dimension to this kingdom (Matt. 13). He taught that the kingdom was part of God's plan from the beginning: 'inherit the **kingdom** prepared for you from the foundation of the world' (25:34). In the end, Jesus was rejected and crucified publicly as 'the **King** of the Jews' (a phrase that appears four times in Matthew 27). Yet He rose from death to affirm that '**all authority** in heaven and in earth' had been granted to Him (28:18)—just as Daniel 7 predicted.

That's a curious mix of kingdom motifs. The kingdom is here yet we are to pray for it to come? Jesus' ministry is proof of its presence, yet we are to seek it? What kind of kingdom is this? And what is its relation to the gospel?

'Jesus went about ... preaching the **gospel** of the **kingdom**' (4:23; 9:35). That '**gospel** of the **kingdom**' is the ongoing message of the church throughout this age until the end (24:14; cf. Acts 28:30-31 below). The gospel is not something to be merely believed, but obeyed (Rom. 10:16; 2 Thess. 1:8; 1 Pet. 4:17). So, what is the 'good news' of a *kingdom*? And how does one *obey* good news? These two questions, and their answers, are intertwined. Think of a herald entering a domain to proclaim that the rightful King has arrived (2:2; 3:2; 4:17) and laid claim to the land previously dominated by an evil interloper and cruel tyrant (4:8-9), and that a new kingdom is poised for a victorious takeover and rule. That is the *gospel* (good news) of the *kingdom*. The question is, will you maintain your allegiance to the old tyrant, or will you bow to the authority of this new King and submit yourself to the rule of His kingdom (18:3-4; 21:31-32)? That is *obeying* the good news of the kingdom. Mere lip service to this Sovereign will not do (7:21; cf. 21:43). On one's *response* to the good news of this kingdom hangs

226

one's kingdom citizenship (25:25:34, 41) and eternal destiny (7:21-23; 25:46). Jesus is not only the long-anticipated King of the Jews (2:2; 27:11, 29, 37, 42); He has been given all authority over heaven and earth (Matt. 28:18). Everyone—Jew and Gentile—is accountable to Him.

In His first coming, Christ claimed sole and sovereign authority over the spiritual dimension of humanity—our salvation, our eternal destiny, our spiritual enemies (demons). He also exhibited His sovereign authority over creation—no illness, animal, element, or substance ever defied His will. His final declaration of universal authority is meant to remind you of Daniel 7:14, but just the first movement of that prophecy. He possesses the authority to rule both heaven and earth; but He has yet to impose His sovereign will on the kingdoms of this world. The day when His full kingdom rights will be claimed and His rule exercised without the human resistance described in Psalm 2 is yet to come.

The Acts

Luke tells us that during the forty days after His resurrection, Christ was teaching the disciples specifically about 'the things pertaining to the **kingdom** of God' (Acts 1:3). That's why the disciples' question whether the time had come for him to 'restore the **kingdom** to Israel' (1:6) was perfectly natural. Jesus' reply confirms what we surmised from our brief survey of the Gospels. Is Christ a present King, or a coming King? Has the kingdom arrived (as Jesus preached in the Gospels), or is it still coming (as the disciples seem to assume)? The answer is yes. Because the kingdom is comprised of multiple dimensions, 'it is both present and future until its consummation at Jesus' return' (Goldsworthy 2000, p. 620).

Acts opens a window on the disciples' understanding and interpretation of what was going on when Jesus, their King, was dying:

> Lord, You are God, who made heaven and earth and the sea, and all that is in them, who by the mouth of Your servant David have said [in Ps. 2]: Why did the nations rage, and the people plot vain things? The kings of the earth took their stand, and the rulers were gathered together against the Lord and against His Christ. For truly against Your holy Servant Jesus,

> whom You anointed, both Herod and Pontius Pilate, with the
> Gentiles and the people of Israel, were gathered together to do
> whatever Your hand and Your purpose determined before to
> be done (Acts 4:24-28).

Putting God to death in the flesh was the consummate expression of humanity's powerbrokers rejecting God's rule over them. Yet even in their rejection, God was ruling over the decisions and actions of human kings and rulers, Jew and Gentile.

The rest of the book of Acts is a record of apostolic testimony not only to the death and resurrection of Christ but to the kingdom of Christ. Paul described the believers at Ephesus as those 'among whom I have gone preaching the **kingdom** of God' (Acts 20:25). When Paul first came to Rome and the Jews wanted to hear from him, 'he explained and solemnly testified of the **kingdom** of God' (28:23). For the next two years while under house arrest, Paul was 'preaching the **kingdom** of God and teaching the things which concern the Lord Jesus Christ' (28:31). I thought Paul preached the gospel! He did. Just like Jesus continued the kingdom preaching of John (Matt. 3:2, 4:17), Paul continued the ministry of Christ, preaching the gospel—the good news—of the kingdom (Matt. 4:23, 9:35, 24:14).

What exactly did that kingdom-preaching sound like? We get a pretty good idea in Acts of what kingdom-preaching to unbelievers sounds like. The preaching of the kingdom is the preaching of the gospel, and vice versa. The call to believe the gospel of Christ is a call to submit to the kingdom of Christ. Gospel ministry is the proclamation of the kingdom of God and a call to people to submit to His King.

But what did Paul's kingdom-preaching to believers sound like? We have no express samples of it in Acts, but we do have examples in the letters Paul was writing concurrently with the events recorded in Acts.

The Epistles

'The unrighteous,' writes Paul, 'will not inherit the **kingdom** of God' unless they become righteous; and that, he continues, is exactly what had happened to the Corinthian believers (1 Cor. 6:9-11). When God saves sinners, He liberates us from 'the **domain** [dominion, authority] of darkness' and transfers us into 'the **kingdom** of his beloved Son' (Col. 1:13 ESV), as we await the return of 'the **King of kings**' (1 Tim. 6:14-15).

Paul describes the final consummation of this kingdom:

> Then comes the end, when He delivers the **kingdom** to God the Father, when **He puts an end to all rule and all authority and power.** For **He must reign** till He has put all enemies under His feet. The last enemy that will be destroyed is death (1 Cor. 15:24-26).

Hebrews 2 is another Himalayan height that juts up suddenly and surprisingly out of its surrounding landscape. It is the New Testament's most concise explanation of the connection between the dominion God intended for us (Gen. 1–2), the marring of that dominion and the loss of our kingdom-inheritance (Gen. 3), and God's remedy for recapturing that lost dominion (Dan. 7). Because this passage is so integral to the original kingdom concept of dominion for which we were created, we need to spend a bit more time here.

The opening argument of Hebrews can be condensed this way: **(1)** Christ is superior to *prophets* because He is the Son of God (1:1-3); **(2)** Christ is superior to *angels* because He is the Son of God (Heb. 1:4-14); but **(3)** Christ is also superior to angels because He is the Son of Man (Heb. 2:1-9). That argument sounds counterintuitive. How does His humanity make Him superior to angels?[2] Aren't humans inferior to angels? In some ways, yes, but in other important ways, no. Angels are never said to be created in God's image, but we are. Angels do not judge us; we will judge them (1 Cor. 6:3). But the main proof given in Hebrews is because God granted dominion over all creation to man, not to angels (Heb. 2:5; cf. Ps. 8:6; 115:16; Matt. 25:34).

> Jesus is superior to angels because, unlike the angels, he assumed the human condition, experiencing, like his human family, suffering and death. He can therefore accomplish something that no angel can do: he can ... bring 'many sons'

---

2. 'Son of Man' is not merely a title of humanity; it is a title of exaltation rooted in Daniel 7. But it is inherently a title of incarnation that incorporates humanity and deity in the person of the God-Man, Jesus the Messiah.

> to the 'glory' God intended for humanity to have over the world
> to come (Thielman 2005, p. 593).

Our decision to distrust God, the King, at the Fall forfeited our right and capacity to exercise righteous dominion over the world God originally ceded to us to rule as His regents and representatives. Because of the Fall, the recovery of that dominion was relegated to a future 'world to come' (Heb. 2:5). *And because it was a privilege promised only to man, it is a right that can be reclaimed only by a Man.* Christ the Last Adam (1 Cor. 15:25) righteously obeyed God where we failed, in order to give life to those who are united to Him by faith. Likewise, Christ the Son of Man (Ps. 8:4; Dan. 7:14) will righteously wrest dominion over this world from the unrighteous and win back the inheritance for those who are united to Him. The incarnation not only enabled Christ (as God) to taste death for us and recover the innocence we lost, but also uniquely qualified Christ (as Man) to subdue the earth for us and recover the dominion we lost.

The writer uses Psalm 8 to make a point about *us* in Hebrews 2:6-8; he does not apply it to Christ until 2:9, and only because He became man. Becoming man qualified Christ to fulfill a destiny uniquely given to (but lost by) man. Redemption is not about God's trashing what He lost to sin and Satan, and starting over with something new; that would be to admit the defeat of His original purposes. Redemption is God's victory over sin and Satan through the Man Christ Jesus. He had to become flesh not only so He could die for our sins, but also so He could reclaim this world for human dominion.

When exactly, then, is this 'world to come' (Heb. 2:5) to come? Where is this future kingdom actually described as finally arriving? God gave us one more book to answer that question. Like the beacons of Gondor in Tolkien's grand tale *The Lord of the Rings*, a series of scriptural beacons light the way for the trajectory of the theme of human dominion over this creation for which we were originally fashioned. You can trace that dimension of the kingdom motif as it spans from Genesis 1–2 to Psalm 8 to Daniel 7 to Hebrews 2 to Revelation 20–22.

The Apocalypse

The book of Revelation is the reversal of the Creation, Fall, Redemption storyline. On the basis of His redemptive work (Rev. 5) Christ is authorized as the only one worthy to execute cosmological judgment on this fallen and unrepentant world (Rev. 6–18), clearing the way for righteous human dominion over this present creation (Rev. 19–20) before establishing the new creation (Rev. 21–22). Revelation is about the full and final establishment of the kingdom, and the imposition of God's good and righteous will on the final frontiers of His creation. Unsurprisingly, the kingdom theme abounds in the book of Revelation.

John immediately introduces the reader to Christ as '**the ruler over the kings of the earth**' (1:5) and to himself as a 'brother and companion in the ... **kingdom** ... of Jesus Christ' (1:9). On the threshold of unveiling the fiercest fulfillment of Christ's kingdom claims, Revelation 4 re-orients us to a worldview-shaping reality: there is 'a **throne** ... in heaven' and God is on it (4:1-2). 'Throne' is a kingdom image with a message. Above all of earth's evil and chaos, God is serenely in control. Satan is a squatter, a pretender who has posted his petty little potentates here and there—little men who are kinging and lording, all the time thinking they're in charge. Revelation 4–5 informs us that they are in for a serious reality check.

God has sworn this earth to His Son: 'Ask of Me, and I will give You the nations for Your inheritance and the ends of the earth for Your possession' (Ps. 2:8). The transfer of the scroll from the Father seated on the throne to the Lion-Lamb (5:1-9) portrays the transfer of authority over the earth—including the right to judge it—from the Father to the Son. Everything in Revelation 6–20 flows from this throne-vision and scroll-granting, and sets in motion the final realization of all the dominion promises ever made. Though Revelation contains not a single formal Old Testament quotation, John's prophecy is drenched in Old Testament language. The celebrated arrival of the true King drips not only with Old Testament language but specifically with kingdom vocabulary.

> Now I saw heaven opened, and behold, a white horse. And
> He who sat on him was called Faithful and True, and in

righteousness **He judges and makes war** [Isa. 11:4]. His eyes were like a flame of fire, and on His head were many **crowns.** He had a name written that no one knew except Himself. He was clothed with a robe dipped in blood [Isa. 63:2], and His name is called The Word of God. And the armies in heaven, clothed in fine linen, white and clean, followed Him on white horses. Now out of His mouth goes a sharp sword, that with it He should strike the nations [Isa. 11:4]. And He Himself will **rule** them with a rod of iron [Ps. 2:9]. He Himself treads the winepress of the fierceness and wrath of Almighty God [Isa. 63:3]. And He has on His robe and on His thigh a name written: **KING OF KINGS AND LORD OF LORDS** (Rev. 19:11-16).

Christ's people 'reign with Him' over the earth (Rev. 20:4, 6), followed by a last Psalm 2 bid to throw off the cords of His righteous rule (20:7-10), and His final judgment (20:11-15). That kingdom transitions into a new heaven, a new earth, a new Jerusalem ... and a throne (21:1-5). Don't miss the physicality of all this. We were formed in God's image as physical beings to cultivate and rule in righteousness over a sinless and unfallen physical world. The new earth, apparently, will be our chance to do that—this time with no serpent snooping around. It is God who has chosen to make physicality eternal. The final picture Revelation leaves with us is not a glimpse into the clouds, but a look at the surprisingly tangible, material new earth we will inhabit in resurrected bodies alongside Christ in His resurrected body. Forever.

The kingdom motif persists right up to the very end:

> And he showed me a pure river of water of life, clear as crystal, proceeding from the **throne** of God and of the Lamb.... And there shall be no more curse, but the **throne** of God and of the Lamb shall be in it, and His servants shall serve Him.... And they shall **reign** forever and ever (22:1-5).

Christ closes His revelation with this self-identification: 'I am the Root and the Offspring of David' (22:16). Why is this so important that He would end with a reminder of it? Jesus' physical connection not just to humanity but to David is significant because it is His kingdom connection. John's closing prayer (22:20) echoes the request Jesus taught him to pray six decades earlier: 'thy **kingdom** come.'

Even So

From 1954–1955, a thousand-page epic tale was published in three separate volumes. Those volumes were actually subdivided into six 'books.' You could jump into the final 150 pages of Book 6, figure out to some degree what was going on, and still enjoy a great read about a massive battle between good and evil, with monsters and madmen, a last-minute cavalry charge against incredible odds that saves the good guys from death and defeat, and the challenge of putting the world back together again. But to really understand and appreciate the breadth of what was happening in those final pages, and what led to it all, and what was at stake, you'd have to go back and read the first five books of Tolkien's masterpiece, *The Lord of the Rings*.

Revelation is the last book in a two-volume, sixty-six book series. It is the last 'chapter' of a story as old as the human race. You can jump right into it and enjoy a great read about a massive battle between good and evil, with monsters and madmen, and a last-minute cavalry charge against incredible odds that makes good triumph and sets history to rights. But to really understand and appreciate the historical magnitude and cosmic breadth of the events described in Revelation, you need to see it in the context of the first sixty-five books.

God became Man in Christ not only to enable Him to die but to qualify Him to reign.

The biblical theme of the kingdom of God over this earth is not just a theological concept—it is a Christological concept. The Ruler of this kingdom is not God the Father but Christ the Son. The Reign over this kingdom is exercised not indirectly by the Father but by the Son of Man directly. The Realm of this kingdom is this earth and all its kingdoms, under the universal rule of God; that's why 1 Corinthians 15 describes Christ, after His reign, delivering up the kingdom to God the Father, that God may be all in all.

The Creator became a creature—with all the humiliation and suffering and self-sacrifice that entailed—to recapture and restore all that we lost in the Fall. Christ, having conquered all and achieved dominion over creation, will then share the dominion He has won— by both divine grant and human conquest—with His people as fellow partakers in the recovered dominion decree. This creation-kingdom, given to man but marred by the Fall, is rescued and redeemed and returned to man through God's anointed Son and King, the God-Man.

The Bible is the story of the Great King who bequeathed a kingdom to a race created in His own image, how that race rebelled against the King, and what He is doing to bring them back to Himself and to return the kingdom to them through the self-sacrificial death and conquering reign of His own Son. That's the Big Picture storyline of the Bible. Everything you read in Scripture feeds into that storyline in some way. Just being aware that there *is* a Bigger Picture is important for how you read and understand the Bible. And trusting God's narrative of reality is decisive for how you see the world and live life in it.

Review and Reflect

1. What philosophies does the world present that undercut or attempt to rewrite the narrative of reality presented by God in His Word?

2. In what practical, specific ways should trusting God's narrative of reality (i.e., a biblical worldview) impact your priorities, your decisions, and even your speech and actions?

Conclusion

15
Amen: Responding to God's Words

For he has rescued us from the dominion of darkness and
brought us into the kingdom of the Son he loves
Colossians 1:13 NIV

We began with a chapter on trust (*bātach*). We will end with a chapter on its closest synonym.[1] It's a Hebrew word that believers and even unbelievers know well, even if they don't know Hebrew. We use it with regularity, though perhaps not always accurately or with understanding. The word 'amen' is not a translation, but a transliteration. The letters of the Hebrew word are rendered directly into their English equivalents, so that when you pronounce the English word 'amen' you're coming reasonably close to actually pronouncing a Hebrew word.

It occurs pretty regularly in our Bibles, though perhaps not as frequently as we might have thought. The word appears nearly eighty times in my New King James Verson. Interesting where it tends to cluster —Deuteronomy 27, Romans, the Pastoral Epistles, and Revelation. If the two dozen times in John's Gospel where Jesus employs a unique use of the term were also transliterated ('amen, amen') rather than translated ('verily, verily' or 'truly, truly'), it would show up a good deal more.

It doesn't mean 'The End.' It's not just a religious throwaway word, or devout verbal décor for sacred occasions. In some churches it seems to function as a Baptist equivalent for 'That was good!' used to

---

1. When my pastor preached through this idea on a Wednesday night near the beginning of my writing sabbatical, I knew then that it should be my final chapter. I owe the concept and shape of this chapter to him.

punctuate special music or stirring statements from the pulpit. (I say that as a Baptist, by the way.) But that's not what it means either.

As we discussed earlier in this book, the Hebrew verb from which it derives (*'āman*) means *to be reliable, steadfast*. It can also be used in a verbal form that means *to believe* (signifying our response to what we think is reliable). Its noun form (*'emunah*) means *firmness, steadfastness*. A closely related noun (*'emeth*) is the Hebrew word for *truth*.

A common English translation of this family of words is 'faithful' which, to us, usually implies constancy or loyalty. We would describe a dog as a 'faithful' companion. But there's more to the word family than that. It describes something or someone that is constant, unshifting, immoveable. One of the rare physical uses of the word describes Moses' hands—raised in prayer for the Israelites battling the Amalekites, and held up by Aaron and Hur when Moses became weary—as '*steady* until the going down of the sun' (Exod. 17:12). Even our word 'truth' can convey the static entity of objective fact devoid of falsehood. But truth is not just about honesty; it's about *reality*. Think 'real estate' and you have a working image of this idea: firm, unshifting, certain, factual, and therefore reliable, dependable. In other words, trustworthy.

All these words communicate the connection between the reliability of a person and the dependability of his words. Throughout the Old Testament the one predominantly described by these words is God. He is 'rich in ... constancy' (Exod. 34:6 NJB), 'a reliable God' (Deut. 32:4, NET) of 'Great ... faithfulness' (Lam. 3:23). It is so native to His nature that it is one of His names. He is 'the Amen, the Faithful and True Witness' (Rev. 3:14). Anything to which God testifies is 'sure' (Ps. 19:7) because 'the entirety of Your word is truth' (Ps. 119:160). That's why, throughout Scripture, 'Amen' is the right response to anything and everything God says.

When the curses of the Law were read from Mount Ebal, twelve times the Israelites were to affirm them by saying 'Amen' (Deut. 27:15-26) to 'indicate understanding and agreement' (Craigie 1976, p. 331). Likewise, when Nehemiah charged the Israelites to stop exploiting the economically vulnerable among them, he then shook out the fold of his garment adding, 'So may God shake out each man from his house and from his property, who does not perform this promise'—to which 'the assembly said, Amen! and praised the LORD' (Neh. 5:13). 'Amen' affirms prayers for the glory of God (Ps. 72:19, 106:48; Matt. 6:13), and regularly punctuates the contents of each New Testament Gospel and epistle.[2] Paul was full of spontaneous Amens because he was full of spontaneous doxologies to God.[3] Angels add their Amen to affirm the glory of God (Rev. 5:14, 7:12, 19:4). Even when the light of a glorious truth is offset by shadow, it deserves an Amen (Rev. 1:7).

Because God is the Amen, that's what His words are as well: firm, unshifting, certain, real, reliable, dependable. Amen is, therefore, the only right response to God's words. It is our way of verbalizing and certifying our conviction, our belief, our confidence, our trust that whatever God says is reality. Amen is our 'Yes' to the words of God. Amen is a stake that we drive down deep into a statement from God and hang all our weight from it. The words of God are sure, and Amen is my signature that I'm pitching my tent there because I'm sure they are.

Nothing magnifies God more than our Amen to His words even when we can't see how they could possibly come to be. It is your testimony that His words are your reality, that you consider Him worthy to be trusted on the basis of His words alone. And nothing brings the believer more stability and security and, yes, inner peace than grounding all his life's decisions and priorities in the confidence that all His words about everything are Yes and Amen (2 Cor. 1:20).

This book began by talking about inner peace. The path to that inner peace, we have discovered, is learning to trust the trustworthy God. Isaiah pens a confident celebration of this truth:

> You will keep him in perfect peace
> Whose mind is stayed on You,
> Because he trusts [*bātach*] in You.
> Trust [*bātach*] in the LORD forever,
> For in YAH the LORD is everlasting strength (26:3-4).

---

2. The only exceptions are James and 3 John.

3. Excluding those that conclude his epistles, see Rom. 1:25, 9:5, 11:36, 15:33, 16:20, 24; Gal. 1:5; Eph. 3:21; 1 Tim. 1:17, 6:16; 2 Tim. 4:18.

There it is. Not just peace. Perfect peace. The Hebrew literally reads, 'You will keep him in peace peace' because 'Hebrew uses repetition to express superlatives or to indicate totality' (Motyer 1993, 76). 'Peace' is the word *shalom*, a word as broad as it is deep; it refers to wholeness, wellness, health, welfare, security, well-being—in other words, everything is just as it should be. The gist of the repetition ('peace peace') in Hebrew is to emphasize '*true* peace as compared with pseudo-peace, and *total* [peace] as excluding every disturbing element' (Motyer 1993, 213 emphasis added). And the specific promise is that God Himself will 'keep' (guard, watch over, protect, preserve) such a person.

Who enjoys this genuine and unruffled tranquility? The object of the promise is actually not a person, but a certain kind of mind. Again, the Hebrew text reads, 'You will keep in peace peace a stayed/steady mind.' Not the usual word for 'mind,' this term has reference to a mindset, an outlook, a frame of mind, a habitual way of looking at things. It is a mental disposition that is 'steadfast'—an expression that 'carries the idea of "leaning on, depending on, resting on" something' (Smith 2007, 442). On what? The next phrase answers that question: because it (this kind of mind) or he (the person with this kind of mind) trusts in God.

Out of this assurance flows an exhortation. Because God promises to guard with unmixed peace a mindset that leans in total trust entirely on Him, then trust in this God, Yahweh, forever! Because in Yahweh alone is (literally) 'an everlasting rock.' What links this promise specifically to the trustworthiness of God's words? The object of our trust is God Himself. *But the only means we have of knowing the character and purposes of God is through His words.*

Akin to peace, joy is a disposition of delight and settled serenity that is rooted in trust in the character of God. It's like one of those redwoods or live oaks we talked about earlier. The believer is the trunk. The tree grows in the ground of the being and character of God Himself. But the roots represent my trust in all the specific sayings and statements, promises and prophecies of God in Scripture. His words are the only link between us and God Himself, the only truth about God that can nourish and support us amid hurricanes or hot summer days. And the branches bear the foliage and fruit of that stabilizing trust rooted in the words of God: peace, joy, contentment, stability, confidence, patience, boldness, steadfastness. The deeper the roots and the firmer their grip on God's words, the higher and healthier the believer grows.

Appendixes

Appendix 1

(Chapter 3)

Ezekiel—You/They Shall Know Theme

Bold = passages where the *nations* will know the Lord, as a result either of (a) God's judgment on one of the nations, or (b) God's blessing on Israel.

Italics = references that maintain the recognition motif ('you/they shall know') but changes the object from Yahweh or His actions.

( ) = references to past blessing or judgment, rather than future.

* The first reference to the theme does not technically fall under any of the three major categories.

Future Judgment on Israel	Future Judgment on Nations	Future Blessing on Israel
2:5*		
5:13		
6:7		
6:10		
6:13		
6:14		
7:4		
7:9		
7:27		
11:10		
11:12		
12:15		
12:16		
12:20		

Future Judgment on Israel	Future Judgment on Nations	Future Blessing on Israel
13:9		
13:14		
13:21		
13:23		
14:8		
		14:23
15:7		
		16:62
17:21		
17:24		**17:24**
		(20:12)
		(20:20)
(20:26)		
		20:38
		20:42
		20:44
21:5		
22:16		
22:22		
23:49		
24:24		
24:27		
	25:5[a]	
	25:7[a]	
	25:11[b]	
	25:14[c]	
	25:17[d]	
	26:6[e]	
	28:22[f]	
	28:23[f]	
	28:24[f]	
		28:26
	29:6[g]	
	29:9[g]	
	29:16[g]	
		29:21

Future Judgment on Israel	Future Judgment on Nations	Future Blessing on Israel
	30:8[g]	
	30:19[g]	
	30:25[g]	
	30:26[g]	
	32:15[g]	
33:29		
33:33		
		34:27
		34:30
	35:4[c]	
	35:9[c]	
	35:12[c]	
	35:15[c]	
		26:11
		36:23
		36:36
		36:38
		37:6
		37:13
		37:14
		37:28
	38:16[h]	
	38:23[h]	
	39:6[i]	
		39:7
		39:22
		39:23
		39:28

[a] Ammon [b] Moab [c] Edom [d] Philistia [e] Tyre
[f] Sidon [g] Egypt [h] Gog [i] Magog

Appendix 2

(Chapter 3)

Thus Says the LORD (of Hosts): Zechariah's Insertion or God's Exclamation?

Fourteen times in Zechariah 8 God's words are punctuated with the solemn assertion, 'Thus says the LORD (of Hosts)' (8:2, 3, 4, 6 [twice], 7, 9, 11, 14 [twice], 17, 19, 20, 23). The HCSB translates it a bit more freshly: 'The LORD of armies says this.'

If this phrase is Zechariah's addition, his way of emphatically reminding people that he is giving them God's words, that's significant. But what if it is part of what God actually said to Zechariah? That's what the Hebrew construction implies.

Zechariah 8:1 reads, 'Again, the word of the LORD of hosts came to me, saying ....' The word 'saying' (left untranslated by some versions) is a Hebrew infinitive construct which signals that a quotation is about to begin. It functions like an opening quotation mark, implying that everything that follows is part of the word of the Lord that came to Zechariah. So God's words to Zechariah in 8:2 do not begin with 'I am zealous for Zion.' Rather, the first words out of God's mouth to Zechariah are: 'Thus says the LORD of hosts: I am zealous for Zion ....'

For Zechariah to repeatedly alert people that 'This is what the LORD says' is a sober reminder. But for God Himself to preface every detail with 'This is what the LORD says' only magnifies the solemnity and certainty of the message.

Appendix 3

(Chapter 9)

Dābār : Thing or Word ?

The examples below demonstrate that the word *dābār* is often translated 'thing' even when the referent in the context is clearly neither an object nor an abstract, but something spoken, a word, a message. Such examples lend considerable weight to my translation and interpretation of *dābār* in Genesis 18 and Jeremiah 32.

- Gen. 19:21—'I have accepted thee concerning this **thing** …' The 'thing' is clearly Lot's request in 19:18-20. This is so clear that KJV and NKJV are virtually alone in the generic rendering; most versions translate *dābār* as 'request,' a spoken thing.

- Gen. 20:8—Abimelech 'told all these **things**' to his servants. What were 'these things'? All the words God had spoken to him in his dream (20:3-7).

- Gen. 21:11—'the **thing/matter** was very displeasing in Abraham's sight.' What displeased Abraham in 21:11 was not just the general situation with Esau, but specifically what Sarah had said in 21:10. NET picks up on this by rendering *dābār* as '*Sarah's* **demand**.'

- Gen. 41:28—'this is the **thing** which I have spoken to Pharaoh' refers to the dream interpretation Joseph had just communicated (literally, 'this is the word/message that I have spoken to Pharaoh').

- Gen. 41:32—'the dream was repeated to Pharaoh twice because the **thing** is established by God' refers to the *message* communicated via the dream.

- Gen 41:37—'the **thing** was good in the eyes of Pharaoh.' The 'thing' here is the word of counsel Joseph had just given him regarding how to prepare for the coming events that God had revealed. Most translations give it a 'word' sense by translating it as '**advice**' (NET), '**proposal**' (ESV, NASB), or '**plan**' (NIV).

Examples could be multiplied many times over. The point is not that 'thing/matter' is never an appropriate rendering of *dābār*. A generic rendering is the only one that makes sense in many contexts. Frequently, however, when *dābār* is translated in the generic sense of 'thing/matter,' the context indicates that the more specific sense of 'word' (i.e., something spoken) is in view and makes perfect sense (indeed, better sense) in the context. A simple comparison of translations in such passages validates the point. Seeing Genesis 18:14 and Jeremiah 32:17, 27 in that light alerts the reader to fresh implications that are theologically and applicationally significant.

Rhēma : Thing or Word?

Like the Hebrew word *dābār*, the Greek word *rhēma* is sometimes translated 'thing' when the context clarifies that a 'spoken thing' is in view.

- Luke 1:65—'All these **sayings** were noised abroad' (KJV). The sense of verbal content is obvious and correctly captured in all translations.

- Luke 2:15—'Let us now go ... and see this **thing**.' What thing? The shepherds' meaning is clear from the rest of the verse: 'Let us now go to Bethlehem and see this **thing** that has come to pass, **which the Lord has made known to us**.' The 'thing' is the news, report, message of Messiah's birth communicated to them via the angelic announcement.

- Luke 2:17—The shepherds 'made widely known the **saying** which was told them.' Here the translation could just as easily have been 'the thing which was told them' following the example of 2:15; but the translators correctly pick up on the verbal content that the shepherds had received and were passing on.

- Luke 2:19—'But Mary kept all these **things** and pondered them in her heart.' What things? All the words of the angelic messages that the shepherds were reporting about her son (2:17-18). NET translates 'Mary kept all these **words** ....'

- Luke 2:51—Again, Mary 'kept all these **things** in her heart.' This comes at the end of a series of events that feature significant statements: Simeon's prophecy about Christ (2:25-35), Anna's testimony (2:36-38), and Jesus' own elusive (to them) self-testimony (2:46-50, where *rhēma* shows up as **saying** in v. 50). Mary is clearly pondering statements about her son, verbal information that she has been receiving about him through a variety of sources.

Again, the fact that *rhēma* is used to refer to specific verbal content much more often than the impression created by common translation, lends additional weight to my interpretation and application of Luke 1:37.

Appendix 4

(Chapter 11)

Fulfillment of 'The Word of the LORD' in 1, 2 Kings

Shaded entries do not expressly include *the word of the Lord* fulfillment formula, though they do include some form of *the word of the Lord* pronouncement formula [see endnotes 1 and 2 at end of table].

	Historical Fulfillment	Content	Original Statement	Time Lapse
1	1K 2:27	Eli's descendants removed from priesthood [1]	1S 2:31-35	50 yrs
2	1K 5:12	God gives Solomon wisdom	1K 3:12	-
3	1K 8:20, 24	Solomon reigns and builds the temple	1C 22:6-10	yrs
4	1K 12:15	Jeroboam receives the kingdom of Israel	1K 11:31-37	-
5	1K 13:4-5	Bethel altar splits, spilling its ashes	1K 13:3	-
6	1K 13:26	Man of God dies for eating/drinking in Bethel	1K 13:9, 17	-
7	1K 14:18	Jeroboam's son dies and is mourned	1K 14:12-13	-
8	1K 15:28-29	Jeroboam's descendants cut off	1K 14:7-11, 14	yrs
9	1K 16:12	Baasha's descendants cut off	1K 16:1-7	yrs
10	1K 16:34	Hiel lost his children in building Bethel	Josh. 6:26	600 yrs

	Historical Fulfillment	Content	Original Statement	Time Lapse
11	1K 17:5-6	Elijah sustained by ravens at Cherith Brook	1K 17:2-4	-
12	1K 17:10 ff.	Elijah sustained by widow at Zarephath	1K 17:8-9	-
13	1K 17:16	Widow's food miraculously sustained	1K 17:14-15	-
14	1K 18:45	God sends rain	1K 18:1	-
15	1K 20:20-21	Ahab defeats Syrians	1K 20:13-14	-
16	1K 20:29-30	Ahab defeats Syrians again	1K 20:28	7 days
17	1K 20:36	Man killed by lion for not striking prophet	1K 20:35	-
18	1K 22:37	Ahab forfeits life for disobedience	1K 20:42	-
19	1K 22:29-37	Ahab killed in battle	1K 22:19-28	-
20	1K 22:38	Dogs licked up Ahab's blood	1K 21:19	-
21	2K 9:36	Dogs eat Jezebel in Jezreel	1K 21:23; 2K 9:10	~15 yrs
22	2K 9:25-26	Judgment/loss of kingdom on Ahab's sons	1K 21:28-29	yrs
23	2K 1:17	Ahaziah dies from injury	2K 1:4, 6, 16	-
24	2K 2:22	Bad water cleansed	2K 2:21	-
25	2K 3:20	God provides water for armies	2K 3:16-17	1 day
26	2K 4:17	Shunammite woman has a son	2K 4:16-17	1 yr
27	2K 4:44	God multiplies bread for Elisha's followers	2K 4:43	-
28	2K 5:14	Naaman washes and is cleansed of leprosy	2K 5:10	-
29	2K 5:27	Gehazi becomes leprous	2K 5:27	-
30	2K 6:18	Syrians struck with blindness per Elisha's word	2K 6:18	-

	Historical Fulfillment	Content	Original Statement	Time Lapse
31	2K 7:16	Miraculous provision in siege-famine	2K 7:1	1 day
32	2K 7:17-20	King's officer dies because of unbelief	2K 7:2	1 day
33	2K 9:13ff.	Jehu becomes king of Israel	2K 9:1-12	-
34	2K 10:10-11	Ahab's seed exterminated by Jehu	1K 17:21-24, 29	yrs
35	2K 14:25	Jeroboam II restores Israel's territory	2K 14:25	-
36	2K 15:12	Jehu's dynasty lasts exactly four generations	2K 10:30	100 yrs
37	2K 19:35-37	God delivers Jerusalem from Sennacherib	2K 19:21-34	-
38	2K 20:4-6	Hezekiah given 15 more years to live	2K 20:4-6	15 yrs
39	2K 23:15-16	Josiah burns priests' bones on Bethel altar	1K 13:1-2	~300 yrs
40	2K 23:28-30	Josiah dies 'in peace'[2]	2K 22:18-20	13 yrs
41	2K 24:2	Babylon over-runs Judah	2K 23:27 et al.	yrs
42	2K 25:11-21	Babylon carries away Jerusalem's wealth/people	2K 20:16-17	yrs
43	2K 25:1ff.	Babylon over-runs Judah	2K 21:12-15	yrs
44	2K 25:1ff.	Babylon over-runs Judah	2K 22:15-17	yrs

1 In 1 Kings 2:27, an apparent anomaly exists between the original statement and the fulfillment that seems to be ignored by most commentators: How is removing Abiathar from the priesthood (at the age of no less than fifty), but not executing him, a fulfillment of the statement that Eli's descendants would never live to old age (like Eli)? The resolution seems to lie in the prophetic words in Samuel, 'The days will come.' Either, (a) the universality of the judgment did not commence immediately, but commenced with the deposition of Abiathar, or (b) Abiathar's deposition was one more example of the cutting off of Eli's descendants (like Hophni & Phineas, and like Saul's slaughter of the priests at Nob, from which Abiathar escaped as a young man). In light of the 1 Kings statement, it seems that (a) fits best as the 'fulfillment' that is implied in the Samuel statement. Deposition from the priesthood may not seem equivalent to being 'cut off,' but we do not know what happened to Abiathar after this; neither he nor his sons (Jonathan,

Ahimelech) are mentioned again. Some assume that the Samuel prophecy simply announces that Eli's line would be cut off from the priesthood, in which case the fulfillment is clearer; but there are two problems with that explanation: (1) the assumption doesn't seem to fit the language in Samuel, and (2) it seems Abiathar's son, Ahimelech, later served as priest (1 Chron. 24:6).

2   The fact that Josiah died in battle at the hand of Pharaoh-Neco does not contradict the prophecy that he would die 'in peace.' The point of 2 Kings 22:20a (that he would be 'gathered to his grave in peace') is clarified in 22:20b—'your eyes shall not see all the calamity which I will bring on this place' (described in 20:15-19). Josiah died while the kingdom was still at peace, and never saw the Babylonian calamity that God brought on Judah shortly after Josiah's death, just as He said.

Bibliography

à Brakel, Wilhelmus. 1993 (Reprint). *The Christian's Reasonable Service*. Trans. Bartel Elshout. Ligonier, PA: Soli Deo Gloria Publications.

Alexander, Joseph A. 1991 (Reprint). *Commentary on Psalms*. Grand Rapids: Kregel.

Anthony, Lawrence with Graham Spence. 2009. *The Elephant Whisperer: My Life with the Herd in the African Wild*. New York: St. Martin's Press.

Baron, David. 1988 (Reprint). *Commentary on Zechariah*. Grand Rapids: Kregel.

Barrett, Michael P. V. 2003. *God's Unfolding Purpose: The Message of Daniel*. Greenville, SC: Ambassador-Emerald..

Bascomb, Neal. 2002. *Hunting Eichmann: How a Band of Survivors and a Young Spy Agency Chased Down the World's Most Notorious Nazi*. Boston: Houghton Mifflin Harcourt.

Bell, Robert D. 2010. *The Theological Messages of the Old Testament Books*. Greenville: Bob Jones University Press.

Berg, Jim. 2002. *Created for His Glory: God's Purpose for Redeeming Your Life*. Greenville: BJU Press.

Blaising, Craig L. 2014. 'Israel and Hermeneutics.' *The People, the Land, and the Future of Israel*. Eds. Darrell L. Bock and Mitch Glaser. Grand Rapids: Kregel.

Block, Daniel L. 1997. *The Book of Ezekiel*. 2 volumes. New International Commentary on the Old Testament. Grand Rapids: Eerdmans.

_____. 1999. *Judges, Ruth*. New American Commentary. Nashville: Broadman & Holman.

Bock, Darrell L. 1994. *Luke*. The IVP New Testament Commentary Series. Downers Grove: IVP.

_____. 1996. *Luke*. NIV Application Commentary. Grand Rapids: Zondervan.

Bruce, F. F. *The Epistle to the Hebrews*. 1964. The New International Commentary on the New Testament. Grand Rapids: Eerdmans.

Burroughs, Franklin. 1998. *Billy Watson's Croker Sack*. Athens, GA: University of Georgia Press.

Bunyan, John. 1990. *The Pilgrim's Progress*. Reprint. Carlisle: Banner of Truth.

Butterfield, Rosaria Champagne. 2015. *Openness Unhindered: Further Thoughts of an Unlikely Convert on Sexual Identity and Union with Christ*. Pittsburgh: Crown & Covenant Publications.

Calvin, John. 1960 (Reprint). *Institutes of the Christian Religion*. Ed. John T. McNeill. Trans. Ford Lewis Battles. Louisville: Westminster John Knox Press.

Carson, D. A. 1984. 'Matthew' in *The Expositors Bible Commentary*. Vol. 8. Ed. Frank E. Gaebelein. Grand Rapids: Zondervan.

_____. 1991. *The Gospel According to John*. Pillar New Testament Commentary. Grand Rapids: Eerdmans.

Chambers, Oswald. 1941. *The Philosophy of Sin and Other Studies in the Problems of Man's Moral Life*. London: Simpkin Marshall.

Craigie, Peter. 1976. *The Book of Deuteronomy*. Grand Rapids: Eerdmans.

Cranfield, C. E. B. 1985. *The Gospel According to St. Mark*. Cambridge Greek Testament Commentary. Cambridge: Cambridge University Press.

Crockett, Nathan. 2013. 'This Is That? An Evaluation of Cessationism Contrasting Biblical Tongues and Miracles with Contemporary Phenomena and Examining

Foundational Hermeneutics.' PhD diss., Bob Jones University Seminary.

Davis, Dale Ralph. 2007. *1 Kings*. Fearn: Christian Focus.

_____. 2008. *Joshua*. Fearn: Christian Focus.

Delitzsch, Franz. 1982 (Reprint). *Biblical Commentary on the Book of Isaiah*. 2 Volumes. Trans. James Martin. Grand Rapids: Eerdmans.

DeYoung, Kevin. 2014. *Taking God at His Word: Why the Bible is Knowable, Necessary, and Enough, and What That Means for You and Me*. Wheaton: Crossway.

Edersheim, Alfred. 1976 (Reprint). *The Life and Times of Jesus the Messiah*. Grand Rapids: Eerdmans.

Edwards, James R. 2001. *The Gospel According to Mark*. Pillar New Testament Commentary. Grand Rapids: Eerdmans.

Erickson, Millard J. 2013. *Christian Theology*. 3rd Edition. Grand Rapids: Baker Academic.

Evans, G. Blakemore and J. J. M. Tobin, eds. 1997. *The Riverside Shakespeare*. Second Edition. New York: Houghton Mifflin.

Ferguson, Sinclair B. 2014. *From the Mouth of God: Trusting, Reading, and Applying the Bible*. Carlisle, PA: Banner of Truth.

Frame, John. 2010. *The Doctrine of the Word of God*. Phillipsburg: P & R Publishing.

_____. 2013. *Systematic Theology: An Introduction to Christian Belief*. Phillipsburg: P & R Publishing.

Goldsworthy, Graeme. 2000. 'Kingdom of God' in *New Dictionary of Biblical Theology*. Ed. T. Desmond Alexander, Brian S. Rosner, D. A. Carson, Graeme Goldsworthy. Downers Grove: InterVarsity.

Goslinga, C. J. 1986. *Joshua, Judges, Ruth. Bible Student's Commentary*. Trans. Ray Togtman. Grand Rapids: Zondervan.

Gould, Stephen Jay. 1995. *Dinosaur in a Haystack: Reflections in Natural History*. New York: Three Rivers Press.

Green, Joel B. 1997. *The Gospel of Luke*. New International Commentary on the New Testament. Grand Rapids: Eerdmans.

Griffith-Thomas, W. H. 1976 (Reprint). *Genesis: A Devotional Commentary*. Eerdmans: Grand Rapids.

Grudem, Wayne. 1994. *Systematic Theology*. Grand Rapids: Zondervan.

Hamilton, Victor. 1995. *The Book of Genesis*. New International Commentary on the Old Testament. Grand Rapids: Eerdmans.

Helm, Paul and Carl R. Trueman, eds. 2002. 'Introduction.' *The Trustworthiness of God: Perspectives on the Nature of Scripture*. Grand Rapids: Eerdmans.

Helm, Paul. 2002. 'The Perfect Trustworthiness of God.' In *The Trustworthiness of God: Perspectives on the Nature of Scripture*. Ed. Paul Helm and Carl R. Trueman. Grand Rapids: Eerdmans.

Henry, Matthew. n.d. *Commentary on the Whole Bible*. 6 Volumes. McLean, VA: MacDonald.

Jacobson, Rolf. 2014. *The Book of Psalms*. New International Commentary of the Old Testament. Nancy L. deClaissé-Walford, Rolf A. Jacobson, and Beth LaNeel Tanner. Grand Rapids, Eerdmans.

Jaeggli, Randy. 2004. *More Like the Master: Reflecting the Image of God*. Greenville: Ambassador Emerald International.

Johnson, Dennis E. 2013. *Philippians*. Reformed Expository Commentary. Phillipsburg: P & R Publishing.

Kaiser, Walter C. Jr. 1998. *A History of Israel*. Nashville: B & H.

———. 2008. *The Promise-Plan of God: A Biblical Theology of the Old and New Testaments*. Grand Rapids: Zondervan.

Kalland, Earl S. 1980. '*Dābār*' in *Theological Wordbook of the Old Testament*. Ed. R. Laird Harris, Gleason L. Archer Jr., and Bruce K. Waltke. Chicago: Moody.

Keil, C. F. and F. Delitzsch. 1982 (rpr). *Commentary on the Old Testament*. Trans. James Martin. Grand Rapids: Eerdmans.

Kent, Homer A. Jr. 1978. 'Philippians' in *The Expositor's Bible Commentary.* Volume 11. Ed. Frank E. Gabelein. Grand Rapids: Zondervan.

Kershaw, Alex. 2010. *The Envoy: The Epic Rescue of the Last Jews of Europe in the Desperate Closing Months of World War II.* Cambridge, MA: De Capo Press.

Kidner, Derek. 1967. *Genesis: An Introduction and Commentary.* Tyndale Old Testament Commentary. Downers Grove: IVP.

_____. 1973. *Psalms: An Introduction and Commentary.* Tyndale Old Testament Commentary. Downers Grove: IVP.

Koukl, Gregory. 2017. *The Story of Reality: How the World Began, How It Ends, and Everything Important That Happens in Between.* Grand Rapids: Zondervan.

Lane, William L. *Hebrews.* 2 volumes. Word Biblical Commentary. Nashville: Thomas Nelson, 1991.

Lange, John Peter. 1980 (Reprint). *Commentary on the Holy Scriptures.* Trans. Philip Schaff. Grand Rapids: Zondervan.

Laskin, David. 2004. *The Children's Blizzard.* New York: HarperCollins.

Lau, Peter H. W. and Gregory Goswell. 2016. *Unceasing Kindness: A Biblical Theology of Ruth.* Downers Grove: InterVarsity Press.

Leupold, H. C. 1942. *Exposition of Genesis.* Grand Rapids: Baker.

_____. 1969. *Exposition of the Psalms.* Grand Rapids: Baker.

Lewis, C. S. 1970. *The Horse and His Boy.* New York: Collier Books.

_____. 1970. *The Last Battle.* New York: Collier Books.

_____. 1976. *The Weight of Glory and Other Essays.* New York: Harper One.

Liefeld, Walter L. 1984. 'Luke' in *The Expositor's Bible Commentary. Volume 8.* Ed. Frank E. Gaebelein. Grand Rapids: Zondervan.

Marshall, I. Howard. 1978. *The Gospel of Luke.* New International Greek New Testament Commentary. Grand Rapids: Eerdmans.

McComiskey, Thomas Edward. 1985. *The Covenants of Promise.* Grand Rapids: Baker.

Merrill, Eugene. 2006. *Everlasting Dominion: A Theology of the Old Testament*. Nashville: Broadman and Holman.

_____. 2008. *Kingdom of Priests: A History of Old Testament Israel*. Grand Rapids: Baker Academic.

Morgan, G. Campbell. 1936. *The Crises of the Christ*. Old Tappan, NJ: Fleming H. Revell.

Morris, Leon. 1971. *The Gospel According to John*. New International Commentary on the New Testament. Grand Rapids: Eerdmans.

_____. 1992. *The Gospel According to Matthew*. Pillar New Testament Commentary. Grand Rapids: Eerdmans.

Motyer, J. Alec. 1993. *The Prophecy of Isaiah: An Introduction & Commentary*. Downers Grove: InterVarsity.

Oehler, Gustav. 1978 (Reprint). *Theology of the Old Testament*. Reprint 1873. Minneapolis: Klock & Klock.

Oswalt, John. 1980. '*bāṭaḥ*' in *Theological Wordbook of the Old Testament*. Ed. R. Laird Harris, Gleason L. Archer, Jr., and Bruce K. Waltke. Chicago: Moody.

_____. 1998. *The Book of Isaiah, Chapters 40–66*. New International Commentary on the Old Testament. Grand Rapids: Eerdmans.

Packer, J. I. 1973. *Knowing God*. Downers Grove: InterVarsity Press.

Payne, J. Barton. 1962. *The Theology of the Older Testament*. Grand Rapids: Zondervan.

Perowne, T. T. 1878. *Jonah*. Cambridge: University Press.

Peterson, David G. 2009. *The Acts of the Apostles*. Grand Rapids: Eerdmans.

Piper, John. 2006. *God's Passion for His Glory*. Wheaton: Crossway.

_____. 2016. *A Peculiar Glory: How the Christian Scriptures Reveal Their Complete Truthfulness*. Wheaton: Crossway.

Reymond, Robert L. 1998. *A New Systematic Theology of the Christian Faith*. Nashville: Thomas Nelson.

Rydelnik, Michael. 2010. *The Messianic Hope: Is the Hebrew Bible Really Messianic?* Nashville: B & H Academic.

Ryle, J. C. 1986 (Reprint). *Expository Thoughts on Luke.* Carlisle, PA: Banner of Truth.

Sailhamer, John H. 1990. 'Genesis' in *The Expositor's Bible Commentary.* Volume 2. Ed. Frank E. Gaebelein. Grand Rapids: Zondervan.

Sanders, John. 2007. *The God Who Risks.* Downers Grove: InterVarsity Press.

Schaff, Philip, ed. 2007 (Reprint). *Nicene and Post-Nicene Fathers.* Volume 4. New York: Cosimo Books. 1886.

Smith, Gary V. 2007. *Isaiah 1–39.* New American Commentary. Nashville: Broadman & Holman.

Sproul, R. C. 1995. *Faith Alone.* Grand Rapids: Baker.

Spurgeon, C. H. n.d. *The Treasury of David.* Mclean, VA: Macdonald Publishing.

Steinmann, Andrew E. 2019. *Genesis.* Tyndale Old Testament Commentaries. Ed. David G. Firth. Downers Grove: IVP Academic.

Tada, Joni Eareckson and Steve Estes. 2000. *When God Weeps: Why Our Sufferings Matter to the Almighty.* Grand Rapids: Zondervan.

Talbert, Layton. 2001. *Not by Chance: Learning to Trust a Sovereign God.* Greenville, SC: BJU Press.

_____. 2007. *Beyond Suffering: Discovering the Message of Job.* Greenville, SC: Bob Jones University Press.

Tanner, Beth. 2014. *The Book of Psalms.* New International Commentary of the Old Testament. Nancy L. deClaissé-Walford, Rolf A. Jacobson, and Beth LaNeel Tanner. Grand Rapids, Eerdmans.

Thielman, Frank. 2005. *Theology of the New Testament: A Canonical and Synthetic Approach.* Grand Rapids: Zondervan.

Thompson, J. A. 1980. *The Book of Jeremiah.* The New International Commentary on the Old Testament. Grand Rapids: Eerdmans.

Thompson, Mark. 2006. *A Clear and Present Word: The Clarity of Scripture.* Downers Grove: IVP.

Trueman, Carl R. 2002. 'The God of Unconditional Promise.' In *The Trustworthiness of God: Perspectives on the Nature of Scripture.* Ed. Paul Helm and Carl R. Trueman. Grand Rapids: Eerdmans.

Turner, David L. 2008. *Matthew.* Baker Exegetical Commentary on the New Testament. Grand Rapids: Baker Academic.

Turretin, Francis. 1994 (Reprint). *Institutes of Elenctic Theology.* Volume 2. Ed. James T. Dennison, Jr. Trans. George Musgrave Giger. Phillipsburg: P & R Publishing.

VanGemeren, Willem A. 1991. 'Psalms' in *The Expositors Bible Commentary.* Volume 5. Ed. Frank E. Gaebelein. Grand Rapids: Zondervan.

Walker, W. L. 1982. 'God, Names of.' *International Standard Bible Encyclopedia.* Ed. Geoffrey Bromiley. Grand Rapids: Eerdmans.

Wallace, Daniel B. and M. James Sawyer, eds. 2005. *Who's Afraid of the Holy Spirit? An Investigation into the Ministry of the Spirit of God Today.* Dallas; Biblical Studies Press.

Waltke, Bruce. 2007. *An Old Testament Theology.* Grand Rapids: Zondervan.

Ward, Mark L., Jr., Brian Collins, Bryan Smith, and Gregory Stiekes. 2016. *Biblical Worldview: Creation, Fall, Redemption.* Greenville, SC: BJU Press.

Warfield, Benjamin B. 1948. *The Inspiration and Authority of the Bible.* Phillipsburg, NJ: Presbyterian and Reformed.

Wenham, John. 1994. *Christ and the Bible.* Grand Rapids: Baker.

Wessell, Walter W. 1984. 'Mark' in *The Expositor's Bible Commentary.* Volume 8. Ed. Frank E. Gaebelein. Grand Rapids: Zondervan.

Young, Edward J. 1981. *The Book of Isaiah.* 3 Volumes. Grand Rapids: Eerdmans.

Zimmerli, Walther. 1979. *A Commentary on the Book of the Prophet Ezekiel, Chapters 1–24.* Trans. Ronald Clements. Philadelphia: Fortress.

Scripture Index

This index does not include the charted references in Appendix 1 and 4. An *n* after the page number indicates that the reference is in the notes on that page.

Also available from Christian Focus Publications...

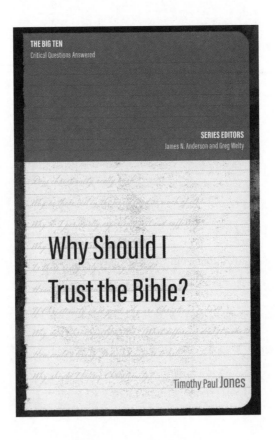

THE BIG TEN
Critical Questions Answered

SERIES EDITORS
James N. Anderson and Greg Welty

Why Should I Trust the Bible?

Timothy Paul Jones

ISBN 978-1-5271-0474-7

Why Should I Trust the Bible?

Timothy Paul Jones

The Bible is a cobbled-together selection of ancient writings that have been changed so many times by so many people over hundreds of years that surely the text can no longer be trusted – right? Certainly, there are plenty of people who take this view. Timothy Paul Jones here addresses the fact that the Bible is a difficult book to believe. It is full of incidents that seem highly improbable, if not impossible. Written for people who are sceptical of its accuracy, and of its authority, this book takes a reasonable look at the claims made about the Bible.

This is Timothy Paul Jones at his best. Witty. Transparent. Always wrestling with the hardest of questions while holding out the faith once for all delivered to the saints. This is an essential resource for contemplating and critiquing contemporary attacks on the trustworthiness of the Bible.

Dan DeWitt
Author of *Life in the Wild* & Associate Professor of Applied Theology and Apologetics, Cedarville University, Ohio

Christian Focus Publications

Our mission statement —

STAYING FAITHFUL

In dependence upon God we seek to impact the world through literature faithful to His infallible Word, the Bible. Our aim is to ensure that the Lord Jesus Christ is presented as the only hope to obtain forgiveness of sin, live a useful life and look forward to heaven with Him.

Our books are published in four imprints:

CHRISTIAN
FOCUS

Popular works including biographies, commentaries, basic doctrine and Christian living.

CHRISTIAN
HERITAGE

Books representing some of the best material from the rich heritage of the church.

MENTOR

Books written at a level suitable for Bible College and seminary students, pastors, and other serious readers. The imprint includes commentaries, doctrinal studies, examination of current issues and church history.

CF4•K

Children's books for quality Bible teaching and for all age groups: Sunday school curriculum, puzzle and activity books; personal and family devotional titles, biographies and inspirational stories — because you are never too young to know Jesus!

Christian Focus Publications Ltd,
Geanies House, Fearn, Ross-shire,
IV20 1TW, Scotland, United Kingdom.
www.christianfocus.com